High-Level Languages and Their Compilers

High-Level Languages and Their Compilers

Des Watson

School of Cognitive and Computing Sciences, University of Sussex

Addison-Wesley Publishing Company

Wokingham, England · Reading, Massachusetts · Menlo Park, California
New York · Don Mills, Ontario · Amsterdam · Bonn
Sydney · Singapore · Tokyo · Madrid · San Juan

The programs presented in this book have been included for their instructional value. They have been tested with care but are not guaranteed for any particular purpose. The publisher does not offer any warranties or representations, nor does it accept any liabilities with respect to the programs.

Many of the designations used by manufacturers and sellers to distinguish their products are claimed as trademarks. Addison-Wesley has made every attempt to supply trademark information about manufacturers and their products mentioned in this book. A list of the trademark designations and their owners appears on page vi.

Cover designed by Marshall Henrichs and
printed by The Riverside Printing Co. (Reading) Ltd.
Illustrated by Chartwell Illustrators.
Typeset by CRB Typesetting Services, Ely, Cambs.
Printed in Great Britain by The Bath Press, Avon.

First printed 1989.

British Library Cataloguing in Publication Data
Watson, Des
   High-level languages and their compilers.
   1. Computer systems. High level languages.
   Design
   I. Title
   005.13

   ISBN 0-201-18489-3

Library of Congress Cataloguing in Publication Data
Watson, Des.
   High-level languages and their compilers.

   Bibliography: p.
   Includes index.
   1. Programming languages (Electronic computers)
2. Compilers (Computer programs)   I. Title.
   QA76.7.W38   1989   005.13   88-16613
   ISBN 0-201-18489-3

To Helen

Preface

The study of high-level languages and of compilers form a central theme in the field of computer science. Being able to carry out an objective analysis of the design of a programming language can help a programmer choose the right language for a particular application, as well as motivating the design of new languages. An understanding of the techniques used by high-level language compilers can give the programmer a set of skills applicable in many aspects of software design – one does not have to be a compiler writer to make use of them.

Aims of this book

The purpose of this book is to introduce the design and development of high-level languages and to show how they can be implemented on computer systems. It is not intended as an introduction to high-level language programming, nor is it a book for the seasoned compiler writer. It presents a wide-ranging study of the essential features of a fairly large group of high-level languages and then describes some of the more important techniques for their implementation. A familiarity with the material in this book should give the student a broad insight into the study of high-level languages, together with enough information to write and implement a complete compiler for a language of moderate complexity. Specialized techniques are not covered and the compiler design sections concentrate on the implementation of imperative languages.

Intended audience

This book is primarily intended for use in introductory courses in high-level language and compiler design. Such courses often appear in the second year of a traditional computer science degree programme, although this may be in the third year for students who specialize less in computer science. This book can also be used for self-study, with references to the computer science literature identifying directions for further study.

Readers are expected to have some competence in a block-structured high-level language, such as Pascal or C, together with a very basic grounding in computer architecture and machine-level programming. Although most of the examples in this book are coded in Pascal, a knowledge of Pascal is not a prerequisite, since it is a language whose syntactic details should not hide the underlying algorithms.

Structure of the book

This book is made up of three parts. Part One covers the design and characteristics of high-level languages.

- **Chapter 1**: **High-Level Languages** puts programming languages into a historical context, shows some of the major differences between high-level languages and low-level languages, and gives an overview of language definition. [pages 3–17]

- **Chapter 2**: **Technical Characteristics of High-Level Languages** looks at a number of technical characteristics of languages that can be used as the basis of a comparative study of programming languages. It also shows ways in which languages can be classified into different groups. [pages 19–44]

- **Chapter 3**: **A Survey of High-Level Languages** describes the characteristics of languages that are either popular or incorporate features of special interest and shows how these languages can be inter-related. [pages 45–93]

Part Two describes some of the theory and practice of compiler design, which forms the major part of the book.

- **Chapter 4**: **Syntax, Semantics and Translation** describes the structure of a typical compiler and covers the ideas of syntax specification and grammar classification, together with an overview of parsing techniques. [pages 97–125]

- **Chapter 5**: **Lexical Analysis** looks at lexical analysis and describes some of the characteristics of regular grammars and finite-state automata on which the design of a lexical analyzer can be based. [pages 127–158]

- **Chapter 6**: **Syntax and Semantic Analysis** covers syntax and semantic analysis, concentrating on several popular parsing techniques. [pages 159–211]

- **Chapter 7**: **Code Generation** shows how target machine code can be generated. It also examines the problems of run-time storage management, covers some of the issues relating to the designs of the target hardware and describes some methods for code improvement. [pages 213–275]

Part Three describes some of the approaches for implementing a high-level language.

- **Chapter 8**: **Approaches to Language Implementation** examines hardware issues that can influence the implementation plan and looks at some of the major issues of compiler and interpreter implementation. [pages 279–299]
- **Chapter 9**: **Software Tools** describes Lex and Yacc, compiler construction tools that can greatly simplify the implementation of a compiler. [pages 301–311]

Finally, an appendix presents a simple example of the use of the lexical analyzer generator Lex and the parser generator Yacc.

How to use this book

The three parts of this book are to some extent independent. So, for example, a course in comparative languages could use Chapters 1, 2 and 3 and skim the rest of the book. However, a compiler course is not really complete without at least a brief survey of the characteristics of high-level languages, and so the first part should not be totally ignored in such a course.

If time is limited, it may be necessary to restrict the topics covered. Chapter 3 is not a prerequisite for subsequent chapters and so could be omitted in a first reading. Similarly, sections such as the descriptions of finite-state automata (Section 5.3) and code optimization (Section 7.5) could be squeezed out if necessary. The details presented in Chapter 9 may be of somewhat limited relevance to students without access to implementations of Lex and Yacc.

Each chapter contains a synopsis, outlining the major topics to be covered, a concise end-of-chapter summary and a set of exercises. Some of these exercises are intended to provoke thought rather than a written answer, while others form the basis of a major programming project. The material presented in this book will make very much more sense if the course incorporates a significant practical component. The reader is strongly advised to use a computer system to experiment with the algorithms presented in the text and to program some of the exercises. The coding of a compiler for a simple language is a feasible project for a student using this book and it can be of enormous educational value. The questions following Chapter 9 include several relating to material from throughout the book. In particular, some compiler-writing projects are to be found here. Solutions to selected exercises are provided at the back of the book.

Acknowledgements

This book arose from a series of undergraduate courses taught at the University of Sussex. I am grateful to all the students on these courses who shared my enthusiasm for compilers and helped me to decide which topics to include in this book. Many improvements and corrections were made on the advice of the reviewers – in particular, Dr J. P. Bennett made many valuable suggestions, very few of which I could ignore. All the remaining errors and obscurities are, of course, my own responsibility.

I would also like to thank Debra Myson-Etherington, Sarah Mallen and Simon Plumtree of Addison-Wesley for their extraordinary patience, good advice and unflagging encouragement. Finally, I must thank Wendy for her support and forbearance, and Helen – who has grown up much faster than this book!

Des Watson
November 1988

Contents

PART ONE

Languages

Part One of this book is concerned with the design of high-level pro-gramming languages. There are now many high-level languages in widespread use and it is worth examining the characteristics of some of these languages. This helps in making useful comparisons between high-level languages and hence facilitates the selection and use of high-level languages. These characteristics are also important to the compiler writer, since a compiler must perform a complete analysis of the structure of a high-level language program input to it.

CHAPTER 1

High-Level Languages

Communication is the essence of computing and languages provide the means for communication. The degree of success or failure of communication is thus influenced by the characteristics of the language used. Unless rules are carefully prearranged, the communication is bound to fail.

There are many different languages used in the context of computing. When talking about their work, computer scientists may use a conventional spoken language incorporating the liberal use of specialized terminology, thus making parts of the communication unintelligible to the uninitiated listener. Inter-computer communication also involves the use of a specialized vocabulary and grammar. Here, the rules of the interchange are somewhat easier to specify than the rules of the natural language used by humans but, again, both parties must be aware of the rules and their meanings.

Specialized languages are also used to enable humans to communicate with computers. There are many hundreds of different languages being used today for this purpose. Such languages are usually referred to as programming languages, but others such as command languages, job control languages and database query languages have to be included in this category.

This chapter introduces some of the fundamental concepts of programming languages and outlines the important role of the language definition. The development of software in a high-level language rather than in a low-level language can offer numerous advantages, and it is these advantages that help motivate the study of high-level languages.

1.1   Programming Languages

Programming languages are used to describe **algorithms**; that is, sequences of steps that lead to the solution of problems. A programming language has to support the definition of dynamic courses of action. Not only must it provide a means for specifying basic computer operations, but it must also allow its user to specify how these steps should be sequenced to solve a particular problem. A programming language can be considered to be a 'notation' that can be used to specify algorithms with precision.

Computer programming languages can be broadly classified into two groups: low-level languages and high-level languages. **Low-level languages** are close to machine languages and have a strong correspondence between the operations implemented by the language and the operations implemented by the underlying hardware. **High-level languages**, on the other hand, are closer to languages used by humans for expressing problems and algorithms. Each statement in a high-level language may be equivalent to many statements in a low-level language. This classification of programming languages into two groups is of course a simplification, as, in practice, there is a continuum between low-level languages and high-level languages, with some languages possessing features from both groups. Nevertheless, this distinction is useful.

The range of operations directly implemented by the hardware of a computer is usually very limited; hence, the coding of complex algorithms using only these operations is a major task. Coding can be tedious, protracted and prone to error. It is the aim of programming languages, especially high-level programming languages, to provide the programmer with a much friendlier environment so that the task of coding the algorithm is greatly simplified. The algorithm, once coded in the chosen programming language, is translated, normally without human involvement, into an equivalent set of basic machine instructions. These instructions are executed by the hardware and, if all is well, the desired effect of the algorithm is produced.

The key advantage offered by high-level languages is **abstraction**. This is the process by which the essential properties required for the solution of a problem are extracted while hiding the details of the implementation of the solution from the programmer. As the level of abstraction increases, the programmer needs to be concerned less and less about the hardware on which the program runs. In other words, the ideas of programming can be separated from hardware design. For example, at the level of abstraction of a high-level language, the programmer can refer to symbolic variable names rather than numerical memory addresses. Data abstraction allows memory locations to be regarded as storage cells for higher-level data types; for example, the Pascal programmer does not need to be concerned with the method of representation for Boolean variables. Control abstraction allows the high-level language programmer to express algorithms in terms of structures such as **while** loops, **if** statements and procedures. Again, the mapping of these structures on to the hardware implementation is of no concern to the programmer. The composition of a program as a set of subprograms is another example of the idea of abstraction.

A high-level programming language is translated into its equivalent machine code by means of a program called a **compiler**. This book is concerned with these high-level languages and also with the design of their compilers.

1.1.1   A little history

Programming language history really started with the work of Charles Babbage in the early nineteenth century. Motivated by his observation that the printed tables of mathematical functions available at that time were full of mistakes, he developed an automated technique for their calculation. The **difference engine** was a mechanical device that used the theory of finite differences to calculate polynomial functions. Although a small prototype was both built and demonstrated successfully, the full-size system was never completed. As Babbage's interest in the difference engine waned, he became increasingly involved in the much more ambitious **analytical engine**. This machine was intended to have a much wider application area than the difference engine with the capability to execute any form of numerical computation. Babbage produced very careful designs for this extraordinarily complex mechanical device. It contained a large store based on a column of wheels, a 'mill' responsible for the execution of arithmetic operations and a printing device to avoid the possibility of any human transcription errors in the presentation of the results. The engine was controlled by punched cards: some of these cards (the operation cards) controlled the mill, while others (the variable cards) were responsible for the transfer of numbers into and out of the store. Again, this project was never completed. The sad story is recounted in Morrison [1961] and Hyman [1984].

With hindsight, the analytical engine project was far from being a failure. Of special interest are the techniques that were proposed for the engine's control and the sequencing of calculations. Ada Augusta, Countess of Lovelace, who worked with Babbage on this project, wrote 'programs' for the machine using a very sophisticated notation. Although this notation was a long way from the high-level languages of today, the programs do bear a strong resemblance to today's microprograms, which are used for the low-level control of a computer's operations. Ada Augusta wrote very clear notes on the engine and its programming (also reprinted in Morrison [1961]), emphasizing that the machine's programmability gave it the overwhelming advantage of generality. She is regarded by many as the first programmer.

The history of computing then progressed through several electromechanical stages. Punched card machinery, pioneered by Hollerith in America, was developed and used widely for many applications, including census data analysis. Although many more uses were introduced, these systems did not directly contribute much to the development of programming languages.

The advent of the wholly electronic computer in the late 1940s prompted a dramatic rise in the rate of development of programming tools. Assembly languages soon became available, some having a very impressive specification. Many slightly higher-level languages were implemented, some being aimed at specific application areas while others were intended for use in more general-purpose fields, such as numerical computation. By 1959, the list of available automated programming systems was surprisingly long [Sammet, 1969]. However, these languages, some of which were called **autocodes**, were comparatively simple by today's standards. For example, some autocodes did not permit the programmer to specify arithmetic expressions in a compact and readable algebraic form, while others imposed severe restrictions on the complexity of these expressions. Such needs gave rise to a further phase of language development, which resulted in high-level languages appearing on the scene.

1.2   The Need for High-Level Languages

Almost all current digital computers operate on binary representations of data using instructions that are also coded in a binary form. In the early days of computing, all programmers had to be familiar with this binary representation because programs were expressed in terms of sequences of low-level machine instructions, which were then translated by hand, using a conversion table, into a string of binary digits (1s and 0s) for loading into the computer. For example, the instruction 'increment the value in the accumulator' might be represented as 101001000000.

However, this early form of programming, known as **machine code programming**, had many major disadvantages:

- There was a high probability of error in all stages of the programming process.

- Programming anything but the simplest of algorithms resulted in long programs, since each machine operation could only perform a comparatively simple operation. These long and involved programs were also difficult to debug and validate, thereby placing an enormous burden on the programmer.

- Memory address calculations also had to be performed by hand, which was hard work and error prone. In addition, a very careful record had to be kept of the precise storage locations of all instructions and data so that, should the program require modification, the address arguments could be easily altered.

Some of the disadvantages of machine code programming can be overcome by making the computer responsible for the translation stage. The program is still written in terms of the basic machine operations, but the translation into binary notation is performed by the computer. The program performing this translation is called an **assembler**. Even the simplest of modern assemblers can recognize symbolic addresses and **mnemonics** representing machine operations. So, for example, the programmer need only write:

```
ADD ival
```

to specify an instruction to add the contents of location ival to the accumulator. The assembler then performs the translation to the equivalent string of 1s and 0s. The assembler also copes with the problems of address calculation, using text names for addresses as well as for other data. Hence, the programmer does not need to be concerned with the alteration of address arguments, due to the addition or removal of instructions or data during the development of the program, as this is done automatically by the assembler. The consequence of this automated translation is that assembly language programs are much easier to write and to debug than machine code programs.

Although the introduction of assemblers in the early 1950s was a significant step forward in the history of programming, neither assemblers nor **macro assemblers**, with their increased level of abstraction, solved the problem common to all forms of low-level language programming. This was that 'real' programs tended to be long, complex and hard to write, debug and maintain. A major reason for this was that a large proportion of the instructions were concerned with managing, sequencing and other housekeeping duties, rather than with the actual solution to the problem. What was needed was a much better system of notation with which to specify the tasks to be performed by the computer. Higher-level languages were required.

1.3   Characteristics of High-Level Languages

Having seen what led to the development of high-level languages, let us now look at those characteristics of high-level languages that make them more useful than low-level languages. In this context, it is also necessary to consider what characteristics make languages easy to use. This is a very wide-ranging question that goes well beyond the consideration of technical characteristics.

1.3.1   High-level languages versus low-level languages

High-level languages can offer major advantages over low-level languages. The primary motivation for their use is that most problems can be solved much more quickly and easily. This comparative ease with which problems can be solved is due largely to the fact that the problem may already be at least partly specified in a notation not too far removed from the high-level language being used. For example, a high-level language designed for numerical computation has the ability to express arithmetic expressions in the conventional and universally understood infix notation. Many other characteristics of high-level languages are important in this respect, such as the availability of data- as well as program-structuring facilities, powerful and relevant functions and operators, and the ability to break programs up into distinct modules.

A related advantage is that high-level languages are generally much easier to learn and understand. The high-level language programmer does not need to know the detailed structure of the underlying hardware. The programming environment provided by the high-level language should be much more comfortable than that provided by the bare machine or by the assembler. In other words, the high-level language is offering abstraction (see Section 1.1).

High-level language programs are usually much easier to follow than those written in an assembly language for several reasons:

- They are more likely to be self-documenting.
- The structure of the program can be made to reflect the structure of the original problem.
- Meaningful names can be chosen for variables and subprograms.
- The solution of the problem need not be obscured by the level of detail necessary in a low-level language program.

Nevertheless, it is still possible for the determined programmer to write obscure programs in a high-level language! For example, the Obfuscated C

Code Contest is held annually and entrants aim to write the most obscure C program conforming to a set of simple rules.

Improved portability is another motivation for writing in a high-level language. If a program is written in a 'standard' high-level language, a high degree of machine independence is possible. This is in contrast to low-level languages which are very machine specific and so programs written in these languages are not very portable. Portability is achieved as a result of high-level language abstraction. It is an important aspect of programming and is considered again in later chapters.

High-level language programs are usually much easier to debug for several reasons:

- As a high-level language program is generally easier to follow and understand than a low-level language equivalent, the programmer is more likely to spot errors on a careful visual inspection.

- The compiler can provide a useful debugging facility. If the compiler offers a comprehensive set of compile-time checking operations, the probability of errors in the compiled code can be reduced significantly. Operations such as type checking and testing for parameter compatibility between the definition of a subprogram and its call can be very useful. The nature and extent of the checking that can be carried out at compile time depends on the language. Languages such as Pascal, Ada and ALGOL 68 allow a great deal of checking at compile time and, in fact, it has been commented that if a program can be passed through an ALGOL 68 compiler with no compilation errors, then there is a good chance that it will run correctly. This contrasts with languages such as C where a program declared to be valid by the compiler may yield many run-time errors.

- Depending on the nature of the language, the compiler may optionally include instructions in the generated code for the detection of run-time errors such as numerical overflow and violation of array bounds. Such checks can dramatically reduce debugging time.

- Some languages inherently support interactive debugging. For example, in BASIC, it is very easy to stop a running program at any point and print out the values of key variables. Alternatively, some language implementations incorporate a debugging package that allows the programmer to examine the run-time behaviour of the program using names and structures defined in the original high-level source program. Ideally, the compiler should allow the generation of run-time debugging code to be switched on and off under the control of the programmer. For example, in circumstances where the programmer may feel that a section of code or even a complete program is most unlikely to fail and run-time efficiency is important, the programmer should instruct the compiler not to produce debugging code, thus reducing run-time overheads.

Because of the comparative ease with which high-level languages can be learned, used and debugged, it follows that high-level language programs are easier to modify than low-level language programs. This is an important advantage since most programmers seem to spend more of their time modifying existing programs than writing new programs. A major factor providing the potential for easy modification is the ability to localize the side effects of a modification. However, some languages, especially the low-level languages, are poor in this respect. For example, where all variables are assumed to have global scope, a modification that alters the value of one of these variables can have repercussions throughout the program. Other languages provide information-hiding facilities so that the scope of variables can be strictly limited and the side effects of a modification contained.

Despite all these advantages of high-level languages, low-level languages are still being used for some applications. There are several possible reasons for their continued use:

- It may be necessary to perform some low-level machine-specific hardware function not directly supported by the high-level language. A conventional technique allowing such functions to be carried out under high-level language control is to provide a subroutine library written in a low-level language, callable by high-level language programs. In programming language implementations, the machine-specific aspects of high-level language functions, such as input and output, and storage allocation, are often provided by such a low-level language subroutine library. For some applications, the poor low-level control offered by most high-level languages can be a major difficulty. Some high-level languages offer good exception-handling facilities, allowing control to be retained by the program after faults, interrupts or other 'external' asynchronous events. This can improve matters but is far from being a complete solution.

- Advantages of efficiency are often bestowed on low-level languages. For some applications, it may be vital that the program should be very small and/or execute as rapidly as possible. Some people claim that the only way to achieve this is via a low-level language. However, comparatively recent developments in compiler design – in particular, in the techniques of code generation – make it possible for a compiler to generate extremely high-quality code, which is just as good as, if not better than, a handwritten attempt.

One should not be dogmatic about the superiority of one type of computer language over another. The actual choice of a language for the writing of a program to solve a problem depends on a vast number of factors, only a few of which can be presented here. A summary of some of

Table 1.1 Advantages of high-level languages and low-level languages.

High-level languages	Low-level languages
Easy to learn and understand	Access to low-level, machine-specific operations
Programs can be self-documenting	
Rapid solution of problems	Time/space efficiency (not universally true!)
Improved portability	
Simplified debugging	
Simplified modification and maintenance	

the advantages of high-level languages and low-level languages is shown in Table 1.1.

1.3.2 Choosing and using high-level languages

The most obvious factor determining the choice of language for any particular application is the set of languages currently implemented on the computer or computers to be used. Only under the most extreme circumstances is it advisable to implement a new language system for a single application!

Another factor that must be considered is the intended application areas for the proposed language. Languages do not have universal applicability. For example, COBOL is more suited to portable business data processing applications while FORTRAN is intended primarily for portable numerical scientific computation. However, it is possible to use languages for applications far removed from those for which they were designed. For example, FORTRAN has been used to solve a wide range of problems, including the writing of compilers. The use of a language in an unexpected application area may well result in some coding difficulties and, in addition, the run-time efficiency may suffer. Several of the more recent languages have tended to be somewhat broader in application, but specialized languages are still being developed.

The basic type of the language is also important. It may be appropriate to abandon the conventional imperative programming languages, like Pascal, and use a functional language like LISP. Or at another level, an inherently interactive language like BASIC may be well suited to some applications.

The attitudes and abilities of the programmer are also significant. In some cases, it may be worthwhile for a programmer to learn a new language, even to implement a single program. On the other hand, it may be easier to struggle with a familiar language, using it for an application for which it was not primarily designed. Very broadly, computer programmers can be divided into two categories:

(1)   Those whose primary interest is in programming and computing.
(2)   Those who use computers and programs to solve problems from other applications.

There are many languages suitable for both categories of programmer, but some are clearly directed towards the first category since they incorporate features that offer great power and flexibility at the expense of clarity or ease of debugging.

Finally, portability must be considered. If it is known that a program has to be implemented on a wide range of computers, then care should be taken in the choice of a language for its implementation. This language should be well defined and standardized over the range of computers on which the program is to be implemented.

Once a program has been written, it is a good idea to carry out some form of evaluation, even if only informally, to determine whether the program meets its original objectives. Such an assessment may also serve to highlight mistakes and thus prevent them being made again. If a program does not satisfy the original requirements, then the reasons for failure should be examined. These may include a fault of the programmer, a bad choice of programming language, or specific problems in the design of the programming language, the compiler, the operating system or other systems software, the computer or the original objectives. In some cases, it may even be necessary to rewrite the program.

1.4   Language Definition

The definition of a programming language is a very important document. It has to fulfil many functions:

- It must serve as a reference document for users of the language so that details of the syntax of statements can be checked rapidly.

- It must also specify the semantics – that is, the meanings of valid programs.

- Ideally, it should also serve as an introduction to the language, especially for programmers experienced in other languages.

- It is also the starting point for the compiler writer.

It is comparatively easy to state the requirements of a language definition:

- It should be clear and comprehensible, so that potential users of the language are not frightened away.
- It should be precise and free from ambiguity.
- It should be complete, leaving no room for guesswork.
- And, of course, it should be accurate.

These are extremely stringent requirements and few, if any, programming language definitions fulfil them all.

1.4.1 Syntax, semantics and pragmatics

At this stage, it is important to realize exactly what the language definition is trying to define. A large part of the theory of language definition is concerned with the specification of syntax. The **syntax** of a language defines the sequences of characters that can make up a valid program. Hence, this definition requires a statement of the set of characters that can be used in valid programs, together with a set of rules that show the permissible ways in which these characters may be strung together. For example, it is the Pascal syntax rules that state that:

$$a := a + 0.2$$

is a valid statement and that:

$$a := a + .2$$

is invalid. Powerful formal methods exist for specifying the syntax of programming languages.

A language definition should also be concerned with the **semantics** of the language. These semantic rules define the 'meaning' of each of the possible valid programs allowed by the syntax rules. So, for example, the Pascal semantic rules will specify that the effect of the (valid) Pascal statement above is to increase the value of the real number stored in the variable a by 0.2.

Specifying semantics is much harder than defining syntax, although formal methods are now available. Many language definitions resort to the use of a natural language, such as English, to explain the meaning of language constructs and hence complete programs. Fortunately, for most of the commonly used programming languages, a large proportion of the semantic definition can be omitted, since it is intuitively obvious. For example, a programmer would be justifiably concerned if the Pascal statement:

> *write('Hello')*

resulted in the string *Goodbye* being output! However, it should never be assumed that meaning is always obvious and that semantics need not be specified. For example, in the Pascal example:

```
for i := 1 to j * k do
begin
  .
  .
  .
  j := j + 1;
  .
  .
  .
end;
```

the effect of the **for** statement depends on whether the expression defining the maximum value of the loop variable (*j* * *k*) is evaluated just once or every time the loop is executed. Fortunately, the Pascal definition does not permit any ambiguity in this case and insists that implementations should evaluate the *j* * *k* term once only.

Language definitions may also include **pragmatic** information; that is, information relating to the implementation and use of a programming technique or programming language. For example, a programming language definition may state that an integer constant has its conventional meaning, resorting to common sense rather than providing a formal definition of the interpretation of an integer constant.

1.4.2   Techniques for language definition

Before looking at the definition of programming languages, consider the vastly harder problem of defining a natural language such as English. *The English Language Definition Manual* does not exist as a published document because, as yet, no way has been devised for formally defining exceptionally complex languages which also happen to be in a process of continuous change. It is important to note that these natural languages are 'defined' in terms of themselves. For example, native English speakers are taught English using English while they learn French by defining its vocabulary, grammar and usage in English. A language used to define another language is called a **metalanguage**. So, in this last example, the metalanguage English is used to define the language French.

Metalanguages are also used in the definition of programming languages. Hence, the requirements for clarity, precision and accuracy are also imposed on the metalanguage. Early high-level languages were defined using English as a metalanguage but, not surprisingly, ambiguities and other errors in the definition were not uncommon. A major breakthrough in language definition occurred in the 1960s when a new notation was presented for the specification of the syntax of ALGOL 60. This notation is called **Backus-Naur Form**, or Backus Normal Form (**BNF**). BNF is a very simple but powerful metalanguage for the specification of syntax and is described fully (using English as a metalanguage!) in Chapter 4 together with the other important metalanguages.

The metalanguages just discussed are concerned primarily with syntax specification. The specification of semantics is a somewhat harder problem. Fortunately, some formal techniques do exist. For example, the semantics of PL/I have been defined in terms of the effect of executing a PL/I program on the internal states of a hypothetical abstract machine. A somewhat less formal, and also less satisfactory, method would be to adopt one particular implementation of the language (on real hardware) and state that the semantics are defined by that chosen implementation.

Since the aim of a language specification is to enumerate all valid programs, a language's definition could conceivably consist of all of the possible valid programs. However, no practical programming language is either small enough or simple enough for this to be possible, so a set of rules have to be supplied to indicate how all valid programs can be synthesized. These are the rules that define the language's syntax.

The production of a language definition should not be undertaken lightly. Programming language definitions seem to be the most carefully scrutinized and heavily criticized documents of computer science. Some definitions are quite short and straightforward, such as that for Pascal (29 pages in Wirth [1971]) or ALGOL 60 (17 pages in Naur [1963]). Other languages are defined by somewhat larger documents; for example, the Ada programming language reference manual [United States Department of Defense (US DoD), 1980] covers 242 pages. Further examples are given in McGettrick [1980].

A final point concerns the precise meaning of the term 'syntactically correct program'. As has been seen, the syntax of a language defines the set of 'syntactically correct programs'; however, the syntax definition says nothing about what happens when the programs are run. Consequently, problems can arise, as illustrated by the following Pascal statement:

write(1/0)

The question as to whether the language syntax should prevent programmers from writing unreasonable programs or should be somewhat less constraining seems to be largely dependent on personal taste.

SUMMARY

- There is a clear development path from machine code via assembly languages and autocodes to high-level languages. One of the key features offered by high-level languages is abstraction.

- High-level languages offer many advantages over low-level languages, and there are many issues to be considered when choosing a high-level language for a particular application.

- The advantages of high-level languages include: support for the ideas of abstraction so that the programmer can concentrate on the solution of the problem, rather than on the low-level details of data representation; the comparative ease of learning; the more rapid solution of problems; improved portability and simplified debugging, modification and maintenance. These all lead towards lower software costs and more reliable software.

- A language definition must specify both the syntactic and semantic aspects of the language. Languages are often defined with the aid of simpler formal metalanguages.

EXERCISES

1.1 Table 1.1 lists some of the relative advantages and disadvantages of high- and low-level languages. Extend this table.

1.2 List the features that you feel would be essential in a language designed for (a) numerical computation and (b) character string manipulation. Do you know of any real languages that support both these sets of features, or at least a large subset of them?

1.3 Would the Obfuscated Pascal Code Contest be a success? What language features help in the writing of obscure code?

1.4 To what extent is it possible to design a high-level language that incorporates the advantages of low-level languages?

1.5 Try to assess the efficiency of the code generated by a high-level language compiler on a computer system to which you have access. Some compilers can produce an assembly language listing showing the code that has been generated and careful inspection of this code can yield interesting information about the compiler. But it is always possible to run simple benchmarks to compare the run-time efficiencies of, say, compiled code and handwritten assembly language.

1.6 Babbage's analytical engine was never completed, although detailed and lengthy descriptions were published. Write a software simulator for the analytical engine to determine whether it could have worked and use this simulator to solve a few simple numerical problems. How does the analytical engine's programming language rate in comparison with more modern languages?

CHAPTER 2

Technical Characteristics of High-Level Languages

Before examining the details of individual high-level languages, it is instructive to take a much broader look at the characteristics of high-level languages. One way of classifying languages is by their application areas, but such classifications overlap so much and do not say a great deal about the languages themselves. A better approach is to specify a set of technical criteria that enable the design of languages to be compared more fully, even though the evaluation of these criteria is sometimes highly subjective. The set presented here is intended to form a basis for the classification of languages and for pinpointing some of the good and bad aspects of any programming language. There are many other non-technical properties of languages that affect their popularity, such as sponsorship by large organizations, quality of available implementations and aesthetic appeal, but these criteria, although very important, are rather elusive.

2.1 Broad Classification

Programming languages can be roughly divided into four groups: **imperative languages**, **functional languages**, **logic programming languages** and others (see Chapter 3). Most of the commonly used languages such as FORTRAN and COBOL fall into the imperative category. In these languages there is a fundamental underlying dependence on the assignment operation and on variables implemented as computer memory locations, whose contents can be read and altered. There is a close correspondence between this model and the design of 'conventional' computer hardware, where the central processor operates on values held in storage locations. This close correspondence allows the efficient implementation of imperative languages on von Neumann architectures.

In functional languages (sometimes called **applicative languages**), the fundamental operation is function application. Perhaps the most famous language in this category is LISP. There is a growing interest in this kind of language, partly fuelled by recent trends in the development of parallel processing and new types of machine architecture.

In a logic programming language, the programmer only needs to supply the problem specification in some formal form, as it is then the responsibility of the language system to infer a method of solution. This represents a very high-level approach to problem solving, based on declarative rather than procedural notions.

Another way of grouping programming languages is to classify them as procedural or declarative languages. **Procedural languages** (or procedure-oriented languages) are those in which the action of the program is defined by a series of operations executed in a sequence defined by the programmer. To solve a problem, the programmer has to specify a series of steps (or statements) which are executed in sequence. In a low-level language, each of these steps is comparatively simple, but in higher-level languages, each step can accomplish a great deal and so fewer steps are required to solve the problem, although an increased burden is placed on the computer in interpreting each step. The logical progression of this approach is for the computer to be given just the statement of the problem, without any indication of how it is to be solved. In such a case, the problem would be expressed in a **declarative language**. Programming in a declarative language (or a **non-procedural language**) involves the specification of a set of rules defining the solution to the problem; it is then up to the computer to determine how to reach a solution consistent with the given rules. Much interest is being shown in the declarative languages because they have the potential of greatly simplifying the programming process. The language PROLOG falls into this category, although it retains some procedural aspects. Another widespread non-procedural system is the spreadsheet program. The spreadsheet is made up of a matrix of cells and the user defines the contents of some of the cells as well as the rules for calculating the contents of other cells. It is then up to the software to resolve the rules and place values consistent with the rules in the matrix cells.

EXAMPLE

The following short examples illustrate program fragments written in (a) a procedural language (Pascal) and (b) a declarative language (PROLOG).

(a) $t := sqrt\ (b * b - 4 * a * c);$
       $root1 := (-b + t)/(2 * a);$
       $root2 := (-b - t)/(2 * a);$
       $writeln(root1, root2);$
       .
       .
       .

(b)   carnivore(X) :- eats(X, meat).
       herbivore(X) :- eats(X, leaves).
       eats(X, leaves) :- eats(X, grass).

       eats(cow, grass).
       eats(lion, meat).

       ?- carnivore(lion).
       ?- herbivore(X).

2.2   Language Structure

When first looking at a programming language, it is important to gain an overview of the structure of programs written in that language. An associated concern is the language's definition – its form and how it is expressed. In this section, we look briefly at language definitions and then consider whether it is possible to write programs as a collection of smaller and simpler units – a recommended approach for productive software development.

2.2.1 Language definition

Any language requires a complete and unambiguous language definition for both the compiler writer and the language user. The compiler writer uses this definition as a means of recognizing programs while the programmer uses it as a means of deriving programs. The definition of a language can be achieved in many different ways. For example, it can be defined in terms of a metalanguage; however, the metalanguage itself also requires careful definition. The topic of language definition has already been introduced in Section 1.4 and is discussed in detail in Chapter 4.

2.2.2 Program-structuring facilities

Software implementation can be simplified if the language supports structuring primitives reflecting those used in a program design methodology, such as top-down design.

In some languages, it is possible to encapsulate an instance of a data structure with the code required for its manipulation. For example, in Smalltalk, a **class** defines an object type together with a set of operations to manipulate such objects. This important aid towards program modularity is also supported in Ada in the form of a **package**, which can encapsulate code and data, supporting data abstraction. A package is divided into two parts:

(1)   The visible specification part, which defines the objects that are accessible from outside the package by its users.

(2)   The package body, which actually defines the details of the package's implementation.

In conjunction with Ada's separate compilation facilities, the package provides a powerful tool for the construction of large software systems. The specification part, the body and the programs using the package can all be compiled separately. Because interfaces can be formally and simply specified, relatively independent development of the program modules of a system can be undertaken.

EXAMPLE

The following is the specification of a simple Ada package:

```
package stack is
    procedure push(n : in INTEGER);
    procedure pull(n : out INTEGER);
end stack;
```

2.2.3 Subprograms and parameter passing

All but the simplest of the high-level languages offer support for the use of subprograms such as procedures or functions. The presence of these facilities is vital for the production of well-structured programs. However, languages vary widely in their support for parameter passing to and from subprograms. For example, ANSI (American National Standards Institute) Standard BASIC only supports parameter passing by the use of global variables. Another important consideration is whether recursion is permitted, as some problems can be solved very clearly and easily using recursive techniques.

Various techniques are adopted by high-level languages for parameter passing:

- call by value,
- call by reference,
- call by name,
- call by value-result,
- call by result.

In the case of **call by value**, the value of the actual parameter is copied into the formal parameter defined within the subprogram, when the subprogram is entered. As this formal parameter is defined locally, any alteration of its value within the subprogram cannot directly alter the value of the corresponding actual parameter. Since call by value implicitly involves a copying operation, the passing by value of large data structures such as arrays can cause a significant overhead in subprogram call. Call by value parameters can pass data into a subprogram but cannot receive data to be passed out from a subprogram.

In **call by reference**, the address of the actual parameter is passed to the subprogram, rather than its value. When the subprogram is called, each formal parameter is bound to the address of its corresponding actual parameter. This implies that values can be passed into the subprogram, since they can be accessed through the formal parameter names, and that updating a formal parameter within the subprogram immediately affects the value of the corresponding actual parameter in the caller's environment. So, call by reference allows data flow into and out of a subprogram. Since only address values are manipulated on a subprogram call, call by reference is efficient, even when used for passing large data structures. It is a very simple mechanism but it does have a drawback: if a value, rather than a variable name, is passed as an actual parameter and the subprogram updates the corresponding formal parameter, then the effect is undefined and potentially dangerous. This action may attempt to store a new value into a constant and may be difficult for the compiler or run-time system to detect.

In **call by name**, a formal parameter is textually replaced by the actual parameter, wherever it occurs in the body of the subprogram. Like call by reference, this mechanism also allows data to be passed into and out of a subprogram. Although call by name is a powerful method, it does suffer from some potential dangers and it can be inefficient and rather difficult to implement. Some of the problems of ALGOL 60's call by name are discussed in Knuth [1967].

A method for removing some of the deficiencies of call by name and call by reference is the technique known as **call by value-result**. Here, the values of the actual parameters are copied into the corresponding formal parameters on subprogram entry. On subprogram exit, the values in the formal parameters are copied back into the actual parameters. In this way, greater checking of parameter/value compatibility can be carried out on subprogram call and return. A simplification of this scheme, known as **call by result**, is obviously possible for parameters used solely for passing back results to the caller.

To maintain maximum security and flexibility, some languages require the programmer to specify whether each formal parameter is a value (input) parameter, a result (output) parameter or both. Languages such as ALGOL W, Pascal and Ada adopt variants of this scheme. Parameter passing is discussed again in Section 7.2.5 where methods for the implementation of these mechanisms are outlined.

EXAMPLE

The following program fragments illustrate (a) call by value (in Pascal), (b) call by reference (in Pascal) and (c) call by name (in ALGOL).

(a)   **procedure** *printsquare*(*i* : *integer*);
      begin
        i := *sqr*(*i*);
        writeln(*i*)
      end;

        .
        .
        .

        k := 3;
        printsquare(*k*);   (* *causes* 9 *to be output* *)
                                  (* *k still has the value* 3 *after the call* *)
        .
        .
        .

(b)   **procedure** *printsquare*(**var** *i* : *integer*);
      begin
        i := *sqr*(*i*);
        writeln(*i*)
      end;

        .
        .
        .

        k := 3;
        printsquare(*k*);   (* *causes* 9 *to be output* *)
                                  (* *k has the value* 9 *after the call* *)
        .
        .
        .

(c)   **real procedure** *sumarray*(*i*, *a*, *b*, *el*);
      value *a*, *b*; **integer** *i*, *a*, *b*, *el*;
      begin
        integer *sum*;
        sum := 0;
        for *i* := *a* **step** 1 **until** *b* **do** *sum* := *sum* + *el*;
        sumarray := *sum*
      end;

        .
        .
        .

        vsum := *sumarray*(*j*, 1, *max*, *k*[*j*]);
        .
        .
        .

The call to *sumarray* has the effect of summing elements $k[1]$, $k[2]$, ..., $k[max]$ and placing the result in *vsum*.

2.2.4   Separate compilation

The design of some languages makes it very difficult to build up a large system from a set of separately compiled modules. On the other hand, some languages, such as FORTRAN, are designed so that each subroutine or function can be compiled separately. This is made possible by the highly controlled methods of data sharing and communication between modules. In theory, separate compilation is always possible if enough information on the environment can be stored and used in the compilation of later modules. Unfortunately, surprisingly cumbersome techniques may have to be used and so simple solutions for the implementation of this important idea are hard to find. In some languages, the support for separate compilation results in a significant increase in compiler complexity. It is worth noting that, despite its age, FORTRAN handles the problem of separate compilation better than many other languages.

2.3   Data Access and Manipulation

The concept of 'data' is fundamental to most programming languages. Imperative programming languages use a sequence of statements to modify data values held in the computer's memory. Here, the concept of a variable can be considered to be an abstraction of the computer's memory locations. The facilities for data access and manipulation offered by a programming language have a great influence on the applicability of the language. In this section, we examine some of the facilities offered by high-level languages for data declaration, data structuring and data manipulation.

2.3.1   Variable declaration, typing and scope

Most programming languages allow names to be given to values used in computations. These names identify particular storage locations. Languages vary a great deal in the flexibility provided by this name-storage association mechanism. For example, in some languages it may be possible for a single name to refer to several different storage locations during the course of the execution of a program. Variable names may need to be explicitly declared and the declaration will explicitly or implicitly associate some attributes with that name. Many languages allow the type of a variable to be specified, indicating the nature of the data that can be stored in its corresponding memory location and also implicitly defining a range of permissible operations on that variable.

The advantage of the explicit declaration of all variables is that the programmer can keep track of variables more easily – misspelled variable names can be detected by the compiler. The main benefit of the typing of variables is the potential for an increased degree of checking at compile and/or run time. In languages like Pascal, the typing is very strict (but there are loopholes!). Every variable is associated with a single type, such as *integer*, *char*, *Boolean*, **array** or **record**, and the compiler ensures that all operations carried out on each of the variables cannot violate the rules associated with the corresponding type; for example, an assignment of the constant value 2 to a variable of type *Boolean* is flagged as an error by the compiler. However, some languages, such as BCPL, manipulate values with no regard for type. Although variables still have to be explicitly declared, no type information is recorded and it is up to the programmer to keep track of the nature of the data referred to by each variable name. The consequential absence of type checking permits conciseness and flexibility, but at the expense of rapid error detection. For example, the compiler does not consider the multiplication of a Boolean value by an integer value to be an error. Although typed and typeless languages have both distinct advantages and disadvantages, the superiority of one approach over the other seems to be largely a matter of personal preference and prejudice, as well as being governed by the nature of the application.

Most of today's commonly used languages are statically typed; that is, the type, if any, of each variable is known at compile time, thereby enabling type checking to be carried out during compilation. APL is an example of a language that supports dynamic typing. In this case, the type of a variable name is determined by how it is used in the program and the type can be changed freely throughout the execution of the program. As type checking has to be done at run time in these languages, run-time efficiency may suffer.

Languages may support automatic **type coercion**; that is, an implied conversion of type depending on the context of the value. For example, Pascal supports the coercion of integer values to real values in some contexts, such as in:

$$x := x + 2$$

where the variable x is declared with type *real*. Here, the integer value 2 is automatically converted to the real value 2.0 before the addition is performed. Type coercion is discussed in Section 6.4 which describes the semantic analysis phase of a compiler.

Another important issue in programming language design concerns the scope of names. The **scope** of a variable is the part of the program during which that particular variable may be accessed. In some languages, the scope rules are very simple and all names have global scope; that is, a name declared within a program can be referred to throughout the program. In other languages, such as those following the ALGOL block-structured tradition, the scope of names may be much more limited. For example, in ALGOL 60, the scope of a variable name is local to the block in which it is declared. Limiting the scope of names in a program has a major benefit in that it allows a much more local view of program development to be taken. For example, names can be used in one section of the program without clashing with names already declared in another section.

A related concept is that of extent. The **extent** of a variable is the time during which the storage associated with that variable is bound to the name of that variable. In other words, it is the time during which the variable has a 'physical' representation.

In the traditional block-structured languages, blocks may be nested. For example, in the block nesting shown in Figure 2.1, the conventional scope rules state that the names declared in block A are accessible within block A and the names declared within block B are accessible within block B (and not within block A). In many languages, the scope rules are extended so that the variables declared in block A are also accessible in block B. This idea of **static scoping** can be generalized by stating that the names in scope in a block consist of those names declared locally within that block together with all those defined in enclosing blocks. However, this general rule has to be qualified slightly: if a name is declared locally in a block and the same name is declared in an enclosing block, then the locally defined name has precedence. In this case, the declaration of the name in the enclosing block is hidden within the local block. To illustrate this, consider the following ALGOL 60 example:

```
begin
  real x, y;
  .
  .
  .
  begin
    integer y, z;
    .
    .
    .
  end;
  .
  .
  .
end
```

In the outer block, there are two **real** variables in scope (x and y). In the inner block, the two local **integer** variables y and z are in scope, but the non-local **real** variable x is also accessible. The **real** variable y is not in

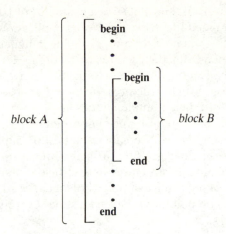

FIGURE 2.1

Example of block nesting.

scope in the inner block, so any reference to the name *y* in the inner block refers to the locally defined variable.

Variables that are not declared within the current block but are declared in an enclosing block are called **free variables**. In some languages, the use of free variables may be restricted to simplify implementation or to improve run-time efficiency. In other languages, such as APL, a technique known as **dynamic scoping** is used. Here, if a name is not declared in the local block, then other blocks are searched for the declaration of that name in the reverse order to which the blocks were invoked. So, in this case, if a name is not found locally, then the first block to be examined for the appropriate declaration is the block that caused the invocation of the current block. Dynamic scoping tends to be used by interpreted languages whereas compiled languages tend to favour static scoping.

A **stack** is the natural choice for the management of run-time storage in a block-structured language. As a block is entered, space for local variables is reserved at the top of the stack. As the block is left, this space is freed. The mechanisms that can be used for variable access, and procedure call and return are described in Chapter 7.

2.3.2 Data structuring

Nearly all high-level languages support data structures more complex than single values. In a sense, data structuring is just as important as program structuring, so the provision of facilities for the straightforward definition of data structures is highly desirable. Most common languages support arrays, sometimes with restrictions on the number of subscripts or the ranges of each subscript value. A very frequently used data structure is the character string. In some languages, the support for character strings is very limited, but built-in support for the manipulation of this data type can be very useful. SNOBOL and ICON are examples of languages that have been expressly designed for string-processing applications.

An increasing number of programming languages support some form of programmer-defined structures or records. Here, a structure can be defined as a collection of simpler objects. There are many benefits arising from the use of such structures, including improved documentation and the potential for efficient implementation.

Linked structures are also very important, the simplest example of such a structure being the list. Languages like LISP can be used to manipulate lists with ease. Languages supporting pointers can be used to manipulate more complex linked structures in an efficient manner, but to retain complete type checking – for example, in languages such as Pascal – the operations allowed on pointer variables must be severely limited.

EXAMPLE

The following fragments illustrate some of the data structures supported by Pascal:

Array

      type *vector* = **array** [1..10] **of** *integer*;

Character string

      type *cstring* = **packed array** [1..20] **of** *char*;

Record

      type *person* = **record**
          age : 0..120;
          sex : (*male*, *female*);
          name : *cstring*
      end;

Linked structures

      type *link* = ↑ *node*;
          node = **record**
          data : *integer*;
          next : *link*
      end;

Table 2.1 Precedence of Pascal operators (operators on the same line have the same precedence).

highest precedence	
	not
	* / **div** **mod** **and**
	+ − **or**
	= <> < <= > >= **in**
lowest precedence	

2.3.3 Operators

A programming language must provide a comprehensive set of operators that are capable of acting on values of all types provided by the language. Different data types require different operators, but some operators may be used for several data types.

All the commonly used programming languages support the conventional set of arithmetic operators, taken from the notation of algebra. The usual representations are $+, -, *, /$ and $\uparrow$ or $**$ (raising to a power). There are several important considerations behind the apparently simple use of arithmetic operators. Firstly, to write involved arithmetic (and other) expressions, some method must be available for directing the order of evaluation of the expression. Most languages, therefore, support the use of brackets, again interpreted in the conventional algebraic manner. Secondly, to make the notation used for expressions in programming languages even closer to that used in algebra, the idea of operator **precedence** is introduced. For example, the multiplication operator (*) is normally given greater precedence than the addition operator (+). So, in the expression $a + b * c$, the multiplication is carried out before the addition and the expression has the expected value of $a + (b * c)$. Needless to say, precedence rules vary slightly from one language to another, but fortunately brackets can nearly always be used if in any doubt. In fact, the precedence rules for the arithmetic operators are fairly similar between languages, but there are many inconsistencies in the treatment of relational operators. For example, the interpretation of the Boolean expression:

$a > b$ **and** $c > d$

depends on the relative precedence of the **and** and > operators. As an example, the relative precedences of the Pascal operators are shown in Table 2.1

A related consideration is the **associativity** of operators; that is, whether the expression $x + y + z$ should be evaluated as $(x + y) + z$ or as $x + (y + z)$. Often, in practice, this would be of no concern, since the final result would be the same no matter how the operator associated. But there are important cases where it does matter, such as in the expression

$x \uparrow y \uparrow z$ where the two possible results $(x \uparrow y) \uparrow z$ and $x \uparrow (y \uparrow z)$ are in general not the same. For most operators, left associativity is usually chosen – that is, the interpretation $(x \uparrow y) \uparrow z$ – but sometimes the exponentiation operator is made right-associative. We will return to the implications of operator precedence and associativity in later chapters.

At this point, it is appropriate to briefly mention the laws of commutativity (as in $x + y = y + x$) and distributivity (as in $x * (a + b) = x * a + x * b$). In some circumstances, the application of these rules at a comparatively late stage in the compilation process can result in somewhat more efficient code. The extent to which these rules can be applied in practice is discussed in Section 7.3.2.

As programming languages allow the manipulation of many other data types, additional operators are required. For example, the combination of Boolean values in Pascal can be achieved by using the operators **and**, **or** and **not**, while the operators $<, >, =, <=, >=$ and $<>$ can be used to derive a Boolean value from other types, such as *integer*, *real* and *char*.

Some operators can be used in different contexts to give quite different meanings. A simple example of this is the use of the $+$ and $-$ operators as both unary and binary operators. Unary operators only operate on one argument, as in the expressions $+a$ and $-a$, while binary operators have two arguments, as in $a + b$ and $a - b$. There are many other examples of different interpretations being required depending on the context of the use of the operator. In some languages, the $+$ operator can also be used to represent string concatenation, while others even allow the use of the usual arithmetic operators for the manipulation of pointer (address) values. The following more complex Pascal example illustrates how the $+$ operator can be used to represent two completely different computer operations.

EXAMPLE

Suppose that i, j and k are declared as integer variables and x, y and z are declared as real variables. Then the following assignments are valid:

```
k := i + j;
z := x + y
```

In the first statement, the $+$ operator is used to represent integer addition; in the second statement, it represents real (floating-point) addition.

This technique of allowing a construct to have different meanings depending on its context is called **overloading**. The operators are termed **polymorphic** because their effects depend on the types of their operands.

The example just given can be used to show yet another important use of the + operator in Pascal; that is:

$$z := x + i$$

Here, the + operator is used to sum a real value and an integer value. However, according to the rules of Pascal, an automatic type coercion must also take place; that is, the value i must be automatically converted to a real value before being added to x and stored in z. In contrast, the Pascal compiler should flag statements such as:

$$i := x + j$$

as being incorrect, since the sum of a real and an integer value yields a real value, and a real value cannot be coerced automatically to an integer.

Languages vary greatly in their support for operator overloading and 'mixed-mode' arithmetic, where operators can be used with operands of mixed types. For example, the + operator in ALGOL 68 can be used to add integers and reals, as well as for various types of string concatenation. Therefore, it is the responsibility of the compiler writer to ensure that the correct machine code is chosen from a large number of possibilities, depending on the types of the operator's operands.

Further complexities are introduced in languages where the type of the result of an operation not only depends on the type of the operands but also on their values. This can cause severe difficulties in type checking. For example, the ALGOL 60 report states that if i and j are integer variables (i non-zero), then $i \uparrow j$ has type **integer** if j is zero or positive and type **real** if j is negative.

2.4 Control Structures and Executable Statements

As well as providing facilities for the representation, structuring and manipulation of data values, programming languages should permit the structuring of executable statements. Control structures define the sequence in which statements are executed and the set of control structures offered by a language has a great impact on the ease with which readable and maintainable software can be written. For example, the long-standing debate concerning the use of the **goto** statement and its effect on program readability has had a considerable influence on the attitudes people have towards programming languages.

2.4.1 Range of executable statements

The range of statement types provided by a language designer obviously affects its ease of use. Exactly which statement types should and should not be provided is of course largely a matter of personal preference. Many languages provide compound statements such as the **begin**...**end** bracketing facility of Pascal and ALGOL 60; a much simpler example is the IF statement of FORTRAN. These compound statements may influence the scope of names; in other words, names declared within a compound statement or block may not be accessible from outside that block. There is also an enormous variation between languages in the syntax of statements used for controlling the sequence of execution of programs.

A related consideration is the technique used by the language to separate statements. In some cases, only one statement per line is allowed; in others, a special character is chosen to delimit or separate statements. The semicolon has been widely adopted for this purpose and is used as a statement delimiter in languages such as C, but as a statement separator in languages such as Pascal.

EXAMPLE

The Pascal compound statement:

```
begin
    a := 1;
    b := 2
end
```

is translated into C as:

```
{ a = 1;
    b = 2;
}
```

The second semicolon in the C program fragment is introduced to terminate the second assignment statement.

2.4.2   Extensibility

The idea of extensibility is very attractive. A simple base language can be implemented and then the programmer can define a special set of data types, operators and other constructs in terms of the base language facilities so that complex data manipulation may be expressed more clearly. Indeed, the language implementor can provide a set of standard definition files to supply 'standard' environments for various application areas. A widely quoted example of extensibility is the provision of a data type for representing complex numbers. The definition of a complex data type containing two numbers, a real and an imaginary part, is within the scope of many languages. However, comparatively few languages allow the construction of expressions containing complex numbers using the standard operators +, −, * and / while retaining the use of these operators with their original scalar operands.

ALGOL 68 is a good example of an extensible language. Ada is a more recent example.

2.4.3   Concurrency

A comparatively recent development of high-level languages is the incorporation of facilities to support concurrent (or parallel) processes. This requirement has arisen as a direct result of the availability of multi-programming operating systems and multiprocessor computer systems, where several processes may appear to be or may actually be executing simultaneously. Some aspects of concurrency are based on the earlier ideas of **exception handling** offered by languages such as PL/I. A programmer can flag a particular piece of code as an exception handler so that it is entered automatically when an unexpected event occurs in the execution of the program. This exception handler can then act on the event in a programmer-specified way. For example, an exception handler may be called whenever a division by zero is executed anywhere within the program. Without an exception handler, this fault may cause the program to be terminated by the language system or operating system.

A concurrent programming language should ideally offer several special facilities:

- It should allow the programmer to split up the program into separate modules or processes, which are the entities that are scheduled for concurrent execution. In some cases, this decomposition may be carried out automatically.

- The language should also offer facilities for **inter-process communication** and **process synchronization**. The communication mechanism allows asynchronous processes to pass data to one another, possibly by the use of globally shared variables. Synchronization is also essential, as particular orderings may need to be imposed on process executions. There are many methods available for achieving these requirements, but specific examples are left for Chapter 3, where individual languages are described.

Concurrency is an important issue in programming language design. Not only does it give the potential for efficient program implementations, particularly on multiprocessor hardware, but it also offers a natural way for expressing the solution to certain problems. Perhaps the most important and obvious example of its use is for the writing of an operating system: a large program dealing with asynchronous events, requiring careful attention to process synchronization and communication, and which can be usefully structured as a collection of communicating processes. The implementation of concurrency poses special problems and it is an area where the compiler writer must be well aware of the facilities offered by the operating system.

2.5   Language Implementation and Debugging

The characteristics of a language's implementation, as well as its design, affect a user's view of a programming language. An important aspect of the implementation is the efficiency of the language, both at compile time and at run time. Yet another concern of the implementation is the means for communicating with the environment. For example, it may take the form of a dialogue between the running program and a user at a terminal. Without such interaction, a running program can have no external effect. Most languages specify the methods by which this communication can take place, but the actual implementation of these facilities is clearly both language and operating system specific. Finally, a related consideration is the provision of debugging facilities. Debugging facilities may be provided by the operating system and thus may be language independent. Also, the language itself may be designed to ease the problems of debugging. Language implementations in which program debugging is difficult are unlikely to be popular.

2.5.1   Efficiency

When a language is structured in such a way that efficient code can only be generated for a special class of computer architectures, the use of the language on other architectures can result in significant overheads. Indeed, the desire to provide efficient implementations of a wide range of languages on a single system has promoted the development of reduced instruction set computer (RISC) architectures. In contrast to complex instruction set computer (CISC) architectures, which tend to favour a fairly small group of language implementations, the RISC approach implements a fast and simple set of instructions that is of potential use to all language implementations (see Chapter 8).

Some languages inherently require a great deal of work to be done during compilation, perhaps requiring the compiler to make several passes over the source text. The choice as to whether a compiler is structured as single pass or multi-pass is influenced by the design of the source language. In languages where names can be used before they are declared, such as in ALGOL 68, a compiler with at least two passes is normally used. One of the tasks for the first pass is to accumulate information on all the name definitions in the program; the second pass then generates the target code. In Pascal, on the other hand, names have to be declared before they are used; so, one-pass compilation is possible. The nature of the interface between the passes has a great effect on the speed of compilation. If the interface is via some form of secondary storage, as is quite common, then one pass has to write an intermediate file which is read by the subsequent pass. If the interface is managed solely via primary memory data structures, then there is comparatively little overhead in splitting a compiler up into multiple passes. Other factors such as the availability of primary memory may also force a compiler to be split up into several passes – the code and data for only one of the passes need be present in memory at any one time. For example, one of the early FORTRAN compilers ran in a minute amount of primary memory (by today's standards) together with drum storage by using 13 passes!

2.5.2   Interaction with the environment

At some stage, most programs will want to carry out some form of input or output or perform some other function controlled by the computer's operating system. Achieving complete computer and operating system independence in the definition of these language aspects can be quite difficult. Avoiding the problem by not specifying any input or output operations, as was done in the case of the original definition of ALGOL 60, is not entirely satisfactory!

Some work has been carried out recently on the preparation of standards for operating system interfaces with the intention of making this widespread problem of communication with the environment somewhat less serious. However, this is still an area that can cause significant implementation incompatibilities, resulting in even more problems for the programmer when moving a program, even when written in a 'portable' language, from one computer system to another.

2.5.3 Debugging

It is an unusual but happy event when a program typed into the computer works first time. Even the simplest of programs usually needs attention to remove errors. As the time spent debugging can far exceed the time spent writing the first version of the program, any aids offered by the computer system to reduce debugging time are most welcome.

We have already seen that the debugging problem can usually be simplified by abandoning the use of low-level languages and using high-level languages instead. However, this has not always been the case, as early high-level language systems tended to be poor at error detection and recovery. For example, an unexpected error in a running program would produce a voluminous hexadecimal memory dump, requiring considerable patience, skill and luck in its interpretation. Furthermore, it would require a knowledge of machine language (and probably something about the internal working of the compiler), which is precisely what the programmer is trying to avoid by using a high-level language. Fortunately, the diagnostic facilities provided nowadays tend to be much more friendly. Packages that allow debugging at the source code level are now widely used.

Some program errors can be detected by the compiler. For example, errors in the program's syntax can (and should) be reported by the compiler. Other errors – for example, an attempted division by zero – may occur at a later stage when the program is running; such errors are known as **run-time errors**. The sooner an error is detected the better; thus, the greater the proportion of errors detected at compile time the better. This is where the design of a language becomes significant and, as we have seen, languages that support extensive compile-time checking are more likely to result in correct running programs. Language design may also assist run-time debugging. The compiler may be able to insert code into the object program to perform run-time checking for values in range, array subscript violations and so on. For example, Pascal supports subrange types such as:

> **var** x : 1..9;

Any assignment to x of a value outside the range 1 to 9 will cause this checking code, inserted by the compiler, to report an error. This declaration of x is safer than the alternative:

> **var** x : *integer*;

if it is known that the values taken by x should never be outside the range 1 to 9. Ideally, it should be possible to cause the compiler to turn off the generation of run-time debugging code when speed of execution is crucial.

Some languages allow the easy insertion of temporary debugging statements. For example, it is a trivial matter to insert PRINT statements in a BASIC program while debugging to display the values of selected variables at critical points in the program.

Good language design is only part of the debugging story. The design and facilities of the compiler and the run-time support software, as well as the nature of the underlying hardware, are all very important. Furthermore, special program design and debugging packages can assist in the production of reliable software.

2.6   Readability and Writability

There are many factors that influence the ease with which programs may be written and subsequently maintained. The assessment of many of these factors is, of course, highly subjective. However, such factors should not be ignored. These subjective factors imply that, even for a specific application area, there cannot be a 'best' programming language. In this section, we look at some of these subjective factors, in addition to some other more concrete aspects of programming languages that influence readability and writability.

2.6.1   Correct programs

Languages should be designed so that it is easy to write correct and reliable software. There are an increasing number of applications where software failure can result in major disaster, so the use of languages that minimize the risk of such failures is strongly advisable. Languages should be designed so that errors can be eliminated at the earliest stage possible. Unfortunately, many of today's commonly used programming languages do not support the early elimination of errors particularly well. For example, a notable deficiency in FORTRAN is that variables need not be declared explicitly and there is an automatic implicit declaration the first time a variable is used. Thus, the compiler rarely detects any misspelled variable names in a program, the consequences of which are that the resulting code may exhibit unexpected effects when run and the program may be very difficult to debug. It is interesting to note that some of the strong supporters of FORTRAN maintain that the non-mandatory declaration of variables is a positive advantage! A simple solution to this problem, but one that is not often adopted, is to cause the compiler to output a warning message whenever a new variable is implicitly declared. Comparatively simple language deficiencies such as this are surprisingly common. In general, low-level languages do not score well, as only minimal automatic checking of the program is carried out. But there is a real danger that increased compile-time checking may reduce the power and flexibility of the language. As strict type checking is not appropriate in all circumstances, a language should, ideally, support a clean mechanism for relaxing the rules at the required points within a program.

A related consideration is whether a language allows, or indeed encourages, the writing of 'obscure' programs. Of course, no matter how hard a language tries to support well-structured and readable programs, a truly determined programmer can always succeed in writing programs that another programmer would find virtually impossible to understand. Most modern high-level languages make use of **reserved words**; that is, words having a special meaning to the language and which cannot be used for other purposes, such as identifiers. But some languages such as FORTRAN and PL/I allow variable names to be identical to language keywords. So, for example, the FORTRAN statement:

```
IF (IF(1)) 5, 6, 7
```

is syntactically correct, with the second IF representing the name of an array of type LOGICAL. FORTRAN also allows space characters to be inserted freely in most contexts. So the statement:

```
DO 10 I = 1.5
```

which looks remarkably like the start of a DO loop (a full stop replacing a comma) is in fact a simple (and legal) assignment statement! A similar line of code was the cause of the failure of a major American space mission. This simple single-character typing error cannot reasonably be detected by the compiler because of the design of the language. The message is therefore that a language should actively support the straightforward construction of readable and correct programs.

2.6.2 Complexity

It is possible to make comparisons between languages based on some informal measure of their 'complexity'. A language could be considered to be complex if it had a long and involved definition, a large number of different statement types, syntax and semantic rules that are difficult to understand or remember, and so on. Some high-level languages are comparatively simple. For example, Pascal only supports a handful of different statement types and its formal definition is comparatively short. Languages such as ALGOL 68 are much more complex, having much more involved rules of syntax and semantics. Simple languages tend to be easy to learn, their compilers (or, more generally, their implementations) can be comparatively small and hence they can be used on small machines. Larger languages are usually intended to be more powerful, with a wider application area.

2.6.3 Portability

The design of a language can have a great effect on the ease with which programs written in that language can be moved from machine to machine.

For example, if a language always assumes a specified number of digits of numerical accuracy, specific methods of data representation, a large address space or any other hardware-based characteristic, machine independence may suffer. The particular character set required to write programs in the language may be large or in some way special, and may cause problems on machines with restricted character sets. Therefore, great care must be taken to ensure that the language definition is at least capable of being implemented on a wide range of machines. The definition must also leave no room for different interpretations, as this results in language implementation incompatibilities.

     If a compiler is written in a transportable manner, then the language it compiles becomes a transportable language. We will return to this important topic when describing techniques of compiler implementation in Chapter 8.

2.6.4 Orthogonality

Orthogonality implies the support of a comparatively small set of basic facilities that can be combined in a logical manner to form more complex and powerful facilities. Lack of orthogonality may result in complex syntax rules, which can lead to difficulties in language learning and understanding. Consequently, orthogonality is an important aspect of programming language design. An example of orthogonality is that in ALGOL 68 there are no restrictions on the data types of the parameters or results of subprograms. This contrasts with Pascal where, for example, functions can only return simple data types.

     Orthogonality can cause implementation difficulties. The complexity of ALGOL 68 compilers is attributable to a large extent to ALGOL 68's orthogonality.

2.6.5 Layout rules

Some languages have very strict layout rules. For example, FORTRAN is strongly oriented towards the 80-column punched card with fixed-length fields each having specific functions, but within each field, spaces are in general ignored. There is also the limitation of one statement per record. In more recent languages, input format is much less constrained. Several statements may appear on each input line (assuming that they are separated or delimited correctly) and layout characters (spaces, tabs and newlines) are usually ignored by the compiler. In the case of occam, the layout characters are not ignored as the layout defines the structure and meaning of a program. Care taken over input layout using blank lines and indentation to reflect the program's structure can greatly assist with readability.

2.6.6 Comments

Ideally, it should be possible to insert comments freely in the source text. FORTRAN only allows complete lines of comments, whereas many assembly languages permit comments to appear on the same lines as statements, but separated from the main part of the statement by a special character. Pascal and other languages support comment 'brackets' which allow comments to be inserted much more freely; they can even appear within a statement or span several lines.

SUMMARY

- Languages can be broadly classified into imperative, functional or logic programming groups. It is also possible to classify languages as being procedural or declarative.

- The formal definition is a very important part of a programming language.

- The usability of a language is greatly influenced by the facilities available for subdividing programs into blocks, packages, procedures and so on, and the methods for passing parameters to and from subprograms.

- Programming languages must support the flexible management of data. What are the rules concerning declarations, type checking, scope and extent? Does the language offer support for structures more complex than single values? Programming languages must also support an appropriate set of operations for the manipulation of data values.

- The programming language must be able to specify actions to be carried out on data and it must also support mechanisms for the control and sequencing of these actions.

- The implementation of a high-level language can affect its use. In particular, a language may support facilities that make debugging especially easy or difficult.

- There are many other characteristics that can affect a language's readability and writability. These factors may also affect the language's suitability for a particular application and also for a particular programmer.

EXERCISES

2.1 When might it be important to know whether a compiler evaluated $x + y + z$ as $(x + y) + z$ or as $x + (y + z)$?

2.2 Write a procedure that has different effects depending on whether the parameters are passed by reference or by value-result.

2.3 What are the advantages offered by strong typing? Suggest some situations where strong typing can be a hindrance and show how strongly typed languages can be persuaded to be a little more lenient.

2.4 Explain carefully why many modern programming languages provide facilities for the encapsulation of a data structure with the code required for its manipulation. Look at the Ada package mechanism and justify the inclusion of the facilities Ada actually offers.

2.5 What facilities should be offered by a systems programming language? If you had to write an operating system, which existing language would you choose, and why?

2.6 Should implementations of programming languages supporting concurrency be confined to multiprocessor computer systems? What are the advantages and disadvantages of these languages on a single processor system?

2.7 Why does Standard Pascal not include facilities for exception handling? Devise a coherent extension to Pascal to support such facilities and consider how they could be implemented on your computer system.

2.8 List the features required for a language to support a large programming project. What particular demands are made when there are many programmers working on the same project?

2.9 Discuss the issues involved when comparing the efficiency of two programming languages.

2.10 Produce a set of guidelines for writing portable software.

CHAPTER 3

A Survey of High-Level Languages

The preceding chapters have presented material of a general nature about programming languages. They have contrasted the differences between low-level and high-level languages and have presented a set of criteria by which languages can be examined and compared. The time has now come for a more concrete study of a wide range of high-level languages, all of which are in use today. Languages are described in this chapter if they are popular or if they incorporate features of special technical interest. Each language is described in the context of the criteria presented in Chapter 2. As space is limited, the list of languages cannot be exhaustive and neither can the information presented for each language be very detailed. Where appropriate, references to fuller descriptions are given.

To give the chapter some sort of structure, the languages are divided into four groups: imperative, functional, logic programming and others. This is the classification introduced in Chapter 2. Within each group, further subdivisions are made according to groups of languages that share similar characteristics or parentage. Within each of these groups, languages appear in approximate chronological order. As there are no fixed rules for determining to which of the four groups a particular language belongs, there may well be good reasons for including languages in different or several categories. A complete family tree of the languages presented in this chapter is given in Figure 3.1. The arrows in this diagram indicate the flow of ideas, rather than the passage of time or the incorporation of new ideas.

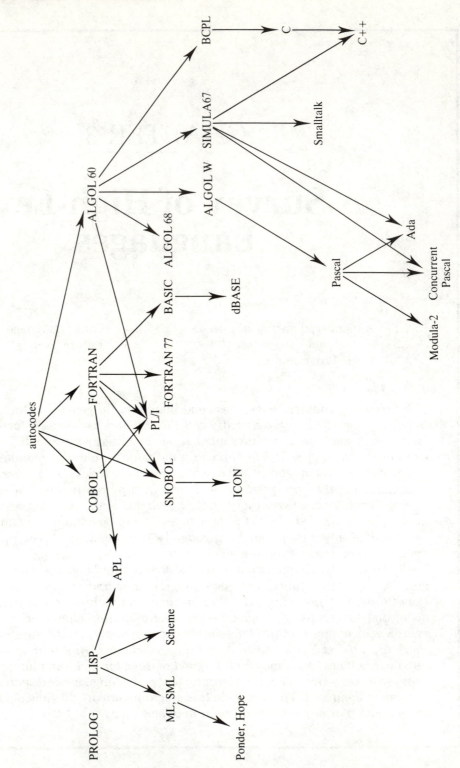

FIGURE 3.1

Family tree of
high-level
languages.

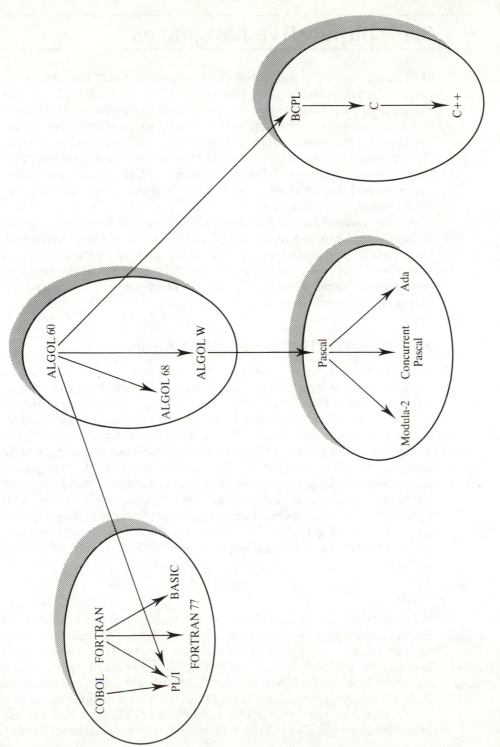

FIGURE 3.2

Family tree of imperative languages.

3.1   Imperative Languages

Most of the languages considered in this chapter fall into the imperative category. A family tree of these languages is shown in Figure 3.2. As well as indicating the passage of time, the arrows indicate the existing languages that have had the most influence on the design of new languages. Note, however, that the location of these arrows is a subjective decision! Even in this simplified diagram, it can be seen that there are complex interrelationships between the designs of different languages. However, as shown in the figure, several distinct clusters can be identified and these form the basis for the subdivision of this section.

The early phases of high-level language development were almost exclusively concerned with the design and implementation of imperative languages. These languages are based on the idea of a program being a sequence of imperative statements. This model is reflected by the design of conventional computer hardware where the processor executes a sequence of 'imperative' instructions.

3.1.1   The FORTRAN and COBOL family

FORTRAN was an early development from the simple autocodes and was one of the earliest high-level languages. Its original definition has changed little in becoming the dialects in use today. The development of COBOL, several years later, was prompted by the need for a language that could be used for business applications. COBOL has comparatively few clear similarities with FORTRAN, which was designed for numerical and scientific computations. PL/I has COBOL, FORTRAN and ALGOL 60 as predecessors and was designed in the hope of incorporating the best features of all three languages. BASIC shares many features in common with FORTRAN and was designed as a simple interactive programming language. Finally, FORTRAN 77 is a product of the continuing development of FORTRAN, incorporating some of the ALGOL family structuring facilities.

FORTRAN

With the advent of the IBM 704 computer, a small group headed by John Backus started work on a new programming language for this system. By the end of 1954, a preliminary specification for the 'IBM Mathematical Formula TRANslating System, FORTRAN' was produced and by 1957 a FORTRAN implementation for the IBM 704 was made available. A significant language revision called FORTRAN II was implemented in 1958 and it was soon after this that FORTRAN III appeared for use primarily within IBM. FORTRAN IV appeared a few years later. Largely because of FORTRAN's fast rise in popularity, the American Standards Association (ASA) commenced standardization work in 1962 and approved two FORTRAN standards in 1966 – ASA FORTRAN and a subset of ASA FORTRAN called ASA BASIC FORTRAN. ASA FORTRAN became a standard on which many implementations were based. (The characteristics of this version are described below.) This standard was published by the US Standards Institute [USASI, 1966], the successor to the ASA and the predecessor of ANSI.

FORTRAN was designed primarily for the solution of problems involving numerical computation. It is an imperative and procedural language. FORTRAN includes a wide range of operators and predefined functions for the manipulation of numerical values. The algebraic expressions used to manipulate these values are written in the conventional infix form. Each statement can be preceded by a unique numerical label and the sequential flow of execution can be altered by the use of the GOTO statement (followed by a label). FORTRAN supports various data types, including REAL and INTEGER. Variables can be explicitly declared and given a type, but if the declaration is omitted, an implicit declaration is assumed the first time the variable is used. In this case, the type of the variable (REAL or INTEGER) is determined by the initial letter of its name. Arrays are also supported.

A FORTRAN program can include user-defined subprograms. Both subroutines and functions can be defined and parameters are passed by reference. Separate compilation of subprograms is permitted, but it is the programmer's responsibility to manage shared data areas. In default, the scope of all variables is assumed to be local to the subprogram (or main program) in which they are used.

FORTRAN offers a variety of input and output statements. A complex FORMAT statement can be used in conjunction with the READ and WRITE statements to control the format in which data is read or written. Such facilities are excellent for the production of most forms of tabulated output, but input and output in less constricted formats is not quite so easy.

The source program layout rules are strict, being based on the 80-column punched card. Program lines are divided into a set of fixed fields: 5 columns for a statement label, 1 to indicate a continuation statement, 66 columns for the statement itself and 8 columns for optional identification information. A statement is treated as a comment if it starts with a C in column 1.

The FORTRAN standard [USASI, 1966] uses English prose to define the language, rather than a special formalized metalanguage. Although this has the distinct advantage that it makes the document readable by anyone having only a basic understanding of computer programming, such an informal presentation does lead to the introduction of errors and ambiguities. However, it should be said that these errors were minor, which indicates the great care with which the standard was prepared.

One of the stated intentions in producing the standard was to simplify the problem of transferring FORTRAN programs from machine to machine. This concern for portability was highly commendable but, to some extent, was negated by another intention stated in the standard; that is, that a 'minimal' language should be accepted by all standard FORTRAN systems. Thus, the implementor of a FORTRAN system was free to add extensions as long as their introduction did not conflict with the published standard. The consequent proliferation of different (and incompatible) sets of extensions has caused many problems in transporting FORTRAN programs.

One of the aims of FORTRAN was that it should be capable of efficient implementation. However, in trying to achieve this aim, many restrictions appeared in the language, such as in the allowable array subscript expressions, the form of the DO loop and the limitation to three-dimensional arrays. FORTRAN's static storage allocation scheme, which requires, among other things, that all array sizes should be known at compile time, is another consequence of this quest for efficiency. The hardware design of the IBM 704 processor also influenced the design of FORTRAN. For example, there is a very close correspondence between the branch instructions supported by the processor and the FORTRAN transfer of control statements. Partly as a result of these language restrictions, several high-quality compilers were soon available. The optimizations implemented by some of the earliest compilers are impressive even by today's standards.

The issue of FORTRAN's efficiency was widely discussed. It was often claimed that the object code produced by a FORTRAN compiler would be far less efficient than that produced by a low-level language programmer. But the advantages offered by FORTRAN and its subsequent revisions partly counteracted these efficiency considerations. It is interesting to note that this objection to high-level languages is still surprisingly widespread today, despite the availability of compilers producing highly optimized code.

More than 30 years have passed since FORTRAN was proposed and, given current knowledge, it is very easy to make criticisms. The poor character-handling facilities, the insecure methods for data sharing between subprograms, the lack of reserved words, some of the syntax restrictions, the absence of dynamic storage allocation, the strict layout rules and the dependence on the GOTO statement have all been used to condemn FORTRAN. Furthermore, the success of FORTRAN has encouraged its use in applications for which it is not particularly suited, resulting in some inappropriate criticism. Nevertheless, the enormous technical contributions made by the development of FORTRAN must not be forgotten. FORTRAN was rapidly accepted and is still in widespread use today. Although its acceptance was due partly to its support by IBM, its efficiency and ease of use were more influential. FORTRAN was indeed a remarkable software development.

COBOL

In 1959, a group coordinated by the US Department of Defense (DoD) designed, at great speed, the language COBOL (COmmon Business Oriented Language). This effort to produce a standard language suitable for business applications was well supported and compilers were soon produced. As usual, there was a long period of language modification and refinement, but eventually a standard COBOL was defined by ANSI in 1968. This standard was revised in 1974 [ANSI, 1974].

One of the design aims of COBOL was that programs should be readable by non-computer specialists. To achieve this, COBOL programs are expressed in terms of ordinary English words and sentences. Data-structuring facilities are provided to allow the hierarchical construction of data records. To ease the portability problem, all the machine-dependent aspects of the program are designed to appear in a single isolated section.

Program statements are expressed in a rather verbose manner, as illustrated by the following example:

```
ADD TAX TO SUPERANNUATION GIVING DEDUCTIONS.
```

Imperative statements contain a verb, such as ADD above, and appropriate operands. Statements can be grouped into sentences, sentences can be grouped into paragraphs and, similarly, paragraphs can be grouped into sections. The verb PERFORM can be followed by a paragraph or section name to achieve a subroutine call. Recursion is not permitted.

COBOL programs are divided into four divisions: the identification, environment, data and procedure divisions. The identification division contains a formal statement of the program's name, the author, the date and similar information. The environment division contains information about the computer on which the COBOL program is being compiled and run. The presence of the environment division is an attempt to recognize the problem of portability. As well as including the salient hardware features of the SOURCE-COMPUTER and OBJECT-COMPUTER, the programmer can specify the correspondence between data files in the program and real files or devices on the object computer. The data division defines the structure of the files to be used by the program. File formats, blocking factors and so on can be specified together with record structures. A hierarchical method is supplied for defining the fields within each record; each field can be named and given a size and data type. Alternative record structures can be specified, depending on the values in specified fields. These COBOL facilities for defining record and file structures are very powerful and contributed a great deal towards COBOL's popularity. Record-based input and output is generally well suited to the requirements of commercial data processing. The final division, the procedure division, contains the actual specification of the program steps – the executable statements.

Compared with more recently developed programming languages, the form and range of COBOL's executable statements is uninspired. In particular, the verbosity of expression and the consequent large number of words with 'special' meanings are easy to criticize. Indeed, modern COBOL compilers also support a more compact FORTRAN-style notation for the specification of some actions, giving two methods for the expression of certain concepts. It is debatable whether COBOL programs are inherently easy to understand by the uninitiated reader.

COBOL derives its strength from other aspects. The strict separation imposed by the four divisions was a major contribution to programming language development. The facilities offered by the data division are particularly important, serving the vital role of unambiguous machine-independent definition of record and file structures. Similarly, the environment division was a significant attempt to address the problems of compatibility and portability.

COBOL is a remarkably popular language and the majority of business applications are still being written in COBOL. Ever since its introduction, it has received enthusiastic support from computer manufacturers and the provision of COBOL compilers has been seen as a priority task. Indeed, some governments have specified in their computer procurement policies that support for COBOL is essential. To some extent, the continued popularity of COBOL is due to inertia; organizations who have a vast investment in COBOL software and expertise are reluctant to change to a different language due to the enormous costs involved. On the other hand, COBOL does offer considerable support for the business programmer and its popularity must be, to a large extent, attributed to its design.

PL/I

The history of PL/I is deeply rooted in the development of FORTRAN. In 1963, a committee was formed by IBM and its users' group to design a new language that would be of use in a wider application area than FORTRAN. In particular, it was noted that FORTRAN was sadly lacking in facilities for character handling. Initial aims of simply extending FORTRAN were soon abandoned in favour of a new language that incorporated ideas from ALGOL 60 and COBOL as well as FORTRAN. Several versions of this language, temporarily christened NPL (New Programming Language), were produced in 1964. NPL was subsequently renamed PL/I by IBM and a PL/I compiler for the IBM System/360 was released in 1966.

IBM's primary motivation in developing PL/I was to produce a language that would be as useful in as many programming applications as possible, including scientific, commercial and systems programming areas. Other design goals were as follows:

- There should be a high degree of machine independence to facilitate portability while, at the same time, allowing access to low-level machine and operating system services.

- There should be a 'default philosophy' so, for example, the programmer need not always code the full form of a statement; that is, default options are automatically assumed. One of the consequences of this approach is that novice programmers can use a subset of the language with the expansion to the full version of the language being performed automatically by the compiler.

An associated aim was that compilers should not reject programs that appeared sensible and unambiguous. Efficient implementations were also required.

Because of the desire to satisfy as many application areas as possible, PL/I has become a large and complicated language, incorporating a wide range of features. Many different types of executable statements are supported, including assignment, procedure call, the DO and DO WHILE statements for repetitive execution, GOTO, IF, input/output and dynamic storage allocation statements. It also offers great flexibility in data typing: arithmetic variables can be declared as decimal or binary, fixed or floating point and a precision may be specified. In addition, bit and character strings are supported, as well as 'picture' data for formatting strings and numbers. Standard operators are available for handling all these data types. Arrays and structured data can be used: the PL/I structure declaration defines hierarchically structured variables using a syntax reminiscent of the COBOL data division. Storage can be declared as static (the FORTRAN style) or automatic (as in ALGOL 60, where storage is allocated at the start of the block in which the declaration appears and is freed on block exit). Explicit dynamic storage allocation can be performed by the statements ALLOCATE and FREE. POINTER variables can be used to create complex data structures.

Statements may be grouped in BEGIN...END blocks or in procedures. Procedures can have multiple entry points and can be written as functions. Recursion is permitted.

Both stream and record-oriented input/output is supported by a large and complex set of PL/I statements. Concurrency facilities are present, allowing the execution of asynchronous tasks. Tasks may be suspended until some specified event occurs in the execution of another task, such as the reaching of a particular point in its code. Interrupt handling is managed by an ON statement, which allows the programmer to specify the action to be taken on the occurrence of a specified error or other event.

Soon after PL/I was introduced, many people claimed that it would replace languages like FORTRAN, COBOL and ALGOL 60 – see, for example, Sammet [1969, p. 542]. About 20 years later, it has become clear that this expectation is far from reality. PL/I certainly still is a fairly popular language, but its use is well shadowed by that of FORTRAN and COBOL. It is instructive to look at the reasons for PL/I's comparative lack of success. It is the set of design aims rather than the design that is primarily at fault. To fulfil the needs of a wide range of users, it was felt that a large number of 'facilities' were required. Thus, PL/I became a complex language with a large number of separate facilities, but with little internal consistency. To lessen the burden imposed by this complexity, the use of defaults was introduced. This has led to many problems where, for example, the default action is not quite what the programmer intended. Supplying default declarations for variables that have been used but not explicitly declared is no longer considered to be a safe action in a programming language. The desire for machine independence clashes with the requirement that PL/I should be useful for low-level systems programming applications. Not surprisingly, PL/I became rather oriented towards IBM hardware and operating systems, and although PL/I was implemented on other manufacturers' systems, there were always problems of portability. Reacting against PL/I's size, several subsets were defined, but they never achieved great popularity. Other approaches were required for languages with wide applicability.

BASIC

As a consequence of the proliferation of the microcomputer, BASIC is one of the most widely known programming languages in use today. It was actually designed well before the microcomputer era in 1965 by J. G. Kemeny and T. E. Kurtz at Dartmouth College as a simple interactive first programming language for students. An essential design aim was that it should be easy to use. This led to the production of 'integrated' BASIC systems containing a language interpreter, an editor and a run-time system. BASIC proved to be very popular and since it was comparatively easy to implement – the syntax of the language makes statement type identification particularly simple – numerous systems appeared. In 1978, ANSI produced a standard for 'minimal' BASIC.

BASIC does not have a rich syntactic structure. It contains a small set of executable statements together with a set of operators for handling numerical and character string data. As can be seen in the following example, each statement is given a number and program execution is normally in numerical statement order. Some statements, such as GOTO, can include a statement number to cause jumps in the flow of control. Arrays are supported.

EXAMPLE

```
10  S = 0.0
20  N = 1
30  S = S + 1.0/N
40  N = N + 1
50  IF S < 5 THEN 30
60  PRINT N
70  END
```

Functions and subroutines are available in BASIC. A subroutine is called by GOSUB followed by the line number of the entry point to the subroutine. Variables have global scope, even if they are only used within a subroutine.

BASIC has several important attractions. Because of the interactive nature of the language, development of simple programs, especially by the 'non-professional' programmer, can be very rapid. If the language is implemented as an interpretive system rather than being compiled, as is usually the case, it is easy to add, modify and delete statements or add debugging code without the effort and time penalty of recompilation. It is an easy language to learn and implement and is suited to many applications, especially in the numerical and scientific area. However, its lack of program-structuring facilities causes difficulties when writing large programs. Other restrictions, such as the fact that subroutines cannot be given meaningful alphanumeric names, may also result in rather obscure code.

BASIC has been given a new lease of life by the advent of the microcomputer. It was chosen as the standard language on these systems because of its ease of implementation on small computers and also because it is well suited to the needs of the new programming community of home computer owners. This proliferation of different BASIC systems has produced a large number of incompatible supersets of the language, with extensions being introduced to offer direct control of special hardware features of the microcomputer. Many of the more recent BASIC implementations incorporate structured statements with limited block structure, local variables and so on.

It is easy to condemn BASIC as a 'toy' language, but this is unfair. BASIC has been used with great success in many large software projects. Perhaps its greatest contribution is that it has introduced computer programming to such a large number of people in a comparatively painless manner.

FORTRAN 77

The development of FORTRAN did not stop with the publishing of the FORTRAN standard documents in 1966. The FORTRAN 66 standard (approximately corresponding to FORTRAN IV) was widely criticized and commented on and various documents were published clarifying aspects of the standard. After a while, however, it was felt that further revisions of the 1966 standard would not be worthwhile and efforts should be directed towards the production of a new version of FORTRAN. This version was called FORTRAN 77 and was approved by ANSI in 1978, at which time the 1966 standards were withdrawn.

Various major improvements were incorporated into the new language, but one of the design aims was that there should be upward compatibility with FORTRAN 66. This aim has been achieved with only a few inconsistencies and most FORTRAN 77 compilers have an option to force FORTRAN 66 compatibility. Among the features added were a character data type, various character-handling facilities, greatly enhanced input/output and symbolic constants. But perhaps more importantly, several new structured control statements, such as IF...THEN...ELSE and WHILE...DO, were added to remove the necessity for routine use of the GOTO statement.

EXAMPLE

The FORTRAN 66 statements:

```
        IF (B.NE.0.0) GOTO 10
        RATIO = 0.0
        GOTO 20
10      RATIO = A/B
20      ...
```

are more clearly expressed in FORTRAN 77 as:

```
        IF (B.EQ.0.0) THEN
          RATIO = 0.0
        ELSE
          RATIO = A/B
        ENDIF
```

As with FORTRAN 66, the FORTRAN 77 standard document [ANSI, 1978] is largely expressed in informal terms. However, it is a significantly larger document and contains syntax diagrams that formally define the syntax. It took several years after the release of the standard for FORTRAN 77 systems to become widely available, but because of the vast established base of FORTRAN programs and programmers, and because of the attractive enhancements, FORTRAN 77 is now being used widely. Many good compilers now exist and manufacturers' support is normally for FORTRAN 77 rather than for the obsolete standard. A FORTRAN standard for the 1980s and beyond is now under development.

3.1.2 The ALGOLs

FORTRAN was not the only influential language to be developed in the 1950s. The roots of the ALGOL family can also be traced to this decade and the characteristics of this family are still alive in many of the programming languages in use today.

The design of ALGOL 60 was influenced by FORTRAN. Both languages were designed for numerical scientific computation, but there were major differences, such as the incorporation in ALGOL 60 of the notions of block structure and type checking. Both ALGOL W and ALGOL 68 are close descendants of ALGOL 60 and are described in this section. However, ALGOL 60 also had a direct influence on the design of other languages, such as PL/I, Pascal and SIMULA67. These languages are described with their closer relations elsewhere.

ALGOL 60

In the mid 1950s, a group was set up to investigate the development of a portable, machine-independent programming language. Proposals passed through various international committees and a language known as IAL (International Algebraic Language) was produced [Perlis, 1958]. This language subsequently became known as ALGOL 58, the word ALGOL being derived from ALGOrithmic Language. It was never intended that ALGOL 58 should become a stable language standard and so a group met in 1960 to produce a new version of the language in the light of the comments and criticisms received. This version became known as ALGOL 60 and the report was published in 1960 [Naur, 1960]. There were only minor differences between ALGOL 58 and ALGOL 60. The ALGOL 60 revised report was published in 1963 [Naur, 1963].

Because of their largely coincident development periods, it is tempting to compare ALGOL 60 with FORTRAN. Despite problems with standardization and definition, FORTRAN rapidly acquired a large number of users. ALGOL 60, on the other hand, never enjoyed such widespread use, but it is undoubtedly one of the most significant developments in programming language history. ALGOL 60 introduced many of the fundamental programming structures on which today's languages are based. In particular, ALGOL 60 is a block-structured language, which is a basic design adopted for many subsequent languages. Furthermore, ALGOL 60's syntax was defined by the use of a formal notation, BNF, reducing the likelihood of errors or ambiguities in its specification.

Like FORTRAN, ALGOL 60 is a language primarily designed for numerical and scientific computation. However, unlike FORTRAN, ALGOL 60 introduced the idea of reserved words; that is, a set of words reserved for specific purposes in the language (see Section 2.6.1). The rules for building up arithmetic expressions are similar to those of FORTRAN, but ALGOL 60 also incorporates many facilities for manipulating numerical values. Statement types supported include conditionals (**if**...**then**...**else**), unconditional branches (**goto**) and repetitive execution (**for**, with or without **while**).

ALGOL 60 supports **real**, **integer** and **Boolean** data types. All variables must be explicitly declared. Arrays are also supported, but with fewer restrictions on the form of the array bounds than in FORTRAN. In particular, ALGOL 60 supports dynamic storage allocation; that is, the size of an array need not be known until run time. ALGOL 60 is a strongly typed language, which means that type compatibility can be checked at compile time. This type checking is very strict and there are few (accidental?) loopholes.

One of the most important aspects of ALGOL 60 is the way in which statements and control structures can be combined. This is the notion of orthogonality. It is possible to nest structures to produce more complex statements. For example, the statement:

> **for** $i := 1$ **step** 1 **until** 100 **do**
> **if** $a[i] > max$ **then** $max := a[i]$

combines a conditional within a repetitive **for** statement. It is also possible to group statements together in a compound statement by preceding the group with **begin** and following it with **end**. ALGOL 60 permits the use of such a compound statement just as if it were a single statement. For example:

> **for** $i := 1$ **step** 1 **until** 100 **do**
> **begin**
>   **if** $a[i] < 0$ **then** $a[i] := -a[i]$;
> $tot := tot + a[i]$
> **end**

In this case, the two statements enclosed by the **begin** and **end** are the target of the **for** statement. The ability to nest statements and to use compound statements greatly reduces the need for the **goto** statement. The use of the **goto** statement has been strongly criticized [Dijkstra, 1968a] as it can result in tortuous and unreadable programs. ALGOL 60 programs are therefore more likely to be readable and hence reliable and maintainable. A very similar structure to the compound statement is the block which has the form:

```
begin
    <declarations>; <statements>
end
```

In this example, the scope of variables declared at the start of the block is the entire body of the block and nowhere outside the block. Since a block is a valid statement, blocks can be nested indefinitely. ALGOL 60 adopts the static scope rules described in Chapter 2.

Functions and procedures are also supported. Their declarations are handled in a very similar way to ordinary variable declarations with the same name scoping rules applying so that their declarations can be nested. The body of a subprogram consists of a block. Functions and procedures can be called recursively and parameters can be passed by value or by name. Separate compilation of subprograms is not supported due to the difficulties in representing the enclosing environment in which the subprogram is declared.

The ALGOL 60 report defines no input or output statements. At the time the report was produced, there was very little standardization of input and output techniques; hence, it was felt that including any such statements in the definition would restrict the portability of the language. It was intended that each implementation of ALGOL 60 should include a set of library procedures to perform input and output in a form tailored to that particular computer system.

ALGOL 60 does not have strict layout rules: blank spaces are ignored, except when in character strings, and newlines are also generally ignored. This free-format input contrasts with the fixed format of FORTRAN. Comments can be introduced by the symbol **comment** and they may be inserted freely between other statements.

The ALGOL 60 revised report [Naur, 1963] is a concise and complete definition of the language. Comparatively few errors and omissions have been discovered in this document – such problems are discussed in Knuth [1967] and McGettrick [1980]. The concise definition reflects one of the design aims of ALGOL 60, which was that regularity should be maintained as far as possible; that is, rules should not have exceptions. To avoid problems of implementation dependence, the ALGOL 60 report took great care over the specification of lexical representations. At the time of the preparation of the report, there was little standardization of character sets, and there was considerable disagreement over the representation of ALGOL 60's symbols and punctuation. To avoid these difficulties, three levels of language were defined. The **reference language** is the one specified and used in the ALGOL 60 report. It uses a character set that is not limited by the computers of the time. The **publication language** is used for publishing ALGOL 60 algorithms using a free choice of typographical representations. The ALGOL 60 report does not specify a publication language, but does state that precise correspondence between a publication language and the reference language must be agreed. The **hardware representations** are also not specified by the ALGOL 60 report. It is left to the ALGOL 60 implementor to define a hardware representation and a correspondence between the hardware representation and the reference language. The form of each hardware representation depends to a large extent on the character set available. The penalty paid for this freedom is of course the difficulty in translating one hardware representation to another when moving an ALGOL 60 program from machine to machine. Depending on the hardware representation, words such as **begin**, **if**, **for** and **end** may become reserved words, thus preventing their use as variable names.

The ALGOL 60 report does far more than simply introduce a new high-level programming language. Its significance lies in the fact that it also presents a technique for the specification of the syntax of programming languages which goes a very long way towards removing the ambiguities inherent in using a natural language for this purpose. Indeed, one of the prime motivations in the design of ALGOL 60 was its use for the specification of algorithms. This contrasts with FORTRAN which was primarily designed as a high-level language initially intended for a single machine – the IBM 704.

ALGOL 60 has never been a widely used language despite its power, simplicity and excellent definition. Probably the main reason for this poor acceptance is the notable success of FORTRAN. Several computer manufacturers promoted FORTRAN rather than ALGOL 60 and FORTRAN's popularity encouraged even greater use. Also, FORTRAN was probably more aligned towards the early uses of computers. Fears of inefficiency were directed towards ALGOL 60 because of its block structure and dynamic storage allocation. Inefficiencies were also introduced because ALGOL 60 made efforts to abolish some of the arbitrary restrictions of FORTRAN, such as the allowable types for the control variable in a DO/**for** statement. Its lack of standard input/output facilities was strongly criticized. Furthermore, the great variation in input/output (I/O) implementations was certainly a drawback. Standards for input and output were eventually produced, but they came too late to make much of an impact on ALGOL 60's popularity.

ALGOL 60's success lies primarily in the revolutionary language constructs and implementation techniques that it introduced. The use of BNF in its definition was also a major milestone. The scoping rules of ALGOL 60 have been copied widely and have been found to be of great assistance when developing large programs; FORTRAN's scoping rules are much less powerful. ALGOL 60 has also had a great influence on the design of subsequent programming languages and to say nowadays that a language is ALGOL-like automatically confers a degree of respectability.

ALGOL W

ALGOL W is an early successor of ALGOL 60 and is in many senses midway between ALGOL 60 and ALGOL 68. Unlike ALGOL 60 and ALGOL 68, ALGOL W never achieved official approval from the International Federation for Information Processing (IFIP), as the committee felt that it did not represent a sufficient advance on its predecessor. The language described in the report [Wirth, 1966] attempted to remove some of the existing trouble spots in ALGOL 60 and to introduce some new features. As well as being useful in the traditional ALGOL 60 areas of numerical and scientific problems, it was hoped that the new facilities would encourage its use for non-numerical applications.

Because of ALGOL W's similarity to ALGOL 60, it is worthwhile examining some of the differences between the two languages. Several new primitive data types were introduced together with appropriate operators, allowing manipulation of values with new types COMPLEX, STRING and BITS (sequences of binary digits). LONG REAL and LONG COMPLEX types are also provided for extended precision calculations. A powerful data-structuring technique called the record was introduced. This allows the programmer to define and name new data types. A **record** is a structure consisting of one or more fields. It is similar to an array except that the fields need not be of the same type. These structures are created dynamically, unlike arrays which are created by declarations. A record class declaration defines the structure of a record: it defines the fields of the record by associating a name and a data type with each field. For example:

```
RECORD PERSON (STRING FORENAME;
               REAL HEIGHT;
               INTEGER AGE)
```

To use a record, a variable has to be declared of type REFERENCE, and the declaration should include an indication of the record class required. Assignment to these variables causes space to be allocated dynamically for the record. This implies that some form of dynamic storage allocation system is required to implement ALGOL W, preferably with some facility for storage reclamation, such as a garbage collector. The power of this record/reference mechanism is enhanced by the fact that fields of a record may be of type REFERENCE, and so dynamic structures such as linked lists and trees may be implemented with ease. Similar facilities have been adopted in many subsequent programming languages.

Several comparatively minor changes were made to some of the ALGOL 60 executable statements. For example, the **for** statement was greatly simplified, making it capable of somewhat more efficient implementation. This was achieved by specifying that the increment and limit expressions were to be evaluated once on entry to the loop and by disallowing assignments to the control variable within the loop.

Various changes were also made to procedures, especially to the specification of formal parameters. When a procedure is declared, its formal parameters can be designated as VALUE or RESULT (or both). This allows much greater flexibility in the parameter passing and return mechanism. If VALUE is specified, then call by value is used. If RESULT is specified, then the actual parameter is given the value of the formal parameter on procedure exit. If neither is specified, then call by name is used, as in ALGOL 60.

ALGOL W's syntax is defined in a similar formal manner to that used for ALGOL 60. Considerable care was taken with the specification of type information so, for example, the contexts were clarified in which an integer expression rather than a real expression was expected. To assist in the specification of type rules, the T-notation was introduced [McGettrick, 1980], which provided a concise method for expressing a set of similar rules that referred to a range of different types. This method of syntax specification was refined in the development of the two-level grammar used for the definition of ALGOL 68.

ALGOL W introduced several important programming constructs, including the record and the flexible parameter-passing mechanism. Stanford University distributed an ALGOL W system for the IBM 360 and 370 series of computers in the early 1970s, and this implementation became quite popular in educational establishments.

ALGOL 68

In 1968, a working group of the IFIP produced a report on the programming language ALGOL 68, which was designed to be a successor to ALGOL 60. As well as the formal report [van Wijngaarden, 1969], an informal introduction was also prepared [Lindsey, 1971]. Great interest was shown in this new language. The report was examined carefully and several groups developed compilers. In the light of the experience gained by these users of the language, a revised report was published in 1975 [van Wijngaarden, 1975]. ALGOL 68 is an extremely powerful programming language that can be used in a wide range of applications.

The executable statements supported by ALGOL 68 are very similar to those provided by ALGOL 60 and ALGOL W, such as assignments, **if**, **while**, **for**, **case** and **goto** statements. However, the syntax of some of these statements is slightly different; for example, **if** statements are terminated by **fi** to avoid any possible ambiguity in matching **if** and **else** statements in a nested **if** statement. Another consequence of the use of **fi** is that **begin**...**end** may not be necessary; for example:

```
if a > b then max := a
else max := b; a := 0 fi
```

Similarly, **od** is used to close a repetitive command to match a starting **do**. ALGOL 68's extreme orthogonality is illustrated by the fact that all ALGOL 68's executable statements are capable of yielding a value. Similarly, groups of statements can yield values. For example, a permissible construct, assuming appropriate declarations of *total* and *pairsum*, is:

$$total := total + (\textbf{int } i, j; read(i, j); pairsum := i + j);$$

This statement increments *total* by the new value of *pairsum*.

ALGOL 68 has some interesting and powerful facilities for the management of different data types or modes. As might be expected, ALGOL 68 allows comprehensive compile-time type checking. ALGOL 68 has a set of predefined data types, called **standard modes**, including **int**, **real**, **bool**, **char**, **compl** (complex numbers), **bits**, **bytes** and **string**. A mode **sema** is provided to enable semaphores to be implemented for process synchronization purposes (see later). There are also methods for specifying non-standard representation sizes for the numerical modes. Arrays can be declared and powerful methods for array use are supported. Structures can also be defined where the data objects being grouped together need not have the same mode. A structured variable can be treated as a single unit or as a collection of individual fields. Manipulation of pointers can be achieved using reference modes; for example, if *mymode* is any mode, then **ref** *mymode* is a new mode of pointers to objects of mode *mymode*. The use of the word **ref** often appears confusing to the newcomer, but its use is consistent and it can help define very versatile structures. Programmers can define their own modes and associate names with them, just as in ALGOL W.

ALGOL 68 treats procedures in a similar manner to data objects. When a procedure is declared, it is given a name, which is associated with a section of program. A procedure is also given a mode, determined by the modes of its parameters and the mode of any value it returns. A procedure declaration can therefore follow a similar syntax to that required for an ordinary variable declaration. By the careful use of reference modes, a comprehensive set of parameter-passing methods may be achieved. Both parameters and results can have any valid ALGOL 68 mode.

One of the difficulties frequently encountered in strongly typed languages occurs during type checking on a procedure call. In many of these languages, it is impossible to write a procedure so that the expected parameter can be any of a range of different types – for example, a procedure to print integer, real or character values. ALGOL 68 does, however, permit the use of united modes so that variables of these modes can have values of any mode stated in the declaration. This facility is not designed to be a method for circumventing mode checking, since mode information is carried with this type of variable at run time and mode checking can be performed dynamically. The current mode of one of these variables can be determined at run time by using a variant of the **case** statement.

As well as being able to define new modes, the programmer can also define new operators. The method used for operator declaration is very similar to that used for procedure declaration. The operator name is associated with the modes of its operands and the mode of its result, as well as with a section of program defining the action of the new operator. One of the special aspects of this mechanism is that ALGOL 68 allows a single operator to be defined with different operand modes. For example, ALGOL 68 defines the + operator for integer and real operands, but the programmer can also use this operator to perform some operation on operands with other, possibly user-defined, modes. The compiler selects which operator definition to use by examining the types of the operands. Operator priorities may also be specified.

ALGOL 68 supports a large number of predeclared operators and procedures for performing standard operations on many data types. These are all defined in the standard prelude, which acts as a form of initialization file for the compiler. A wide variety of formatted and unformatted input/ output procedures are defined in the standard prelude, operating on objects of mode **file**. A separate compilation scheme for ALGOL 68 has been defined.

ALGOL 68 includes the potential for parallel processing. There is a construct called the **collateral clause** that groups a collection of units (loosely, statements). The order in which these units are executed is explicitly left undefined so that there is at least the potential for executing each unit in parallel on separate processors in a multiprocessor computer system. With this facility for parallel execution, there must be some way of performing process synchronization. In ALGOL 68, this is achieved by the support of Dijkstra's semaphores [Dijkstra, 1968b]. A mode **sema** is provided together with operators **level** (to initialize the semaphore), **up** (to 'raise' the semaphore) and **down** (to 'lower' the semaphore).

A brief mention must be made here of the importance and significance of the ALGOL 68 revised report. One of the most significant features of ALGOL 68 is not the language itself but the technique used in the report for its definition. Instead of using the familiar BNF notation, ALGOL 68 was defined in terms of a van Wijngaarden grammar. The aim of the published report was to express the syntax in a clear and complete manner. Elements of a two-level grammar crept into the definition of ALGOL W, but it has been taken much further in the case of ALGOL 68. Two sets of rules are presented. The metaproduction rules are those defining the metalanguage. The hyper-rules make use of the metalanguage and yield the production rules of ALGOL 68. As usual, the semantics are expressed in a natural language. The disadvantage of this new method of definition is that the ALGOL 68 report is an obscure document, being almost impossible to follow except by the initiated. Subsequent readable guides to the language (such as Tanenbaum [1976] and Lindsey [1972]) have improved the situation. We will return to these two-level grammars in Section 4.3.2.

There is no doubt that ALGOL 68 is a complicated language and presents quite a challenge to the compiler writer. However, one of the stated design aims of the language was orthogonality; that is, the number of independent primitive constructs has been minimized. This design principle has played an important part in making ALGOL 68 a pleasant language to use. Extensive checking can be carried out on ALGOL 68 programs at compile time, thereby reducing the burden of run-time debugging. Furthermore, only a very limited amount of mode checking is required at run time, usually when a united mode is used, with all the other mode checking being performed by the compiler.

Despite its many attractions, ALGOL 68 has never been a very popular language. The format of the defining reports certainly had a part to play in this, as did the comparatively slow appearance of reliable and complete compilers. On the other hand, the ALGOL 68 revised report is a remarkable document in programming language history, defining in a formal manner all those aspects of the language that can be checked by a compiler. ALGOL 68 is certainly a language worthy of careful study and, as would be expected from such a milestone in the development of programming languages, has had a great impact on programming language design.

3.1.3   Pascal and its descendants

Although this group of languages has strong connections with the ALGOL family, it is convenient to consider Pascal and its developments in a separate section.

Pascal is a comparatively simple language, but despite this simplicity (or, maybe, because of this simplicity!), it has been used successfully for the implementation of many large software projects. However, its widespread use has been largely confined to the educational sector where it assists in the teaching of the principles of structured programming. Small-scale extensions to Pascal resulted in Concurrent Pascal while somewhat more drastic revisions yielded Modula-2. Ada is also discussed in this section because of its many Pascal-like features.

Pascal

ALGOL 60 had a great effect on the development of programming languages. Wirth defined ALGOL W in 1965 and in 1968 he started work on a new language called Pascal, which was strongly influenced by ALGOL 60 and ALGOL W. The first Pascal compiler was completed in 1970 and the language definition was published a year later [Wirth, 1971]. As usual, various modifications and corrections were made, but most Pascal implementations are based on the second edition of *The Pascal User Manual and Report* [Jensen, 1975]. The International Standards Organization (ISO) published a formal Pascal standard in 1982 and the user manual and report was revised to incorporate the changes imposed by this standard [Jensen, 1985].

The Pascal reports explicitly state two design aims:

(1)   Pascal should be a language suitable for teaching programming in a systematic manner.

(2)   It should be possible to produce reliable and efficient implementations of Pascal.

Although Pascal is used widely as a teaching language, it is in no sense confined to this application. Pascal follows the ALGOL 60 tradition of being of use in numerical and scientific programming, but it is often applied in many other areas, such as symbolic computation, text processing, compiler writing – the first stable Pascal compiler was written in Pascal – and process control.

Pascal supports a range of executable statements similar to those available in ALGOL 60 and ALGOL W. The simple statement types include assignment and **goto**; the structured statement types include compound statements (bracketed by **begin** and **end**), **if** and **case** statements, and **while**, **repeat** and **for** statements. Words such as **if**, **for**, **while**, **begin** and **end** are reserved words in Pascal.

Pascal has several predefined data types together with appropriate operators. Users can define and name their own types. The simple types available are *integer*, *real*, *Boolean* and *char*. Arrays, sets, files and records, similar to those of ALGOL W, are also supported. Pointer types can be defined so that dynamic data types may be manipulated. Subrange types are available so, for example, it is possible to declare variables that can only take integer values in the range -100 to 100. All variables have to be declared before use.

Programs can be divided into a main program and a set of, possibly nested, functions and procedures. Pascal offers two types of parameter passing: call by value, where the value of the actual parameter is passed to the function or procedure, and call by reference, where the address of the actual parameter is passed and hence the function or procedure can both read and update the actual parameter. For example, the procedure heading:

> **procedure** $p(x : integer;$ **var** $ans : real)$;

introduces a procedure that passes the parameter x by value and *ans* by reference.

Scope rules are fairly simple: declarations are local to the procedure or function in which they appear. Declarations in the main program have global scope. There are of course some additions and exceptions to these rules but, in general, the scope rules follow the ALGOL pattern. Pascal does not offer facilities for separate compilation, although some implementations include extensions to support it. Also, Pascal does not include direct support for concurrent programming.

Input and output is managed by a set of predeclared functions and procedures. Pascal supports I/O for both conventional text files and binary files. Pascal files are normally conventional sequential files on secondary storage. Simple facilities for output formatting are supplied.

Pascal programs are not coded in a fixed format. The compiler ignores spaces, tabs and newlines in most contexts, with the obvious consequence that these layout characters cannot appear within identifiers or numbers. Comments may be inserted freely.

Pascal is a very simple language. In fact, there is a formal description of its syntax expressed as syntax diagrams in Jensen [1975] that covers just three pages. Pascal is defined in BNF in Jensen [1975] and in EBNF (Extended Backus-Naur Form) in Jensen [1985]. The simplicity of its syntax and semantics has given it many advantages. It is easy to learn and implement, yet it offers a very rich programming environment. Implementations can be made very efficient and compact and can be run on a wide range of computer hardware. Because of the simplicity of the language and its implementations, Pascal is a good starting point for the writing of reliable software.

It is worth noting at this point that the design of Pascal simplifies its compilation. A single-pass compiler can be used: apart from one minor exception all identifiers have to be declared before they are used. Various other features (or restrictions, depending on one's point of view!), such as the prohibition of dynamic arrays (the size of all variables must be known by the compiler), further simplify the compilation process. We will be looking at the influence of language design on the compiler in later chapters.

Pascal's popularity rose rapidly during the 1970s, probably partly as a reaction against the complexity of languages like ALGOL 68 and PL/I. Many programmers encountered Pascal for the first time at college or university and continued using it in their working lives. However, Pascal is not without its faults; for example, its character-handling facilities are often criticized. Several of these failings are described in Welsh [1977], but these seem minor when compared with Pascal's successes. Pascal is still popular today, despite the development of new languages in the same family, and because of its readability, power, simplicity and widespread familiarity, it is used for most of the programming examples in this book.

Concurrent Pascal

In 1972, Brinch Hansen started work on a set of enhancements to Pascal to permit the specification of concurrency. The result was a language called Concurrent Pascal, which is described in Brinch Hansen [1975].

Concurrent Pascal introduces a new data type called the **process**. A process consists of a set of formal parameters, local declarations and a body defining the actions of the process. By declaring a variable of process type, an instance of that process is defined which can be initiated using the **init** statement together with a set of actual parameters. There are close parallels between these structures and the ideas of object-oriented programming. Similarly, monitors can be defined. A **monitor** consists of a shared data structure, the code to handle it, together with some form of synchronization operations to ensure that the monitor has exclusive access to the data structure. The monitor also includes some initialization code, which is executed the first time the monitor is entered. Procedures within the monitor may be specified as entry points and a monitor is instantiated and started in a similar way to a process. When **init** is used to start a monitor, the initialization code is executed. Another data type called the **queue** can be used by monitors to **delay** a calling process or to **continue** a previously delayed process. A further type provided is called the **class**. The class is a simplified form of the monitor, containing a data structure together with a set of operations, but it cannot be called simultaneously by several callers. These are the same classes as those introduced by SIMULA.

The checking imposed by the compiler ensures the consistent use of variables in these concurrent constructs. The scoping rules are such that processes may only access their local variables and parameters, and the shared variables of monitors can only be accessed via the designated set of monitor procedures. Concurrent Pascal is a simple and attractive language for concurrent programming.

More recent work by Brinch Hansen has produced a language called Edison [Brinch Hansen, 1982]. Edison is based on Pascal and Concurrent Pascal but includes many simplifications. In particular, the underlying mechanism for providing process scheduling is the **when** statement, based on Hoare's conditional critical region.

Modula-2

In the light of the success of Pascal, Wirth went on to design a language called Modula [Wirth, 1977]. Modula was designed for the programming of real-time systems and incorporates comprehensive facilities for concurrent programming. However, it never became very popular. Wirth then became involved in a project to design a powerful personal workstation, which required a single language for all the software development. Neither Pascal nor Modula were suitable, so a new language called Modula-2 was defined. About a year later, in 1979, a compiler was implemented. The language report is included in Wirth [1982] and more general information on the history and goals of Modula-2 appears in Wirth [1984].

As well as introducing facilities for concurrent programming, Modula-2, unlike Pascal, supports modules and separate compilation. In most other respects, Modula-2 is very close to Pascal. In particular, the structure of the executable statements is very similar, the major difference being that Modula-2 requires an explicit termination of structured statements. For example, the WHILE statement has the structure:

WHILE <expression> DO <statement sequence> END

in Modula-2 rather than Pascal's:

while <expression> **do** <statement>

A LOOP statement is added to provide infinite looping together with EXIT (to jump out of a loop) and RETURN (to exit from the current procedure and return to the caller).

The data type CARDINAL has been added to Modula-2 to represent an unsigned integer. The type BITSET is also supported, providing a restricted replacement for the set type of Pascal. Pascal's data types are carried over virtually unchanged. Also, the structure of procedures is very similar, except that Modula-2 uses the keyword PROCEDURE to introduce a function as well as a conventional procedure.

Modula-2 programs can be divided into separately compiled modules. Modules contain declarations of types, constants, variables and procedures. These declarations can be split into a definition part and an implementation part. The details of the implementation part are hidden from the user of the module. The definition part consists of declarations that can be exported to other modules. Modules have to state explicitly which declarations are being exported and which are being imported. These mechanisms are of benefit to the implementation of large software systems, since once interfaces have been defined, the coding of the implementations in each module may be done independently. Library modules can be implemented in this way.

EXAMPLE

The definition part of a module providing stack operations could take the form:

```
DEFINITION MODULE Stack;
    VAR empty : BOOLEAN;
    PROCEDURE push (e : CHAR);
    PROCEDURE pull (VAR e : CHAR);
    PROCEDURE init;
END Stack.
```

The data structure containing the stack, together with the code implementing the three procedures, is contained within the implementation part.

A standard module offers concurrency facilities. Since Modula-2 was primarily designed for software implementation on single processor systems, these concurrency facilities are rather limited. Essentially, they support a coroutine mechanism with control being explicitly passed from one process to another. Basic functions are provided for dynamic process creation. It is possible to construct higher-level concurrency facilities using the low-level operations provided.

Modula-2, like Pascal, is attractive because of its simplicity. It incorporates just the facilities to make it a powerful systems implementation language. Modula-2 systems are available on many computers and it is becoming quite popular, attracting many Pascal users. It has been used successfully in several large software projects. International standardization is currently being sought.

Ada

In the early 1970s, the proliferation of programming languages was accompanied by an increasing concern about the costs of producing software. The US DoD was spending enormous sums on software and was using a large variety of programming languages. Consequently, the DoD decided that standardization was essential and they produced a set of requirements, which were gradually refined over a period of a few years. Existing languages were assessed against these requirements, but it was found that none met the specifications sufficiently well, although the languages ALGOL 68, Pascal and PL/I emerged as possible starting points for the design of a new language. Four competing contractors were selected to design a new language and, in 1979, the winner was announced: a team from CII Honeywell Bull led by Jean Ichbiah. The language was based on

Pascal and was called Ada, named after Ada Augusta, Countess of Lovelace – her second notable appearance in the history of programming languages. Various modifications were made to the language specification during an evaluation exercise and the DoD standard for Ada was published in 1980, becoming an ANSI standard in 1983 [US DoD, 1980].

Since all DoD-sponsored software projects are to be written in Ada, it has a wide application area. Ada is based on the simplicity and elegance of Pascal, but incorporates a large number of additional powerful features that make it more easily applicable to programming in the 1980s, such as concurrency, exception handling and data abstraction. However, it is often claimed that Ada threw away Pascal's simplicity together with much of its elegance!

The structures of Ada's executable statements are very similar to those of Pascal and ALGOL 68. The **if** statement is terminated by **end if** and **case** by **end case**. Ada only supports a single iterative statement, the **loop**, but it can be preceded by a **for** or **while** clause.

Again, Ada's facilities for data typing are similar to those of Pascal. Standard types (*integer*, *float*, *Boolean* and *character*) are provided together with programmer-defined types, such as enumeration types, subranges (subtypes), arrays, structured records, strings and access types, which correspond to Pascal's pointer types. The programmer can also specify the range and precision of numerical types, facilitating the transfer of mathematical software from machine to machine. There is no restriction that the size of all variables be known at compile time; hence, dynamic arrays are supported. Comprehensive type checking can be carried out by the compiler.

Ada supports procedures and functions. Yet again, the syntax is very similar to that of Pascal, but the facilities for parameter passing are somewhat more advanced. Ada allows the programmer to specify the parameter modes **in**, **out** and **in out**. The effects of these modes have already been discussed in the last chapter. Scope rules are also in the ALGOL 60 and Pascal tradition.

Ada incorporates facilities for the splitting up of a program into a set of modules. A module may be implemented as a package, which allows the hiding of internal implementation details. Just as in Modula-2, a package consists of two parts. The specification part contains all the declarations for variables, types, constants and subprograms that can be exported for use by other packages. The implementation part is local to the package and all declarations in this section are hidden from the user of the package. The implementation part contains code defining how the facilities listed in the specification part are implemented. Ada's separate compilation facilities allow the independent compilation of the specification and implementation parts.

The package supports the concept of data abstraction. For example, a data structure can be encapsulated with a set of associated operations so that the user only accesses the data structure through the supplied operations.

Similarly, Ada supports type abstraction. This is achieved by a generic unit which acts as a template and can be instantiated by supplying the missing type information. Using these techniques, it is possible to construct packages of easily reusable software. Development of large programs becomes much simpler due to the explicit stating of the package interface details in the specification part and the facilities for separate compilation.

A related facility supports concurrent execution. The **task** construct allows the specification and use of asynchronous processes. The task is very similar in form to the package, containing the same two parts. The specification or interface part of the task defines a set of entry points, while the implementation part or task body defines the unit that can be independently scheduled for execution. Communication between tasks is normally achieved through entries. Associated with each entry point definition, there must be a corresponding **accept** within the task body. Suppose *task*1 calls *task*2 via one of its entry points. There are two possible situations: either *task*1 is executing or it is waiting on an **accept** for that particular entry. If *task*2 is busy, then *task*1 is suspended until *task*2 executes the appropriate **accept**. Once *task*2 has passed this **accept**, both *task*1 and *task*2 can continue. Similarly, if *task*2 executes the **accept** and there is no pending call on that **accept**, *task*2 is suspended waiting for such a call. This 'meeting' of *task*1 at the call and *task*2 at the **accept** is called a **rendezvous**. As it is possible for several calls to be made to call a task via the same entry point, there has to be a queue of pending calls associated with each entry point. These pending requests are handled on a first-come-first-served basis.

On its own, the **accept** statement is rather restrictive, since the order in which the **accept** statements in a task are executed cannot be influenced by the pattern of arrival of calls. The **select** statement permits greater flexibility by potentially permitting more than one **accept** statement to be 'open' at any one time. For example, it is then possible to write a task with two entry points such that the bodies corresponding to the entry points are activated in the order in which the calls are made. Without **select**, the two branches are executed in the sequence defined by the internal logic of the task. These **select** statements can be qualified by conditions introduced by **when**: these guards are evaluated whenever the **select** is executed and only those branches of the **select** for which the guard is true are considered for entry.

There are other facilities associated with tasks but these are not all unique to Ada. For example, it is possible to write interrupt handlers in Ada by associating an entry with a hardware address. Ada also includes facilities for exception handling. It is possible to cause user code to be executed when a specified error or other exceptional condition is encountered. These facilities allow the error handling code to be physically separated from the rest of the program.

Input and output is not built in to the language as in Pascal, but is defined as a generic package. Ada is a sufficiently powerful language to allow the writing of such an I/O package in Ada.

The Ada standard is a long but quite readable document. It is not a formal definition in the sense of, say, the ALGOL 68 report, but such definitions are being prepared. The US DoD have stated that Ada is the single language defined by the standard; that is, there are no subsets or supersets, which is a great aid to portability.

There is no doubt that Ada is an impressive language. It is powerful and offers many facilities suited to solving today's software problems. The package and task constructs aid in the writing of large programs for software engineering problems and the language is an excellent tool for the writing of embedded and real-time systems. However, Ada has been strongly criticized because of its size and complexity – see Hoare [1981], for example. It is claimed, therefore, that it is difficult to write reliable software in Ada, and since it will doubtless be used for 'critical' applications, the consequences may be serious. It may be significant to note in this context that it was reported that the first Ada compiler to be formally validated found more bugs in the validation suite than in the compiler. This debate over Ada's complexity continues and the experience gained in the next few years will indicate just how great an impact Ada will make on the development of programming languages.

3.1.4 BCPL and C

Another ALGOL-like family includes BCPL, C and C++. Although these languages have been used in many different application areas, their real home is in the broad field of systems programming.

BCPL

Most current programming languages support a variety of data types, often with strict type checking to ensure that type compatibility is maintained. BCPL is a language that goes against this philosophy by supporting only one data type and offering no type checking.

In the early 1960s, a language called CPL (Combined Programming Language) was developed at the Universities of Cambridge and London [Barron, 1963]. CPL was an extremely complex language and a full compiler was never completed. BCPL (Basic CPL) emerged as a result of the simplification of CPL to produce a language capable of efficient implementation. After the author of the language published its description [Richards, 1969], various changes were made, but then the language stabilized as it became increasingly popular. The current version of the language is described in Richards [1980].

BCPL is another imperative, block-structured, procedural programming language. It was originally developed as a language for writing compilers – indeed, the BCPL compiler is written in BCPL – but its application area has grown to include general systems programming, operating systems (the Tripos operating system was written in BCPL), text processors, database systems and graphics. Support for floating-point arithmetic was a comparatively late addition to the language, but because of the way in which floating-point numbers are managed, it is not a very suitable language for numerical problems.

BCPL is based on an idealized object machine that contains a store made up of an array of storage cells such that the addresses of adjacent cells differ by one. Each of these storage cells can hold a value, which corresponds to the single type that BCPL can manipulate. The interpretation of this value is up to the programmer. It can represent an object such as an integer, a real value, a character, a logical value or a function. An essential feature of this object machine is that each storage cell must be able to contain an address. BCPL implements the fundamental operation, called **indirection**, whereby the address of a storage cell is supplied and the operation returns the contents of that storage cell.

Given a single internal type, a set of operators have to be provided so that the programmer may make use of the values. Included in this set are the four standard arithmetic operators (+, −, * and /). They are implemented so that they give the result expected from treating arguments as integers. A full set of relational and bit-manipulating operators is also available. Other facilities allow the representation of single-dimensional arrays, functions and labels.

All variables have to be declared. There are many different ways of achieving this and the form of the declaration determines whether the variable has static or dynamic extent, whether it has global or local scope, or whether it is initialized. Vectors (single-dimensional arrays) are supported by BCPL, but the capability of manipulating address values (pointers) enables arbitrarily complex data structures to be used.

A wide range of executable statements are available, such as assignment, IF statements, a range of repetitive commands such as WHILE, FOR, UNTIL...DO, REPEAT, REPEATUNTIL and REPEATWHILE, the GOTO statement and the SWITCHON command for multi-way branching. BCPL systems come complete with a library of standard functions and procedures. This library contains facilities for input and output, byte manipulation, run-time storage allocation in addition to other miscellaneous functions. Some implementations also support floating-point operations; however, the standard integer operators cannot normally be used, so new operators (#+, #−, #* and #/) have to be provided. In other words, there can be no overloading of the operators because of the absence of typing.

BCPL is a block-structured language and supports the compound command, which is a set of statements enclosed by the $(and $) section brackets. As in ALGOL 60, the compound command can contain declarations. This construct is called a block and the scope of the declarations is limited to the extent of the block, as expected. Functions and procedures can be declared and parameter passing is always by value. Since it is possible to pass addresses as arguments, a procedure is capable of updating its actual parameters, despite the restriction to just call by value. An example of a procedure updating its actual parameter is:

```
LET UPDATE(PX) BE
$(   // PX contains the address of the location to be updated
    !PX := !PX + 1   // !PX is the location pointed to by PX
$)
    .
    .
    .
    UPDATE(@A)   // will increment the value of A by 1
```

Dynamic free variables are not allowed. Dynamic free variables are dynamic variables declared within enclosing procedures. This restriction simplifies the compilation process and the representation of the run-time environment. Separate compilation can be managed very easily. Each module is compiled in an environment supplied by a set of global declarations, which refer to locations in a special area of storage, called the **global vector**. Modules can communicate via these shared storage locations since the global vector is shared between modules.

BCPL programs are written in a free format. Thus, the compiler ignores layout characters in most contexts, although there are specific exceptions. For example, a newline is treated as a statement terminator wherever syntactically possible. Comments can be inserted freely.

BCPL is a language capable of straightforward implementation. If the idealized object machine is similar to the real target hardware, then implementation is simplified. There can be no run-time type checking. One of the most well-known features of BCPL is its portability. The language definition carefully avoids machine-dependent constructs and the BCPL implementation kit is designed so that systems on new machines can be produced rapidly. The techniques used for implementing BCPL systems are discussed in later chapters. This high degree of portability has resulted in BCPL systems being available on a wide range of machines, ranging from personal microcomputers to mainframes. However, certain features of the language make the generation of very efficient code difficult. For example, BCPL's word addressing may result in the need for multiplication and division (or, more likely, shifting) to translate between BCPL addresses and machine addresses on byte-addressed machines.

Most of the users of BCPL tend to be very enthusiastic about the language. Its lack of type checking has both advantages and disadvantages. On the disadvantage side, it obviously limits the checking that can be carried out during compilation and so may defer some awkward debugging to run time. BCPL programs may also be somewhat harder to read as the programmer is not compelled to state the type of each variable and may even indulge in 'dirty tricks'. On the other hand, it does offer a freedom that many programmers find most welcome. This freedom may be essential for some applications, such as in some parts of an operating system, but when used with respect BCPL can simplify the solution of many problems. The lack of overloading of the operators can cause confusion, but floating-point arithmetic is rarely found in BCPL applications. Another attractive feature of BCPL is its orthogonality. BCPL's portability is also a great advantage. By following a simple set of basic guidelines, BCPL programs can be written so that they can be transported from machine to machine with ease. And since the compiler and a large part of the run-time library is written in BCPL, the BCPL system is portable too.

BCPL remains a widespread language whose use is by no means confined to educational establishments. Despite the recent increase in the use of C, which developed from BCPL, the use of BCPL continues.

C

The language C incorporates many of the ideas introduced by BCPL. It was developed from BCPL via another language called B in 1972 by D. M. Ritchie at Bell Laboratories, primarily for the implementation of the UNIX operating system. The reference manual contained within Kernighan [1978], which describes C, has been widely adopted as the standard definition for C. C is a general-purpose programming language and has been used for a wide range of applications. Its most famous application is the UNIX operating system, where C has been used not just for coding the operating system but also for its associated utilities.

The range of executable statements provided by C is very similar to that available in BCPL. The syntax, however, is significantly different, although the underlying ideas remain the same. Statements are grouped by { and } characters to form compound statements. Many operators are supported for arithmetic, logical, bitwise and address operations. State-ments must be terminated by semicolons, which is in contrast to BCPL where the semicolon is syntactically rarely necessary.

A major difference between BCPL and C is that C is a typed language. C supports several data types; for example, integers, characters and floating-point numbers with various lengths. Limited type checking can be done by the compiler, but it cannot be as strict as that provided by a language such as Pascal. A powerful feature of C is the use of variables to hold addresses (pointers). Arrays and structures can be defined. Also, unions are supported that permit a variable to store values of different types.

C supports the use of functions and they can be called recursively. Argument passing is always by value, but call by reference can be achieved by passing addresses of arguments, as in BCPL. Variables can be static (declared at the outermost level), automatic (declared within functions) or external. Static variables stay in existence throughout the execution of the program; automatic variables only exist during the execution of the function in which they are defined; and external variables are static and accessible by other programs. This external variable mechanism is of use in separate compilation.

Input and output as well as other standard operations are supported by a set of externally defined functions. Most C implementations follow the pattern of the UNIX C library.

C is a relatively portable language, despite the set of comparatively low-level operations it supports. Implementations of C are available on most computers and operating systems, ranging from supercomputers down to 8-bit microcomputers. Implementations are often very efficient with the compiler producing code of higher quality than that normally written by hand. C is a concise language, but does contain pitfalls for the unwary programmer. It lacks some of the important features found in more recent languages, such as support for concurrency, although such facilities are normally available via calls to standard run-time libraries. C is a popular language and, since it is so closely associated with the UNIX operating system, will probably continue to be popular for quite some time to come.

C++

An interesting development from C, which is rapidly increasing in popularity, is the language C++. C++ is a superset of C (with a very small number of exceptions) and has new features incorporated to support the ideas of data abstraction.

C++ was developed in the early 1980s at the AT & T Bell Laboratories. The aim was to add to C to produce a language that included structures to aid the development of large software systems while retaining C's advantages of low-level control and conciseness. It is described in detail in Stroustrup [1985].

C++ supports a construct called a **class**, analogous to the class of Smalltalk (see Section 2.2.2). This implements the idea of data abstraction by associating a list of functions with the representation of a data type. The only way in which the data declared within a class may be accessed is via the functions defined within the same class. For example, a class called *stack* can be defined as being made up of an array to hold the data making up the stack, and three functions *push*, *pull* and *initialize*. The stack data structure may then only be accessed via these three routines.

A wide variety of facilities are available for the definition of classes with different characteristics. One attractive feature allows the overloading of operators to manipulate new data types. For example, it is possible to define a class *complex* that includes a specification of how the conventional arithmetic operators are interpreted when used with complex arguments.

Complex expressions can then be written using the conventional algebraic form.

C++ has much in its favour. Since it is a superset of C, existing C programs need little or no modification to run in a C++ environment. In addition, the extensive support for classes greatly assists in the construction of large and easily maintained systems. C++ is also capable of efficient compilation. It seems likely, therefore, that the popularity of C++ will increase at the expense of C.

3.2   Functional Languages

Imperative programming languages are a natural consequence of the use of computers with von Neumann architectures. This is the architecture of the conventional computer with a processing unit both extracting instructions and operating on data held in a memory. There is a close parallel between the step-by-step execution of statements in a program written in an imperative language and the step-by-step execution of machine instructions by the processor. However, this is not the only possible style of programming. Functional programming languages rely on the idea of function application, rather than on the notions of variables and assignments. A program written in a functional language consists of function calls together with arguments to the functions. In the past, the popularity of these languages was greatly affected by the difficulty in achieving efficient implementations on conventional processors. But there are now signs that this problem is being overcome as specialized computer architectures are being developed and as implementation techniques improve.

Only two functional languages are presented in any detail here: LISP and APL. LISP is one of the oldest and most famous of the functional programming languages. APL, on the other hand, is an interesting language with many functional aspects. Many other functional languages have been developed since the introduction of LISP. These include:

- FP, which has an APL-like syntax.

- ML, which is the command language of a system for proving the correctness of programs.

- Hope, which offers facilities for data abstraction and strong typing.

- Standard ML, which is a development of ML based on some of the ideas of Hope.

- Miranda, which is another strongly typed language offering data abstraction.

3.2.1 LISP

The development of LISP started in the late 1950s. A group led by McCarthy in the Artificial Intelligence Group at the Massachusetts Institute of Technology realized the potential of a recursive list-processing language and, in 1960, their ideas were published [McCarthy, 1960]. A LISP system was then implemented on the IBM 704 computer. Various improvements yielded LISP 1.5 [McCarthy, 1965] and many popular dialects have since been developed. A dialect called COMMON LISP is now in widespread use [Steele, 1984].

LISP is an applicative language that achieves its aims by function application. It is a very simple language based on only a few fundamental ideas. LISP's power comes primarily from the equivalence of code and data, from its conditional expression and from the use of recursion.

The fundamental data structure handled by LISP is the list. Data is represented as lists and, perhaps rather disturbingly at first sight, so are programs. There are no inherent differences between LISP programs and data, a factor that makes it both easy for LISP programs to modify or generate other LISP programs and for LISP interpreters to be written in LISP. All data handled by LISP is in the form of **S-expressions**. S-expressions can be atoms, lists of atoms or lists whose elements are lists (a recursive definition). For example:

A, (A), (A B), (A B (C D) (E F) G (H (I J)))

are all S-expressions. There are other forms of S-expressions, but these need not concern us here.

An **atom** is either a number or an atomic symbol made up of a sequence of letters and digits, starting with a letter. LISP atoms cannot be divided into anything smaller. Atoms can be grouped into lists by separating them by spaces and enclosing them in parentheses – for example, (A B C D).

LISP supports three basic functions, which can be applied to S-expressions:

(1) The CAR function extracts the head of a list; for example:

(CAR '(P Q R))

has the value P. Note here that the single quote prevents evaluation of the list that follows.

(2) The CDR function extracts the tail of a list.

(3)   The CONS function allows the construction of new lists. It takes two S-expression arguments and produces a new list whose CAR is the first argument and whose CDR is the second argument. For example:

(CONS 'A '(B C))

yields (A B C). This function has to make use of dynamic storage allocation facilities provided by the LISP system.

There are two other low-level functions which are very useful when writing more complex functions. The function EQ takes two atomic arguments and yields true if they are the same atom, false otherwise. For example:

(EQ 'A 'B)

yields F while:

(EQ 'A 'A)

yields T. The function ATOM yields true if its argument is an atom, false otherwise. These last two functions are called **predicates**: they yield values that are either true or false.

LISP provides a conditional expression written as:

(COND (p1 e1)
       (p2 e2)
          .
          .
       (pn en))

where the pi are conditions and the ei are actions. The action of the complete expression is to evaluate the conditions in sequence until one is found that does not yield the value NIL (the empty list). The actions corresponding to this condition are then executed.

Using these few facilities, it is possible to write a vast range of new functions to manipulate S-expressions. A simple example is the function EQUAL which determines whether two S-expressions are identical. Note that EQ does not fulfil this requirement, since it is only defined for atomic arguments.

(DEFUN EQUAL(X Y)
   (COND ((ATOM X) (COND ((ATOM Y) (EQ X Y))
                          (T NIL)))
          ((ATOM Y) NIL)
          ((EQUAL(CAR X)(CAR Y)) (EQUAL(CDR X)(CDR Y)))
          (T NIL)))

The use of recursion within the conditional expression makes functions like this very compact and easy to write. LISP systems are always supplied with the basic functions described here, but others are normally supported for arithmetic operations and so on.

One of the strengths of LISP is that programs, as well as data, are expressed as S-expressions. The motivation for expressing LISP programs as S-expressions arises from the desire to write a pure LISP interpreter in LISP. Such an interpreter is coded as the LISP function EVALQUOTE, whose definition is remarkably simple, requiring about 20 lines [McCarthy, 1965]. One of the important aspects of this interpreter is that it constitutes a formal definition of the semantics of LISP; in other words, the semantics of the language is being defined by an implementation of the language. Since the LISP interpreter is so short, such an approach seems reasonable, but for more complex languages and implementations, the merits of this approach would be more questionable.

LISP is a notable language in many respects. The use of the same representation for programs and data, the provision of simple but very powerful facilities for symbol manipulation and list processing, its extensibility and its simple implementation all make it a very successful language. LISP is widely used in the realm of artificial intelligence. Several artificial intelligence research groups have developed extremely powerful LISP programming environments, simplifying the process of writing complex LISP programs. The ideas of LISP also have great relevance in the study of theoretical aspects of computer science.

LISP is often criticized for two reasons. Firstly, it is widely believed that LISP implementations are inherently inefficient. Many LISP systems are interpretive and certainly there are some implementations that are extremely slow. However, more recent LISP systems, especially those implemented on special hardware with support for LISP operations, offer very high performance. The second criticism arises from the proliferation of parentheses in LISP programs. Great care must be taken with the layout of LISP programs to maintain readability. Alternatively, a program formatter or prettyprinter should be used. To some extent, this problem with parentheses is alleviated by the facilities offered by the various LISP programming environments available.

It is often thought that LISP is a difficult language to learn. One reason for this might be that its underlying concepts are so different from other more conventional programming languages that exposure to these languages can reduce the ease with which LISP can be learned. Nevertheless, LISP's syntax is so simple that even the most sceptical could be writing LISP programs after only a very short period of study.

This criticism of the syntax of LISP has resulted in the development of several other related functional programming languages. For example, Scheme, as used in Abelson [1985], is a dialect of LISP and has inherited the ideas of scoping and block structure from

ALGOL to produce a powerful yet simple language that is easy to learn.

3.2.2 APL

The language APL (A Programming Language) was developed by Iverson [1962]. It was originally intended to be used for purposes of algorithm description, but subsets were defined and actually implemented. Perhaps the most famous of these implementations is APL/360, running as an interactive interpretive system on the IBM 360 series of computers; indeed, one of APL's most attractive features is its interactive nature.

APL's most striking feature is its notation. It makes use of a special character set which necessitates the use of special techniques for its implementation and for inputting and displaying programs. APL has a comprehensive range of facilities for the handling of arrays. Arrays can be created, reshaped and manipulated in many different ways. The facilities provided by APL are at a higher level of abstraction than most other programming languages, which means that the programmer need not be concerned with how arrays are represented or manipulated.

Another slightly unusual feature of APL is that the type of a variable may change during the execution of a program. APL implementations must, therefore, associate both a current type and a value with each variable, so that the operations carried out on the variables are consistent with their types. The scoping rules for names are also rather unusual. The names used in languages like the ALGOLs, Pascal and Ada have scopes that are determined by the static structure of the source program – in particular, by the way in which the blocks are nested. But in APL, the scope is determined dynamically. The variables that can be accessed within an APL subprogram depend on the chain of calls made to that subprogram. To resolve a variable name, the sequence of calls is retraced and the latest declaration of that name is chosen. These scope rules imply that APL is better implemented as an interpreter, rather than a compiler, as it is difficult to achieve the efficient late binding of names to types and to storage locations in a compiled language.

APL has been used successfully in many areas of scientific and business data processing. It supports powerful operations in a concise form and, because of the availability of many good interactive implementations, software can be developed rapidly. There are many enthusiastic programmers who strongly support the use of APL. On the other hand, APL is heavily criticized because of its notation and its lack of block structure. But whether or not APL is used as a programming language, it will remain of interest because of its powerful and consistent notation.

3.3   Logic Programming Languages

The third broad division of programming languages is the group known as the logic programming languages. These languages offer a radically different approach to problem solving by a computer. Only one such language, PROLOG, is described here since it illustrates the characteristics of this category very well.

3.3.1   PROLOG

PROLOG (PROgramming in LOGic) was developed in the early 1970s by Roussel at the University of Marseilles. Since then, many implementations have been produced and it has become an essential language in the artificial intelligence field, although it has also been used in many other application areas.

PROLOG is one of the most famous non-procedural languages available today, although it does retain some procedural aspects. One of the reasons for this fame was its selection as the programming language for the Japanese fifth-generation project. It can be considered to be a language at a very much higher level than the FORTRANs, ALGOLs and their relatives. Programming in PROLOG involves the specification of a set of facts and rules to form a collection of knowledge on a subject. Then, questions may be asked of this knowledge or data base via PROLOG. It is the PROLOG system, rather than the programmer, that is responsible for the techniques used to structure and access these facts and rules. PROLOG is also responsible for making inferences from this knowledge. A PROLOG program consists of a set of **clauses**. A clause can be a **fact**, a **rule** or a **question**. Questions can be answered by applying the rules to a set of facts.

PROLOG's syntax is simple. Facts are expressed in a natural form. For example, the fact that Pooh eats honey can be written in PROLOG as:

```
eats(pooh, honey).
```

The relationship eats is followed by the objects of the relationship, pooh and honey, enclosed in parentheses. PROLOG systems are normally implemented so that they operate in a conversational manner. Thus, once a few facts like the one above have been entered, it is possible to start asking questions. Questions are prefixed with ?-. So, by typing:

```
?- eats(piglet, thistles).
```

the PROLOG system replies with **yes** or **no**. PROLOG also supports variables that can be used, among other things, to ask more general questions. For example:

?- eats(X, honey).

and PROLOG replies:

X = pooh.

Rules can be specified in a similar manner. For example, the rule that all who eat honey also eat condensed milk can be written:

eats(X, condensed_milk) :- eats(X, honey).

In this way, it is very easy to build up involved sets of facts and rules. It is then the responsibility of the PROLOG system to make the required inferences. PROLOG systems support backtracking to allow all possible search paths to be examined when attempting to satisfy a goal.

These examples are only intended to give a flavour of PROLOG. For a complete treatment, readers should refer to Clocksin [1981] or Bratko [1986]. PROLOG offers simple and rapid solutions to a wide range of problems, and it is easy to write accurate and readable programs. The power of PROLOG often comes as a shock to programmers used to more conventional programming languages.

PROLOG is now implemented on many different computer systems but the development of PROLOG software is still in its infancy. Perhaps not surprisingly, it is difficult to produce efficient implementations, but techniques are improving rapidly. PROLOG programs can execute extremely slowly if the programmer is unaware of the general techniques used for implementation. It is easy to write PROLOG programs requiring extensive backtracking, which thus result in long execution times.

3.4   Other Language Types

There are many high-level languages that do not fall neatly into any of the three language categories already mentioned. In this section, three language types are introduced whose precise classification is impossible as they have numerous links with the language families already described.

3.4.1   Object-oriented languages

The object-oriented style of programming is becoming increasingly popular and several languages, most notably Smalltalk, have been developed to support this methodology. A brief description of SIMULA67 is also included in this section, despite its close association with ALGOL 60, since it was the forerunner of many of the ideas of object-oriented programming. Object-oriented constructs also appear in the language C++, which is described in Section 3.1.

SIMULA67

One of the many members of the ALGOL family is SIMULA67, a language developed primarily for simulation applications [Dahl, 1966; Birtwistle, 1973]. Simulation problems involve the use of interacting processes, which SIMULA67 represents using structures called classes. A **class** declaration encapsulates declarations and procedures and can include parameters; it is syntactically very similar to an ALGOL 60 procedure declaration. Structures similar to SIMULA67's classes have already been seen in Modula-2, Ada and Concurrent Pascal. Reference variables are used to access class objects and classes can be created dynamically. Access to the declarations within a class is via a reference variable 'pointing' to that class object. A class can form the complete definition of an object by associating the representation of the object with the code to manipulate it. SIMULA also has powerful facilities for allowing one class to inherit properties from another, permitting the hierarchical structuring of a software system. SIMULA is well suited for use in the field of simulation as it makes use of coroutines, which allow the apparent simultaneous execution of instances of classes.

As well as being a useful simulation language, SIMULA is notable because it was the first language to make use of the class concept. This concept was later developed into the more general ideas of data abstraction and object-oriented programming. SIMULA also incorporates ideas of language extensibility. SIMULA67 is no longer a frequently used language, having been overtaken by other more modern languages, which are not necessarily designed primarily for simulation applications.

Smalltalk

Smalltalk's development started in the late 1960s as a result of the idea to produce a language suitable for programming personal computers for non-specialist applications. A research group at Xerox Palo Alto Research Center developed this idea in a language called Flex, designed by Alan Kay, producing several versions of the Smalltalk system. Smalltalk-80 is probably the most widely known version, having been described in several articles in *Byte* [1981]. The development of Smalltalk was part of the Dynabook project, whose aim was to design a compact and powerful personal computer, incorporating a mouse and a display made up of windows.

Smalltalk is an object-oriented programming language. This contrasts with more conventional programming languages which are based on a strict separation between data and procedures operating on the data. Smalltalk manages a single entity, called the **object**, which is a combination of both data and procedures. Smalltalk is based on communication with objects: messages are sent to objects and objects can return other objects in reply. The strength of Smalltalk lies in the fact that all entities are objects and all objects are handled in a consistent way. The class concept of SIMULA is an early predecessor of the ideas of object-oriented programming, which have also been carried over into the design of the package in Ada.

Smalltalk's message expression identifies the receiver, the selector and the arguments. On evaluation of the message, it is sent to the receiver. The selector describes the operation the receiver is required to perform. Unary messages have no arguments. For example, the expression 'window erase' sends a message to the window object with the selector 'erase'. Binary messages, on the other hand, contain a single argument and a selector taken from a set of special binary selectors. For example, a binary message is $a + 2$ where the selector is $+$, the argument is 2 and they are passed to the object a. Mechanisms like this enable arithmetic, logical and similar operations to be performed using conventional syntax. Assignment expressions are provided to allow variables to assume values returned by objects. Several other control structures are also available, such as blocks, conditional statements and repetitive statements. Concurrent execution is easily specified.

A description of an object is called a class. A class is named and contains a set of methods. Each method is identified by a pattern. When the object receives a message, the method selected by the selector of the incoming message is invoked. Each method is responsible for handling any arguments accompanying the message.

The Smalltalk language is only part of a large programming environment. The Smalltalk environment consists of utilities such as editors, debuggers, program development tools and graphics support. The system is highly interactive and user friendly. For example, the use of windows makes it much easier for the user to keep track of the progress of multiple tasks, while the use of a mouse to move a cursor on a high-resolution graphics screen helps reduce the use of the keyboard. Most of the Smalltalk system is written in Smalltalk and the user can easily modify this code to support special personal requirements. This feature makes the Smalltalk system portable. To implement Smalltalk on a new machine, it is only necessary to implement a version of the 'virtual environment' for that machine, usually in assembly language. This provides low-level support for storage management and interaction with the machine and operating system. It also provides an interpreter which controls the execution of Smalltalk programs by operating on an intermediate code program derived from the Smalltalk source program. This approach to language implementation is described in Section 8.3.

Smalltalk aims to be simple and uniform and, unlike some other languages, seems to achieve this aim quite successfully. Smalltalk supports data abstraction through classes and, although the ideas of objects and message passing may be rather unfamiliar to programmers used to traditional languages, it forms a powerful tool for the development of complex software projects. The interactive Smalltalk environment is another most attractive feature.

3.4.2   String-processing languages

The language SNOBOL was designed to offer powerful string-processing capabilities. It was first described in 1964 [Farber, 1964] and was subsequently developed into the popular version called SNOBOL4 [Griswold, 1971]. SNOBOL4 has been used for many non-numerical applications, such as text processing, symbolic mathematics, syntactic analysis and simulation.

SNOBOL4 provides a powerful set of facilities for manipulating character strings. It also has limited support for integer and floating-point arithmetic. Strings and numbers can be assigned to variables. Other data types can be defined if required. One of the simplest statements in SNOBOL4 performs pattern matching. It examines a string and determines whether a specified pattern of characters appears in it. The form of this statement is:

```
label subject pattern goto
```

where the label and goto fields are optional. The subject is examined and if the pattern matches, the statement succeeds, otherwise it fails. The goto field can contain one or two labels, indicating the next statement to be executed on pattern match or failure to match. For example, the statement:

```
LINE 'ZZ' :S(FOUND)F(ABSENT)
```

will cause control to be transferred to the statement whose label is FOUND if the string 'ZZ' is contained in the value of the variable LINE and to ABSENT if the string 'ZZ' is not contained in the variable. The power of SNOBOL4 comes from its ability to specify complex patterns with alternatives, patterns matching only selected portions of a string, patterns matching strings with balanced parentheses and so on. A variation of this statement allows the replacement of the matched string by another specified string. So the statement:

```
LOOP LINE 'A' = 'Z' :S(LOOP)
```

converts all occurrences of 'A' in LINE to 'Z'.

Arrays and tables are supported by SNOBOL4. The programmer can define new structured data types and dynamic data structures can be created. Functions can be defined.

There are many, usually interpretive, implementations of SNOBOL4 and it has enjoyed considerable popularity, especially in the academic computing community. SNOBOL4's elegance, simplicity and powerful pattern-matching operations make it an attractive and interesting language.

Several other languages such as Spitbol and ICON have been designed for string-processing applications. ICON [Griswold, 1983] was a development from SNOBOL4 which retained many of its string-processing features while having a syntax closer to that of more conventional languages such as Pascal.

3.4.3 Software packages

Mention must be made in this chapter of the command languages used for controlling the execution of software packages. Programs such as statistical packages and database management systems are becoming increasingly sophisticated and, as a consequence, require powerful methods for their control, allowing input files, operations required and output formats to be specified. Some designers take the view that control should be via menus or by the user answering explicit questions. But packages can be controlled by user-written commands that have a form very similar to conventional programming languages. Some of these languages are complete with variables, block structure, subprograms and other powerful control constructs. In other words, new high-level languages are being developed for these specialized applications.

Such languages have to be designed with great care to enable the packages to be used effectively by non-specialist users. Detail has to be hidden to allow the user to express the problem in a concise and natural way. Providing such a user interface becomes a major part of the effort required in implementing such a package. These interface languages are sometimes called **fourth-generation languages**. Generations one, two and three are associated with machine code, assembly languages and conventional high-level languages, respectively. An alternative approach, which is often favoured, is to implement the package so that it integrates with an existing language. For example, it may be possible to implement a database management system as a set of functions and procedures that can be called from users' programs. Preprocessors are sometimes used to convert from the package's language to a more conventional compiled or interpreted high-level language.

An example of a high-level control language that provides the user interface to a software package is the dBase series of database management packages produced by Ashton–Tate. Here, the user can issue commands of the form:

        list for (name = 'Smith').and.(age >= 65)

to list the selected records in a database. These commands may be issued interactively or may be contained within a 'program' of such commands. These packages provide additional forms of user interface, making the use of the package even easier for the inexperienced user.

   Another area of contact between packages and high-level languages is the group of packages called **application generators** or **program-writing tools**. These packages operate on some form of user-specified description and produce a program, usually in a high-level language, to accomplish the user's requirement. Some of these packages are quite restrictive and are designed solely for the purposes of generating software to perform formatted input and output or other comparatively simple tasks. Other packages are much more powerful and may take some form of graphical program specification, such as a flowchart or a Jackson design, as input and produce a complete program as output. These packages are gradually improving and are becoming more popular. They are essentially attempting to implement very high-level languages. We will look at a package of this type, especially designed for writing compilers, in Chapter 9.

   The popularity of off-the-shelf software packages is increasing rapidly. Many organizations are entering the world of computing by buying a microcomputer system together with a set of packages to perform various functions, such as word processing, accounting and database management. The fact that these computers also support conventional programming languages is of no concern to most of them. The use of prewritten software packages is in general very sensible, as it saves a great deal of time and money that may have been spent on implementing something that has already been implemented. In some cases, all goes well and the packages fulfil the organization's requirements. But in a surprisingly large number of cases, the packages do not offer quite what is needed and, since no source code is supplied with the packages, they cannot be modified to perform as required. One way of achieving greater flexibility may be to integrate these packages with high-level languages so that customization can be easily achieved. The end user should not always be shielded from programming languages!

3.5   Future Trends

It is interesting to speculate on the future of programming languages. Without doubt, novel and interesting programming languages will continue to be developed and implementations of older languages will continue to improve. In addition, the use of the fourth-generation programming languages will doubtless become more widespread. However, the list of the most widely used languages is unlikely to change very much over the next few years due to the investment in the production of programs and training of programmers in these languages. Today's most popular languages, COBOL, FORTRAN, LISP and BASIC, are now all between 20 and 30 years old, which is a long time in the history of computer science. LISP, in fact, seems to be even more popular than ever in the field of artificial intelligence. At the time of writing, the future of Ada was under debate. It will doubtless succeed, but the extent to which it will displace other languages remains to be seen. An interesting observation is that the number of different high-level languages in widespread use continues to increase. The dream of the early computer scientists for a 'Computer Esperanto' has not yet been fulfilled. It remains to be seen how successful Ada will be in becoming this universal language.

Current programming languages are still a long way from natural languages. Although the problems of a computer understanding natural languages are severe, much useful and interesting work is being done in this area. An individual view of the future of programming languages is given in Adams [1979], where the 'deep-thought computer' is asked to produce the answer to 'Life, the Universe and Everything'. The programming effort in stating the problem is minimal, but the resulting burden on the computer turns out to be rather large.

SUMMARY

- There is no real sign that procedural languages will be displaced from their position of almost exclusive use. The less traditional language types, such as the declarative, object-oriented and applicative families, have yet to make an impact on most of the non-specialist users of computers.

- The problem of how to construct correct programs has been greatly eased by several recent trends in language design; for example, language simplicity, information hiding and extensive compile-time checking. Portability, modern implementation techniques as well as the production of formal and unambiguous language definitions have also helped to alleviate this problem.

- Modern languages have much better data-structuring facilities than those available in early languages like ALGOL 60 and FORTRAN. Two major milestones have contributed to this situation: the introduction of the ALGOL W and Pascal record with its equivalents in many other languages and the development of data abstraction by the encapsulation of data structures with the programs to manipulate them, such as by Ada's packages. Smalltalk has taken these ideas even further.

- The range of available executable statements does not seem to vary too much from one procedural language to another. The one major exception is the GOTO statement, which is gradually fading away and being replaced by structured loops, conditionals and procedures.

- The ideas of block structure now seem so firmly embedded in the programming scene that it is difficult to envisage alternative program-structuring mechanisms.

- Software projects are continuing to increase in size and scope and, as a consequence, the requirement for separate compilation facilities is essential. Communication between separately compiled modules in a simple, secure and efficient manner is not an easily soluble problem and was ignored to a large extent by the designers of ALGOL 60, Pascal and similar languages. The primitive facilities offered by FORTRAN have been refined, while the clear distinction between interfaces and implementations offered by a language like Ada offers a good basis for the management of large software projects.

- Concurrency is now seen as a major design issue. Structuring software as interacting concurrent processes is useful as a method of program design as well as a way of achieving parallelism on multiprocessor computer systems. It is certainly an area where much work remains to be done; in particular, techniques for structuring the solution of a problem to maximize parallelism need to be developed further.

- There is a developing trend towards the production of complete programming environments – a compiler or interpreter and a whole range of other packages, such as editors, debuggers and libraries, that are supported and integrated with the language – so that the development of software is simplified. The BASIC environment supplied on most home microcomputers is a simple example, while the Smalltalk environment is an example of a much more powerful system.

EXERCISES

3.1   If you are an experienced Pascal programmer, list the troublesome shortcomings you have found and suggest extensions to overcome these shortcomings.

3.2   Discuss the feasibility of the automatic initialization of variables when they are declared. In particular, carefully consider the values to which variables should be initialized.

3.3   Follow the development path from ALGOL 60 to Pascal to Modula-2 and summarize in broad terms what was added and what was taken away at each step.

3.4   Design a formatted I/O system (as provided by FORTRAN) for Pascal. Also consider the implementation.

3.5   Different programming languages vary greatly in the type of support they offer for input and output. Examine the I/O facilities offered by several languages and, for each language, justify the choice.

3.6   Carefully consider why BASIC implementations are so widespread on today's home computers. Are there any other existing languages that could replace BASIC for this purpose?

3.7   Which should be the first programming language taught to:

(a)   primary school children,

(b)   undergraduate computer science students,

(c)   undergraduate mathematics students, and

(d)   company directors?

Consider carefully the aims of programming language education for each of these groups.

3.8   What features are responsible for a language remaining in widespread use for a long time? Illustrate your answer by referring to the historical development of FORTRAN and COBOL.

3.9   Many novice programmers find the use of pointers confusing. Justify their retention in a programming language such as Pascal. To what extent are these problems due to issues of language syntax?

3.10 Show how the use of pointers is restricted in Pascal to avoid data security problems. Why are such restrictions not present in languages such as BCPL and C?

3.11 What are the relative merits in having a database package controlled by:

(a)   function and procedure calls from a conventional high-level programming language,

(b)   a special-purpose programming/command language, or

(c)   a menu-driven system?

3.12 Which is your favourite programming language? Why?

PART TWO

Compilers

The main part of this book describes the design of compilers. It is often useful to divide the compilation process into three distinct phases. The lexical analysis phase reads the high-level source program and divides it into a stream of basic lexical 'tokens'. The syntax and semantic analysis phase then combines these tokens into data structures reflecting the form of the source program in terms of the syntactic structures of the language. These two phases complete the analysis of the source program. Finally, the code generator converts these data structures into code for the target machine.

Part Two opens with a chapter covering some of the ideas of syntax, semantics and parsing relevant to compiler design. This is followed by three chapters reflecting the three-way subdivision of the compilation process.

CHAPTER 4

Syntax, Semantics and Translation

For a programming language to be usable, its definition must be available. This definition should be complete, so that it covers all features and properties of the language, as well as unambiguous and clear. The programmer can use this definition when writing programs to ensure that programs will be accepted by the language system on the computer and subsequently produce the desired results. The language implementor must also ensure that the implementation conforms to this definition.

The importance of this defining document has already been stressed. It has to specify both the syntax and the semantics of the language. It is of course possible to use informal techniques, such as natural language descriptions, for this purpose. However, because of the risk of ambiguities and incomplete definitions, these informal techniques are not to be recommended. This chapter presents some of the formal methods of language specification and shows how they may be used in the analysis of the structure of programs. But first, the structure of a typical compiler must be described to help show where the ideas of syntax and semantics are relevant.

4.1 Language Translation: The Compilation Process

Compilers for all but the simplest of languages are large and complex programs, possibly involving many tens or hundreds of thousands of lines of code. Just as with any large program, it is wrong to look at a compiler as a monolithic structure; decomposition into simpler modules is essential.

The task of a compiler can be divided very broadly into two sub-tasks:

(1)   The analysis of the source program.

(2)   The synthesis of the object program.

This subdivision helps a little in the structuring of a compiler, but further functional divisions are required. In a typical compiler, the analysis task consists of three phases:

(1)   **lexical analysis**,

(2)   **syntax analysis**,

(3)   **semantic analysis**.

The synthesis task is usually considered as a single **code-generation** phase, although it can be separated into a few distinct processes. These four phases operate in sequence as shown in Figure 4.1.

The nature of the interface between these four phases depends on the compiler. It is perfectly possible for the four phases to exist as four separate programs. For example, the lexical analyzer reads the source program, it writes out a suitable transformed version of the source program to a file, the program is input by the syntax analyzer, and so on. This approach results in a four-pass compiler, since four passes are made over various versions of the source text. However, such four-pass compilers are not particularly common. On the other hand, single-pass compilers pass data between the phases a token at a time, without having to write temporary versions to disk. Two- and three-pass compilers are also possible in this model.

The primary advantage of single-pass compilation is efficiency, since program and intermediate data can be contained in primary memory. But such compilers tend to be greedy in their memory needs and, indeed, in some languages the problems of forward referencing make single-pass compilation very difficult or even impossible.

There are many advantages to be gained in decomposing the task of a compiler into distinct phases, as is the case when a large program is split

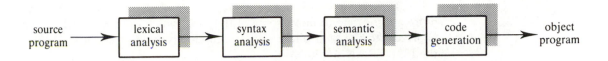

source program → lexical analysis → syntax analysis → semantic analysis → code generation → object program

up into modules; for example, simplification of writing, debugging and modification, and a potential reduction of storage requirements. But there is one other consequence of great significance. A large part of the compiler can be made machine independent, and thus modifying the compiler so that it generates object code for a new computer is not such a difficult task. It is often possible, and indeed desirable, to structure the compiler so that the code generator is the only machine-dependent module. In this way, the same front end – that is, the same analysis part – can be used to drive a whole set of code generators for a variety of target hardware. We will tackle this issue of portability, together with the whole topic of language implementation, in Chapter 8.

FIGURE 4.1

The phases of the compilation process.

4.1.1 Lexical analysis

The lexical analyzer has the task of reading the characters of the source program and recognizing the tokens or basic syntactic components that they represent. The lexical analyzer is able to distinguish and pass on, as single units, objects such as numbers, punctuation symbols, operators, reserved keywords, identifiers and so on. Recognizing such constructs in the lexical analyzer has the effect of simplifying the syntax analyzer, effectively reducing the size of the grammar the syntax analyzer has to handle. In a free-format language, the lexical analyzer ignores spaces, newlines, tabs and other layout characters, as well as comments. For example, the source program line:

   for i := 1 **to** 10 **do** sum := sum + term[i];   (* sum array *)

will be transformed by the lexical analyzer into the sequence of tokens:

   for i :=   1   **to**   10   **do**   sum
   :=   sum   +   term   [i   ]   ;

For a language like Pascal, the lexical analyzer maintains a list of reserved words so that they can be distinguished from identifiers and passed to the next phase of the compiler in the form of, for example, a short integer code. It may be appropriate to store identifiers as they are encountered in a symbol table and return a pointer to the symbol table entry each time an identifier is encountered. Languages in which the same identifier can be declared with different scopes may make management of the symbol table by the lexical analyzer rather difficult.

Lexical analysis is not very easy in some languages and so it may be more appropriate to move some of the functions normally found in lexical analyzers to the next phase – the syntax analyzer. For example, consider the FORTRAN statement:

```
DO 1 I = 1
```

where lookahead is required to determine that the DO does not start a DO loop and that the first token the lexical analyzer should return is an identifier DO1I (see Section 5.1.1).

4.1.2   Syntax analysis

The syntax analyzer or parser has to determine how the tokens returned by the lexical analyzer should be grouped and structured according to the syntax rules of the language. Strictly speaking, the lexical analyzer also has a role in syntax analysis, since it has to determine how the characters of the source program should be grouped according to the syntax of the basic tokens of the language. There are various general techniques that can be used by the syntax analyzer and these are outlined here. The output of this phase is some representation of the syntactic structure of the source program, often expressed in the form of a tree (the 'parse tree').

The choice as to whether a language construct is recognized by the lexical analyzer or by the syntax analyzer is somewhat arbitrary. In practice, the lexical analyzer should be responsible for all the simple syntactic constructs, such as identifiers, reserved words and numbers, while the syntax analyzer should deal with all the other structures. For example, in a language such as Pascal, it would be appropriate for the lexical analyzer to recognize those structures defined by a Chomsky type 3 grammar (see Section 4.3.1), whereas the syntax analyzer would be able to cope with all the remaining type 2 productions. There is, in fact, a sound practical reason for this distinction. Perhaps surprisingly, most compilers spend most of their processing time within the lexical analyzer; so, any improvement in efficiency of the lexical analysis phase is very worthwhile. Parsers for type 3 grammars can be made much more efficient than parsers for type 2 or other more general grammars, and so this partitioning between lexical and syntax analyzers improves the overall efficiency of the compiler.

Error recovery is an important aspect of compiler design, especially in the context of the syntax analyzer. Users of compilers cannot be expected to write syntactically correct programs all the time, so the production of accurate and informative error messages is vital.

4.1.3   Semantic analysis

Loosely, the role of the semantic analyzer is to determine the semantics or meaning of the source program. The semantic analysis phase, sometimes called the **translation phase**, may cope with tasks involving declarations and scopes of identifiers, storage allocation, type checking, selection of appropriate polymorphic operators, addition of automatic type transfers and so on. This phase is often followed by a process that takes the parse tree from the syntax analyzer and produces a linear sequence of instructions equivalent to the original source program. These instructions are for a virtual machine that has characteristics convenient to the translator; for example, a simple stack-based virtual machine may be appropriate. It is called a virtual machine because a physical implementation completely in hardware is unlikely to exist. If this intermediate code is independent of the target machine, then the portability of the compiler is enhanced.

4.1.4   Code generation

The final phase of the compilation process is to take the output from the semantic analyzer or translator and output machine code or assembly language for the target hardware. A thorough knowledge of the target machine's architecture is required to write a good code generator. The code generator is concerned with the choice of machine instructions, allocation of machine registers, addressing, interfacing with the operating system and so on. To produce faster or more compact code, the code generator should include some form of **code improvement** or **code optimization**. This may exploit techniques such as the use of special-purpose machine instructions or addressing modes, register optimization, and the removal of sections of unreachable code. This code optimization may incorporate both machine-dependent and machine-independent techniques. Methods of code optimization have improved a great deal over the last few years and most modern compilers can produce very high-quality object code.

4.2   Syntax Specification

The role of the syntax specification of a language is to define the set of valid programs. There are many techniques available for defining syntax, some of which are very simple but are suitable only for a restricted set of programming languages – for example, the use of sets. For more complex languages, different approaches are required – for example, the use of a metalanguage or a pictorial notation.

4.2.1   Sets

For extremely simple languages, it may be possible to produce a complete list of all the valid strings. However, the languages that can be defined by this notation are of very limited applicability, and certainly no self-respecting programming language falls into this category. Nevertheless, there are constructs within programming languages that can be expressed in this way. For example, a digit in the Pascal language could be defined as:

$$\{0, 1, 2, 3, 4, 5, 6, 7, 8, 9, 0\}$$

As equally simple but much more powerful specification techniques are available, this set notation is rarely used in programming language definition.

Obviously, it is only feasible to enumerate explicitly all the possible strings of the language if the number of those strings is finite. But this set notation is not restricted to the specification of sets with a finite number of members. For example, it is possible to write:

$$\{xy^n \mid n > 0\}$$

This syntax definition is for a language whose strings are xy, xyy, $xyyy$, ..., xy^n; that is, strings that start with a single x and are followed by any number (greater than zero) of ys.

The notation of regular expressions can be used to extend the power of these set specifications. Using a very simple notation, these can be used for the specification of patterns, which can define comparatively complex sets of character strings. Regular expressions are described in Chapter 5 as they are of special relevance to the syntax specification of the basic lexical components of programming languages.

4.2.2 Backus-Naur Form

Backus-Naur Form (BNF) is a formal metalanguage that is frequently used in the definition of the syntax of programming languages. BNF was introduced in the definition of ALGOL 60 and has been widely used ever since. It is a technique for representing rules that can be used to derive sentences of the language. If a finite set of these rules can be used to derive all sentences of a language, then this set of rules constitutes a formal definition of the syntax of the language.

BNF is best explained with the aid of an example. The rule that a sentence, which is interpreted here in its commonplace sense, consists of a subject followed by a predicate can be represented as follows:

<sentence> → <subject> <predicate>

The <angle brackets> are used here to group characters together to form a single indivisible unit while the → character separates the definition from the object being defined. The symbols ::= or => are sometimes used

instead of →. The BNF rule presented here defines a <sentence> in terms
of a <subject> and a <predicate>. So now <subject> and <predicate>
themselves have to be defined. For example:

<blockquote>

<subject> → <noun> | <pronoun>

</blockquote>

This rule defines a <subject> to be a <noun> or a <pronoun>, the |
character being used to indicate alternative definitions. This rule is equivalent to the two rules:

<blockquote>

<subject> → <noun>

<subject> → <pronoun>

</blockquote>

Similarly, <predicate> can be defined as:

<blockquote>

<predicate> → <transitive verb> <object> | <intransitive verb>

</blockquote>

indicating that a <predicate> consists either of a <transitive verb> followed by an <object> or of an <intransitive verb>.

To complete the definition of a <sentence>, a <noun>, <pro-
noun>, <transitive verb>, <object> and <intransitive verb> now have
to be defined:

<blockquote>

<noun> → **cats** | **dogs** | **sheep**

<pronoun> → **I** | **we** | **you** | **they**

<transitive verb> → **like** | **hate** | **eat**

<object> → **biscuits** | **grass** | **sunshine**

<intransitive verb> → **sleep** | **talk** | **run**

</blockquote>

In these five rules, angle brackets are not used for the words on the right-
hand sides as they are to be treated simply as sequences of characters; in
other words, they are not going to be expanded by further rules.

Using this complete set of rules, sentences can be generated by
making random choices. Sentences are generated step by step by substituting any of the alternatives on the right-hand side of the rule for what
appears on the left-hand side; for example:

<blockquote>

<sentence>

<subject> <predicate>

<noun> <predicate>

sheep <predicate>

sheep <transitive verb> <object>

sheep eat <object>

sheep eat biscuits

</blockquote>

Other possible sentences in this language are **I sleep**, **dogs hate grass** and **we like sunshine**. Note that at no stage is the meaning of these sentences considered; for example, the syntactically correct sentence **cats eat sunshine** may not make good sense, but that is of no concern to the BNF rules.

There are two distinct symbol types that can appear in the BNF rules, as illustrated in the foregoing example:

(1) Symbols such as <sentence>, <pronoun> and <intransitive verb> are called **non-terminal symbols**. There are rules indicating how such symbols should be expanded; in other words, any symbol appearing on the left-hand side of a BNF rule must be a non-terminal symbol.

(2) Symbols such as **cats**, **dogs**, **I** and **grass** are called **terminal symbols**, since they cannot be expanded further. They make up the set of symbols of the language being defined.

Given a set of BNF rules, it is important to be able to determine which symbols are terminals and which are non-terminals. In the foregoing example, the distinction was easy since all non-terminals were enclosed by angle brackets, but this convention is not always used. The following conventions will be used in the examples in this book:

- Non-terminals are either enclosed by angle brackets or are single upper-case letters.
- Terminals are represented as single lower-case letters, digits, special symbols (such as +, * or =), punctuation symbols or strings in bold type (such as **begin**).

Let us look now at some different languages. Consider the set of rules:

$$S \rightarrow S + T \mid T$$
$$T \rightarrow a \mid b$$

Here, S and T are non-terminals whereas a, b and + are terminals. In the first production, S is being defined recursively – this is permissible in BNF. An example of the generation of a sentence of this language is:

S
$S + T$ (using $S \rightarrow S + T$)
$S + T + T$ (using $S \rightarrow S + T$)
$T + T + T$ (using $S \rightarrow T$)
$b + T + T$ (using $T \rightarrow b$)
$b + a + T$ (using $T \rightarrow a$)
$b + a + a$ (using $T \rightarrow a$)

The power of BNF is further illustrated by the following example. Productions similar to those shown are often found in the definition of programming languages. Using these productions, sentences such as $a + b * c$ and $a + b + c$ can be generated, as shown in the example.

Notice that at an intermediate step in the expansion of $a + b * c$, the construct $a + $ <term> appears. In other words, the $b * c$ in the final expression is being grouped as a single entity called a <term>. This suggests that the idea of precedence has been introduced by the grammar with the precedence of $*$ being higher than that of $+$. This of course reflects the precedence rules of conventional arithmetic and algebra so that $a + b * c$ is interpreted as $a + (b * c)$ rather than $(a + b) * c$.

In the expansion of $a + b + c$, the construct $a + b + $ <term> appears in an intermediate step. Tracing backwards, it can be seen that the $a + b$ part is derived from <expression> in the second line of the expansion, showing that $a + b$ is considered as a single <expression> distinct from the <term> c. This argument suggests that $+$ is **left-associative** in this grammar, which means that expressions of the form $a + b + c$ are interpreted as $(a + b) + c$ rather than $a + (b + c)$. A similar argument applies to the $*$ operator. For the $+$ and $*$ operators, the associativity rules have little practical consequence (except sometimes to numerical analysts), but for operators such as $-$ (subtraction) and $/$ (division), the order in which the expression is evaluated affects the result. For example, $a/b/c$ may yield $a/(b * c)$ or $(a * c)/b$. This capability for the automatic inclusion of rules of precedence and associativity into the grammar is an attractive feature of BNF. Many languages such as Pascal and ALGOL 60 incorporate BNF rules of this form in their definition of expressions. The ideas of precedence and associativity were introduced in Section 2.3.3.

EXAMPLE

<expression> → <term> | <expression> + <term>
<term> → <primary> | <term> * <primary>
<primary> → a | b | c

$a + b * c$ is generated as follows:

<expression>
<expression> + <term>
<term> + <term>
<primary> + <term>
a + <term>
a + <term> * <primary>
a + <primary> * <primary>
a + *b* * <primary>
a + *b* * *c*

a + *b* + *c* is generated as follows:

<expression>
<expression> + <term>
<expression> + <term> + <term>
<term> + <term> + <term>
<primary> + <term> + <term>
a + <term> + <term>
a + <primary> + <term>
a + *b* + <term>
a + *b* + <primary>
a + *b* + *c*

___

4.2.3 Syntax diagrams

A closely related method of syntax specification makes use of a pictorial notation. Such graphical techniques have been used to represent the syntax of several languages, but perhaps the most famous application is the syntax definition of Pascal [Jensen, 1985]. The complete syntax definition is made up of a set of syntax diagrams, each defining a specific language construct. As an example, the definition of a constant is shown in Figure 4.2.

Each rectangular box contains the name of a non-terminal symbol which is defined by a syntax diagram of its own. The terminal symbols of the language, such as + and − in the example of Figure 4.2, are enclosed in circles or similar rounded shapes. Any path through the syntax diagram, observing the sense of the arrows, expanding non-terminal symbols as they are encountered, yields a syntactically correct construct.

This method of syntax specification is easily understandable and surprisingly compact; in fact, the complete syntax specification of Pascal can be contained on a couple of sheets of paper. This notation allows a simpler and more compact syntax definition than BNF, allowing the use of

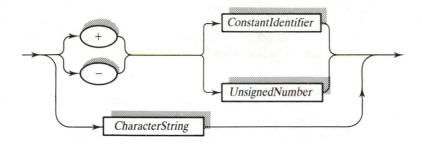

FIGURE 4.2

Syntax diagram defining a Pascal constant.

fewer non-terminal symbols. Furthermore, as we shall see in Chapter 6, it may be possible to construct syntax analyzers directly from this graphical form, just as easily as from a conventional BNF definition.

4.2.4   EBNF

It is not surprising that since its introduction, many extensions to BNF have been proposed. Fortunately, these extensions have in general been minor and, therefore, the elegance and simplicity of BNF has not been lost. One particular set of extensions was used in the ISO Pascal Standard [Jensen, 1985]. The metalanguage used in this document is called EBNF (Extended Backus-Naur Form). EBNF differs from BNF in several ways. One of the principal changes is the set of **metasymbols** – that is, the symbols used for special purposes in the metalanguage. For example, terminal symbols are enclosed in double quotation marks, a full stop (or period) is used to end each production and an equals sign is used to separate the non-terminal from its definition. In addition, parentheses are used to indicate a grouping, as in:

> *AssignmentStatement = (Variable | FunctionIdentifier) ":=" Expression.*

Two methods are used to indicate symbol repetition: [*X*] implies zero or one instance of *X* – in other words, *X* is optional – and {*X*} implies zero or more instances of *X*. These metasymbols can make the definition of the syntax of a programming language very much simpler, perhaps reducing the necessity for the introduction of otherwise unnecessary non-terminal symbols. For example, an identifier could be defined in EBNF as:

> *Identifier = Letter { Letter | Digit }.*

In BNF, it could be defined as:

> <Identifier> ::= <Letter> | <Identifier> <Letter>
> | <Identifier> <Digit>

The advantages of the EBNF definition are that it is much clearer and that it corresponds much more closely to the design of a simple and efficient syntax analyzer. This subject is developed later in Section 6.2 when the topic of top-down syntax analysis is discussed.

4.3   Grammars

The study of grammar started long before the development of programming languages and was based primarily on the study of natural languages. The ideas that had been developed then found direct relevance in the formal study of programming languages. In particular, the work of Noam Chomsky has greatly influenced the study of programming linguistics.

The previous section outlined how BNF and other techniques can be used in the definition of a language. But, formally, a set of BNF rules is only part of the definition of the grammar of a language. Furthermore, BNF and its relations can only be used in the definitions of grammars of a very restricted class of languages.

The **grammar** (G) of a language can be formally defined as a 4-tuple $G = (N, T, S, P)$ where N is the finite set of non-terminal symbols, T is the finite set of terminal symbols, S is the **starting symbol**, which must be a member of the set N, and P is the set of **productions**. The starting symbol is the unique non-terminal symbol that is used as a starting point in generating all strings of the language. A production is simply a rule that defines a string transformation. It has the general form:

$$\alpha \to \beta$$

Any occurrence of the string α in the string to be transformed can be replaced by the string β. For example, the set of BNF productions presented in Section 4.2.2 forms a part of the definition of the grammar of a language. The remainder of the definition is:

N = { sentence, subject, predicate, noun, pronoun, intransitive verb, transitive verb, object}

T = { cats, dogs, sheep, I, we, you, they, live, hate, eat, biscuits, grass, sunshine, sleep, talk, run}

S =   sentence

Unfortunately, the formal definition of a grammar is still not quite complete, since the strings α and β must have some relationship to the sets N and T. Suppose U is the set of all terminal and non-terminal symbols of the language; that is, $U = N \cup T$. The notation U^+ is used to denote the positive closure of the set U; that is, the set of all non-empty strings that can be formed by the concatenation of members of U. U^*, on the other hand, denotes the closure of U; that is, the set $U^+ \cup \{\varepsilon\}$, where ε is the empty string. The restriction placed on the strings α and β is then that α must be a member of U^+ and β must be a member of U^*.

At this point, a few more definitions have to be introduced. A **sentential form** is any string that can be derived from the starting symbol. A **sentence** is a sentential form that does not contain any non-terminal symbols; it just contains terminal symbols and cannot be expanded any further.

Section 4.2.2 showed how sentences can be generated very simply using a set of BNF productions. The reverse process of determining *how* the BNF rules were applied to generate a sentence is much harder. This process of determining the syntactic structure of a sentence is called **parsing** or **syntax analysis** and forms a major part of the compilation of high-level language programs.

Clearly, the major part of a grammar definition is P – the set of productions. It is therefore very important to examine the possible structures of these productions.

4.3.1   Chomsky classification

In the definition of the grammar presented in the previous section, each production has the form:

$$\alpha \rightarrow \beta$$

where there are no restrictions on the sentential forms α and β, other than those already mentioned. A grammar with productions of this general form is called a **Chomsky type 0** or a **free grammar**. These grammars do not have much relevance to today's programming languages because they are too general, requiring restrictions on the form of the productions so that the writing of a compiler is a feasible task.

If the productions are restricted to the form:

$$\alpha A \beta \rightarrow \alpha \gamma \beta$$

where α, β and γ are members of U^*, γ is not null and A is a single non-terminal symbol, then the resulting grammar is of **type 1**. These are the **context-sensitive grammars**. In the production above, A is transformed to γ only when it occurs in the context of being preceded by α and followed by β. These context-sensitive grammars are sometimes defined in a slightly different, but essentially equivalent, way. If all productions have the form:

$$\alpha \rightarrow \beta$$

where $|\alpha| \leq |\beta|$ and $|\alpha|$ denotes the length of the string α, then the grammar is said to be context sensitive. This form of the definition does not visually emphasize the notion of context sensitivity.

Most programming languages have aspects that can only be described by type 1 grammars. In practice, however, the use of a type 1 grammar is conventionally avoided by augmenting the syntax description of the language, which is expressed in a form that is not context sensitive, with additional rules, usually expressed in English. For example, the scope rules of Pascal are not included in the formal syntax definition – they are expressed in informal English.

A further restriction on the form of the productions gives rise to type 2 grammars. If all the productions are of the form:

$$A \rightarrow \gamma$$

where A is a single non-terminal, then the resulting grammar is of **type 2**. Such grammars are also referred to as **context-free grammars**, since A can always be transformed into γ without any concern for its context. This type of grammar is of immense importance in programming language design. It corresponds directly to the BNF notation, where each production has a single non-terminal symbol on its left-hand side, and so any grammar that is expressible in BNF must be a context-free grammar. Hence, languages such as Pascal and ALGOL 60 are defined as context-free (or type 2) languages.

The final Chomsky class imposes yet further restrictions on the productions. If all productions are of the form:

$$A \rightarrow a \quad \text{or} \quad A \rightarrow aB$$

where A and B are non-terminal symbols and a is a terminal symbol, then the resulting grammar is a **type 3 grammar**. These grammars are also called **finite**, **finite-state** or **regular grammars**. This type of grammar is too restrictive for general-purpose programming languages, but it does find application in the design of some of the structures used as components of most programming languages. Structures such as identifiers, numbers and so on can often be described using a regular grammar.

The hierarchy of grammars is represented diagrammatically in Figure 4.3. This figure shows the inclusive nature of the hierarchy so that, for example, all type 3 languages are also type 1 languages. In progressing from type 0 to type 3 grammars, language complexity and hence complexity of recognizers, parsers or compilers decreases. This book concentrates on type 2 and type 3 grammars. Comparatively simple but powerful techniques exist for writing compilers for a subset of type 2 languages. Type 3 languages are even easier, as sentences in these languages can be recognized by **finite-state automata**, and these languages come into their own when considering the design of lexical analyzers. Finite-state automata are described in Chapter 5.

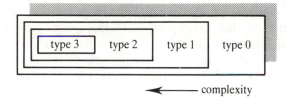

complexity

FIGURE 4.3

Hierarchy of Chomsky
grammars.

4.3.2 Two-level grammars

Compiler writers feel most at home with Chomsky type 2 and type 3
languages. Parsing techniques for these languages are now well understood
and are usually comparatively straightforward. Furthermore, it is of great
benefit to the compiler writer if a formal and complete definition of the
syntax of the language exists. It is a significant disadvantage to have to
resort to natural language descriptions of syntactic constraints that the
compiler must apply. Ideally, it should be possible to specify formally all
the checks a compiler must perform to determine whether a program is
syntactically correct.

Unfortunately, it may not be easy or even possible to produce such a
complete formal specification for a language in terms of a context-free
grammar. For example, a Pascal compiler is expected to check that all
variables and types are appropriately declared before they are used. The
compiler also has to perform extensive type checking and flag any errors;
for example, an assignment statement where the left-hand variable has
type *integer* and the right-hand expression has type *real* should be flagged
as an error. In practice, it is not very helpful to resort to a type 1 grammar
to express these context-dependent rules and so different techniques are
often adopted. The T-notation of ALGOL W was a step in this direction,
but by far the most famous approach is the two-level grammar introduced
in the definition of ALGOL 68 [van Wijngaarden, 1975].

ALGOL 68 is defined by two finite sets of rules: the **meta-
productions** and the **hyper-rules**. These two sets can be used to derive an
infinite set of context-free production rules which define the language. The
fact that this set is infinite distinguishes the definition of ALGOL 68 from
those of the context-free languages, such as Pascal, by allowing the specification of context-sensitive restrictions and also aspects of semantics.

We start with the definition of a **protonotion**. Protonotions are
sequences of "small syntactic marks", composed essentially of lower-case
letters with spaces to improve readability, which are used to represent
terminal symbols in the metaproduction rules. Protonotions ending with
the word 'symbol' are called **symbols** and form the set of terminal symbols
of the grammar. For example, the protonotion *letter a symbol* is a symbol
and has the representation *a*.

At the lowest level, the syntax of ALGOL 68 is defined by a set of production rules. But these production rules cannot be written out explicitly in the ALGOL 68 report, since there is an infinite number of them! Instead, they are derived from the hyper-rules and the meta-production rules using a simple process. Some of these production rules appear in the ALGOL 68 report and are written in a notation reminiscent of BNF. Each rule consists of a protonotion followed by a colon, followed by a sequence of alternatives separated by semicolons. The rule ends with a full stop. A comma is used to separate the individual elements of each alternative. For example, the rules:

> real denotation: variable point numeral; floating point numeral.
> floating point numeral: stagnant part, exponent part

define the protonotions real denotation and floating point numeral. A real denotation is a variable point numeral or a floating point numeral. A floating point numeral consists of a stagnant part followed by an exponent part. The protonotions variable point numeral, stagnant part and exponent part are defined in other production rules.

The mechanism used to generate these production rules is based on the (finite) sets of hyper-rules and metaproduction rules. The form of a hyper-rule is very similar to that of a production rule. Each hyper-rule consists of a **hypernotion** followed by a colon, followed by a non-empty sequence of **hyperalternatives** separated by semicolons. Again, the rule ends with a full stop. A comma is used to separate the individual hyper-notions making up the hyperalternative. For example, the hyper-rule:

> SIZE INTREAL denotation: SIZE symbol, INTREAL denotation.

defines, via a set of other rules, the syntax of real and integer denotations. The words in upper-case letters are called **metanotions** and are defined by the metaproduction rules. A metaproduction rule consists of a metanotion (a sequence of upper-case letters) followed by two colons, followed by a non-empty sequence of hypernotions separated by semicolons. As usual, the rule ends with a full stop. For example, the following metaproduction rules are relevant to the hyper-rule presented above:

> SIZE :: long; short.
> INTREAL :: SIZETY integral; SIZETY real.
> SIZETY :: long LONGSETY; short SHORTSETY; EMPTY.
> LONGSETY :: long LONGSETY; EMPTY.
> SHORTSETY :: short SHORTSETY; EMPTY.
> EMPTY :: .

By using these metaproduction rules to carry out consistent substitution in the hyper-rules, the actual production rules are obtained, an example of which is:

long long real denotation: long symbol, long real denotation.

The substitution has to be consistent so that if INTREAL is substituted by SIZETY integral on the left-hand side of the hyper-rule, then the identical substitution has to be made on the right-hand side. It can be easily seen that this single hyper-rule can give rise to an infinite number of production rules.

It is difficult to convey the power of this syntax specification technique in a simple example. Two-level grammars provide a very convenient notation for the definition of context-sensitive languages. Further information is contained in McGettrick [1980] and van Wijngaarden [1975].

4.3.3 Other approaches to grammar specification

There has been a great interest in the extension of context-free grammars so that they can express some of the semantic aspects of languages. The introduction of the two-level grammar is important in this respect, as it enabled the formal statement of rules of **static semantics**. These are rules for the construction of programs which can be applied by the compiler, but which previously had to be specified in a natural language.

A great deal of interest has also been shown in **attribute grammars**. These extend context-free grammars by the propagation of attributes, which are derived from context information through the parsing process. In these grammars, each context-free production is associated with a set of rules, while each symbol has a set of attribute values associated with it. The rules specify how to evaluate the attributes of symbols in terms of the attributes of other symbols appearing in the same production.

Many other extensions to context-free grammars have been proposed together with corresponding parsing techniques, but these are beyond the scope of this book.

Numerous types of grammar have come from the world of artificial intelligence. One of the major research areas in this field is the understanding of natural language. Indeed, there are many similarities between the techniques used for parsing natural languages and those used for high-level computer languages. The **transition network grammar** can be considered to be equivalent to a context-free grammar. It expresses the grammar as a network, which is traversed as symbols are recognized, and it seems to be more appropriate to the needs of the artificial intelligence community. Approximately equivalent to the attribute grammar is the **augmented transition network grammar**. This allows the accumulation and subsequent use of extra information during the parsing process.

Just as in the field of high-level language parsing, the set of grammars does not end here. New techniques for grammar specification of natural languages are being developed at a rapid rate. Winston [1984] contains an introduction to the techniques being used for natural language understanding.

4.4   Semantics

The syntax of a language defines the set of valid programs, but a programmer or a compiler writer must have more information before the language can be used or a compiler written. The semantic rules provide this information and specify the meanings or actions of all the valid programs. Techniques for semantic specification are very much more complicated than those for syntax specification and, at present, they are not nearly so well developed. In particular, formal semantic specification techniques with wide applicability, simplifying compiler construction, do not yet exist.

A compiler is essentially concerned with two processes: the analysis of the source program and the synthesis of the object program. From the point of view of the compiler writer, syntax is largely concerned with the analysis phase. Semantics, on the other hand, is largely concerned with the synthesis phase. However, semantic specification is sometimes of relevance to the analysis phase; for example, type checking rules are often part of the semantic specification of a language.

It is important to realize the importance of the statement of the semantics. Although the semantics of most high-level language constructs may appear to be obvious, there may be many areas where confusion may arise. Infamous constructs in this respect include the mechanisms for parameter passing to subprograms and the evaluation of **for/do** loop parameters.

4.4.1   Specification of semantics

Early programming languages such as ALGOL 60 used informal, natural language, notations for describing semantics. Consequently, there were many errors and ambiguities in the language definitions and significant incompatibilities between implementations became inevitable. The importance of formal methods then became clear. Several different approaches to the specification of semantics can be identified.

The **operational approach** defines an implementation of the language on which all other implementations should be modelled. This implementation is not normally on real hardware, but instead is based on some idealized abstract machine. The semantics specification states that a particular language construction alters the state of the abstract machine in a specified way; hence, it is possible to deduce the action of any specific program. This approach has been adopted for the specification of the semantics of PL/I using the Vienna Definition Language (VDL) [Wegner, 1972].

At first sight, the operational approach appears very attractive: it is conceptually easy to understand and the flexibility in the design of the abstract machine can simplify the task of specification. However, this technique is usually of limited practical use because it is impossible to make abstract statements about the semantics of programs, in general, since the specification in terms of the abstract machine can only be used to determine the semantics of specific programs with specific sets of input data. Furthermore, it may be very difficult, or even impossible, to relate the implementation on the abstract machine to an implementation on real hardware. To verify an implementation formally, the interpreter on the abstract machine and the compiler or interpreter on the real hardware have to be proved to be equivalent. But, in general, this is not a feasible task. Finally, it should be noted that this technique essentially reduces the problem of specifying the semantics of the original language to that of the specification of the semantics of the operations of the abstract machine.

A second approach makes use of **denotational semantics**. Here, no reference is made to particular implementations. Instead, programs are defined in terms of mappings into mathematical operations and constructs. Formal mathematical techniques can then be used to define semantics. This technique provides an abstract means for defining the semantics of a language. It allows general statements to be made about programs but at a cost, since the mathematics involved is specialized and comparatively complex.

It is also possible to adopt the **axiomatic approach**. Here, axioms are specified that define the way in which data objects (predicates) are transformed by each language construct. This technique has an immediate relevance to the problem of proving program correctness. The semantics of Pascal has been defined in this way [Hoare, 1973].

Many other approaches have been devised, such as the use of attribute grammars, and the problem of semantics specification remains a fertile area of research. Interested readers should consult the bibliography at the back of the book for pointers to further reading.

4.5   Parsing

The rules defining a programming language may be used directly by a programmer to write correct programs but it is not immediately obvious how these rules can be used by a compiler writer. Somehow the compiler must incorporate the rules that define the programming language within its own logic and perform a translation of syntactically correct programs into the appropriate object format. These rules allow the compiler to determine the underlying structure of the program and so deal with all the structural elements in a consistent way.

As an example of a very simple language, consider again the following syntax definition:

<expression> → <term> | <expression> + <term>

<term> → <primary> | <term> * <primary>

<primary> → a | b | c

As was demonstrated in Section 4.2.2, it is a simple matter to show how these productions may be used to generate expressions such as $a * b + c$. However, the compiler has to reverse this process – that is, perform a syntax analysis of the string – to determine whether a string such as $a * b + c$ is a valid expression and, if so, how it is structured in terms of the units <term> and <primary>.

Before looking at the techniques that can be used for parsing, it is important to understand the aims of the parsing process. The syntax analyzer in a compiler has to construct some form of data structure that represents the syntactic structure of the program. For example, the syntax analyzer in a Pascal compiler would have to recognize that the input:

if $a > b$ **then** $n := 0$ **else** $n := n + 1$

represented an **if** statement with the condition being the Boolean expression $a > b$, the **then** part being the statement $n := 0$ and the **else** part being the statement $n := n + 1$. The form of this data structure obviously depends on the language and the whim of the compiler writer, but it is often sensible to use some form of tree, the **parse tree**.

EXAMPLE

Given the three productions defining <expression>, <term> and <primary>, the string $a * b + c$ can be reduced as follows:

a * b + c
<primary> * b + c   (<primary> → a)
<primary> * <primary> + c   (<primary> → b)
<primary> * <primary> + <primary>   (<primary> → c)
<term> * <primary> + <primary>   (<term> → <primary>)
<term> * <primary> + <term>   (<term> → <primary>)
<term> + <term>   (<term> →
                                                     <term> * <primary>)
<expression> + <term>   (<expression> →
                                                     <term>)
<expression>   (<expression> →
                                                     <expression> + <term>)

The example shows how the string a * b + c may be reduced. The production used in each stage is stated in parentheses. For such a simple case, parsing can be carried out comparatively easily by hand, perhaps using some inspired guesswork at certain stages to ensure that the parse follows the correct path. It is vital and also worrying to note that in even such a simple example, the process of parsing may not go quite so smoothly. For example, if the productions were used in a slightly different sequence, the reduction would proceed as follows:

a * b + c
<primary> * b + c   (<primary> → a)
<primary> * <primary> + c   (<primary> → b)
<primary> * <primary> + <primary>   (<primary> → c)
<primary> * <term> + <primary>   (<term> → <primary>)
<primary> * <expression> + <primary>   (<expression> →
                                                     <term>)
<primary> * <expression> + <term>   (<term> → <primary>)
<primary> * <expression>   (<expression> →
                                                     <expression> + <term>)
<term> * <expression>   (<term> → <primary>)
<expression> * <expression>   (<expression> →
                                                     <term>)

and then become stuck, perhaps implying the false deduction that a * b + c is not a sentence of the language. Automating this parsing process is, therefore, not a trivial matter.

The result of parsing the string a * b + c is a data structure that somehow represents the syntactic structure of the string. Figure 4.4 shows

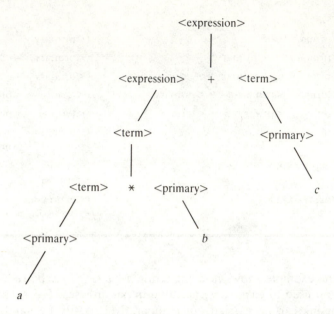

FIGURE 4.4

Syntactic structure of the string *a * b + c*.

a tree representation of the string. This tree combines the relevant information contained in the set of productions, together with the content of the original sentence, in a structure that is self-contained and which can be used by subsequent phases of the compiler. The mechanisms actually used in constructing such a tree will be examined in Chapter 6, but an overview appears in the next section.

4.5.1 Parsing strategies

The sledgehammer approach to the problem of parsing is to take the starting symbol of the language in question and start generating all possible sentences from it. If the input matches one of these sentences, then the input string is a valid sentence of the language. Obviously, this is an impractical approach, since in even the simplest of grammars the number of possible sentences that can be generated is infinite. A more intelligent strategy is required.

Most parsers can be divided into two categories:

(1)   **Top-down parsers**, which construct the parse tree by starting at the root, which is normally the starting symbol, and proceeding to the leaves.

(2)   **Bottom-up parsers**, which start at the leaves and move up towards the root.

The great advantage of top-down parsers is that they are comparatively easy to write, with the actual code capable of being derived directly from the production rules. Unfortunately, the top-down approach cannot always be applied, but the more powerful bottom-up parsers can often be used instead, since they can handle a larger set of grammars.

4.5.2 Top-down parsing

The underlying ideas behind top-down parsing are quite simple, although there are often a few practical difficulties that complicate its implementation. The parsing process starts at the root of the parse tree; in other words, it first considers the starting symbol of the grammar. The goal of the parsing process is to produce, from this starting symbol, the sequence of terminal symbols that have been presented as input to the parser. This goal is successively broken down into a sequence of subgoals, each of which has to be satisfied for the initial goal to be satisfied.

EXAMPLE

Suppose that the starting symbol S is defined in the grammar by the production rule:

$$S \rightarrow AB$$

The goal of satisfying S is then achieved by first recognizing the presence of the subgoal A and then recognizing the presence of the subgoal B. Similarly, if S is defined by the rule:

$$S \rightarrow A \mid B$$

then S would be recognized by recognizing A or by recognizing B. The subgoals of recognizing A and B would then be further subdivided by subsequent rules in the grammar.

Once a subgoal starts with one or more terminal symbols, these symbols can be matched with the input string. If these symbols do not match, then the subgoal has not been satisfied and further decomposition into subgoals is unnecessary. If the symbols do match, then the decomposition has to continue until all the terminal symbols match, in which case the subgoal is satisfied, or until there is a mismatch.

The presence of rules involving alternation may well result in a need for **backtracking**. For example, if the grammar started with the rule:

$$S \rightarrow A \mid B$$

and it was found that the input string did not match the string or strings derived from A, then the parser would have to abandon the A subgoal completely and retrace its steps so that it could try again with the B subgoal. By making use of recursive procedure calls, backtracking may be achieved without too much difficulty, but parsing may become rather inefficient. If it is at all possible, the grammar should be transformed to remove the necessity for backtracking.

4.5.3   Bottom-up parsing

Bottom-up parsers start with the input string and repeatedly replace strings on the right-hand sides of productions by the corresponding strings on the left-hand sides of productions until, hopefully, just the starting symbol remains. The problem faced with bottom-up parsing is that it is necessary to determine which strings should be replaced and in what order the replacement should occur.

Solutions to this problem are suggested in Chapter 6. But first, it is appropriate to look at the process of **derivation**; that is, the process of taking the starting symbol and repeatedly replacing non-terminals according to the production rules. The derivation where the leftmost non-terminal is replaced at each step is called the **leftmost derivation**; similarly, the **rightmost derivation** involves the replacement of the rightmost non-terminal at each step.

EXAMPLE

Using the grammar already defined, the leftmost derivation of $a * b + c$ from <expression> is:

<expression>
<expression> + <term>
<term> + <term>
<term> * <primary> + <term>
<primary> * <primary> + <term>
a * <primary> + <term>
$a * b$ + <term>
$a * b$ + <primary>
$a * b + c$

The rightmost derivation is:

<expression>
<expression> + <term>
<expression> + <primary>
<expression> + c
<term> + c
<term> * <primary> + c
<term> * b + c
<primary> * b + c
a * b + c

The bottom-up parser has to reverse the derivation process and, conventionally, it is the rightmost derivation that is reversed. Consider a bottom-up parser that operates from left to right along the sentential form, applying at each step the production that reduces the characters furthest to the left. The substring that is reduced – that is, replaced by the left-hand side of the corresponding production – is called the **handle**, provided that this reduction corresponds to the next step in the reverse of the rightmost derivation.

EXAMPLE

As an example, consider the parsing of the sentential form $a * b + c$. The parse progresses as shown in Table 4.1.

Table 4.1 Parse of $a * b + c$.

Sentential form	Handle	Production used	Reduced sentential form
$a * b + c$	a	<primary> → a	<primary> * b + c
<primary> * b + c	<primary>	<term> → <primary>	<term> * b + c
<term> * b + c	b	<primary> → b	<term> * <primary> + c
<term> * <primary> + c	<term> * <primary>	<term> → <term> * <primary>	<term> + c
<term> + c	<term>	<expression> → <term>	<expression> + c
<expression> + c	c	<primary> → c	<expression> + <primary>
<expression> + <primary>	<primary>	<term> → <primary>	<expression> + <term>
<expression> + <term>	<expression> + <term>	<expression> → <expression> + <term>	<expression>
<expression>			

Note that the sequence of sentential forms produced during this reduction is that produced in the rightmost derivation in reverse. The reduction performed by this method of parsing is sometimes called the **canonical parse**. The corresponding rightmost derivation is known as the **canonical derivation**.

Unfortunately, the process just outlined does not provide a general bottom-up parsing method – try parsing $a + b * c$, for example. Problems arise in identifying the handle and which productions to use at each step. Detailed methods are presented in Chapter 6.

SUMMARY

- Compilers can often be conveniently structured into four phases: lexical analysis, syntax analysis, semantic analysis and code generation. The first three of these phases are concerned with the analysis of the source program whereas code generation is concerned with the synthesis of the object program.

- There are several widely used techniques for the specification of the syntax of programming languages. BNF is a particularly popular metalanguage used for this purpose.

- The major part of the formal specification of the grammar of a language is the set of productions. The Chomsky classification groups grammars according to the form of their productions.

- It may be possible to make use of two-level grammars to express language features, such as context sensitivity. There are several other approaches to grammar specification which are sometimes used.

- Formal techniques are also available for the specification of semantics.

- Parsers can be broadly classified into two groups: top-down parsers and bottom-up parsers. Top-down parsers try to achieve the goal of recognizing the starting symbol by repeatedly subdividing the goal until terminal symbols from the input string can be matched. Bottom-up parsers work directly on the input string, repeatedly matching symbols on the right-hand sides of productions by the corresponding symbols on the left-hand sides of productions until just the starting symbol remains.

EXERCISES

4.1 Describe the functions and the interfaces of the lexical analyzer, the syntax analyzer and the code generator of a typical compiler. Show how the Pascal statement:

$$total := sum1 + 100 * (a - b); \quad (* \text{ recompute total } *)$$

is transformed by each of these phases.

4.2 Define the terms sentence, sentential form, top-down parsing, bottom-up parsing, handle and canonical parse.

4.3 Although the syntax rules of Pascal have context-dependent aspects, a Chomsky type 1 grammar is not used to define the syntax of Pascal. Why is this?

4.4 Illustrate how a BNF syntax specification can determine the associativity and precedence of operators. Devise a BNF grammar for simple algebraic expressions involving just multiplication and addition, where multiplication has lower precedence than addition and both operators are right-associative. Thus, an expression of the form $a + b + c * d * e$ is evaluated as $(a + (b + c)) * (d * e)$.

4.5 Try expressing other rules of associativity and precedence of the standard arithmetic operators. For example, devise a BNF grammar where all operators ($+$, $-$, $*$ and $/$) have the same precedence and expressions are evaluated from left to right, unless indicated otherwise by parentheses.

4.6 Devise an algorithm for converting EBNF into BNF.

4.7 Using the grammar presented in the text, try the canonical parse of the sentence $a + b * c$.

4.8 Write a set of BNF rules defining a numerical constant of the form defined by Pascal. Use these rules to define leftmost and rightmost derivations of 123, 1.23, 1.23E4 and 1E-2.

4.9 Produce a grammar for the definition of an identifier consisting of one to four letters or digits, where the first character must be a letter.

4.10 Devise a grammar for a simple desk calculator language capable of operating on binary, octal, decimal and hexadecimal values. Try to ensure that the grammar contains no ambiguities. (After studying Chapter 9 and the appendix, this grammar may be transformed comparatively easily into a working program!)

4.11 Write a program that reads a BNF grammar and produces random sentences conforming to that grammar. This can form the basis of a random English language sentence generator or, perhaps more seriously, as a means of generating random programs for testing compilers. If, for example, the BNF specification of Pascal were input to such a program, would the output always be a syntactically correct Pascal program?

CHAPTER 5

Lexical Analysis

The lexical analyzer or scanner has to recognize the basic tokens making up the source program input to the compiler. As these tokens are syntactically simple in structure, they can be recognized by comparatively simple algorithms – the more complex and slower algorithms of the syntax analyzer are unnecessary here. The lexical analyzer relieves the burden on the syntax analyzer.

If the syntax of the tokens can be expressed in terms of a regular grammar, then the construction of a lexical analyzer is straightforward. This chapter describes the characteristics of regular grammars and finite-state automata and shows their relevance to lexical analysis.

5.1   Role of the Lexical Analyzer

Writing an efficient and reliable lexical analyzer demands careful planning and preparation. The syntax of all the structures the lexical analyzer is to recognize must be specified carefully and the analyzer's algorithms have to be matched to the types of grammar being used to specify the symbols. If certain restrictions are placed on the grammar needed for these symbols, it is possible to write efficient parsers by hand comparatively easily. But perhaps more important, it is possible to automate the production of lexical analyzers, thus making significant savings in the effort required for the implementation of a compiler.

Techniques of lexical analysis have application in many fields other than compiler design. For example, almost any program requiring command input from a user requires at least a rudimentary lexical analyzer to separate commands from arguments. Adopting the standard techniques for constructing lexical analyzers for these problems may well simplify their implementation.

The lexical analyzer breaks up the program input into a sequence of tokens – the basic syntactic components of the language. Comments and source program layout information of no relevance to the syntax analyzer are stripped. The lexical analyzer is also responsible for decoding the lexical representation of symbols in the source program. For example, it should be possible to modify a Pascal compiler to accept the character @ instead of ↑ by simply making a minor modification to the lexical analyzer. Similarly, the spelling of reserved words should be of concern only to the lexical analyzer. For example, by changing the lexical analyzer's table of Pascal reserved words, it should be easy to produce a Welsh version of Pascal with all the reserved words replaced by their Welsh translations.

5.1.1   Tokens

The lexical analyzer recognizes the basic syntactic components of a programming language. For example, a lexical analyzer for Pascal would recognize identifiers, reserved words, numerical constants, strings, punctuation and special symbols. These tokens would be passed to the syntax analyzer as single values indicating the nature of the token and, for some types of token such as constants or identifiers, some form of value or identification. So, the lexical analyzer has to perform the dual task of **recognizing** the token and in some cases **evaluating** that token.

The lexical analyzer can be viewed as a collection of simple routines, each responsible for dealing with one particular token type, which are controlled by some program that selects the appropriate routines depending on the characters found in the source program. These individual routines can be very simple – in many cases, their sole action is to return some coded value to the syntax analyzer to indicate which token has been recognized. Other routines have to be slightly more complex. For example, the routine to recognize an unsigned integer constant may include the following code:

```
intval := ord(ch) − ord('0');
    (* first character of the integer already in ch *)
NextCh(ch);
while (ch >= '0') and (ch <= '9') do
begin
    intval := intval * 10 + ord(ch) − ord('0');
    NextCh(ch)
end;
    (* character terminating integer in ch, value of integer read in intval *)
```

In this example, the procedure *NextCh* returns the next character from the input, dealing appropriately with the ends of source lines and the end of the source file. For example, in the case of a lexical analyzer for Pascal, it would be appropriate for *NextCh* to return a space character whenever it reached the end of a source line and to issue an error if end of file is detected – it is not necessary for the compiler to read beyond the terminating full stop of a Pascal program.

At first sight, the writing of a lexical analyzer may appear to be almost trivial. But a significant problem arises from the need for **look-ahead**; that is, it may be necessary to read several characters of a token before the type of that token can be determined. The degree of lookahead required obviously depends on the particular token and on the language. Pascal is a good language in this respect because most tokens can be distinguished using just one- or two-character lookahead. For example, a Pascal lexical analyzer, on reading a + character, immediately returns the symbol to the syntax analyzer (assuming that it is not being read in the context of a comment or a character string). On the other hand, lookahead is required when the lexical analyzer reads the < character, as it may be followed by the = character. A greater degree of lookahead may be required when reading a number; for example, at least six characters have to be read to determine that the token 12345.67 is going to be a real number rather than an integer. A form of lookahead is also required when reading identifiers and reserved words, since it is only possible to distinguish between these token types once the complete token has been read.

Lexical analyzers for other languages may face more difficult problems and so different approaches may be more appropriate. For example, in the FORTRAN statement:

```
DO 1 I = 1
```

the lexical analyzer has to reach the end of the statement before it can determine that it should return the identifier DO1I rather than the DO to start a DO loop. Furthermore, in some languages, the role of the lexical analyzer becomes merged with that of the syntax analyzer. The nature of a token may be determined only in the light of potentially complex context information, which is normally maintained by the syntax analyzer. Languages that do not rely on reserved words, such as FORTRAN or PL/I, fall into this category. For example, the FORTRAN statement:

```
IF(GT.GT.DO) IF = DO + GT
```

requires some careful analysis to determine that the first IF and the second GT are special keywords, not identifiers. Such difficulties can be partially resolved by the syntax analyzer offering context information to the lexical analyzer when required. Alternatively, it may be more appropriate for the bulk of the source analysis to be performed within the syntax analyzer. Such an approach is attractive for several reasons: it reduces the communication required between the two modules, thereby making them less interdependent and hopefully easier to design.

Bearing in mind these comments on tokens and the requirement for lookahead, it is perfectly possible to write a complete lexical analyzer without recourse to formal techniques. But there is a great danger that such a lexical analyzer will turn out to be a poorly structured piece of software, hard to modify and maintain. It may also prove to be an unexpectedly difficult project, full of special cases to be attended to. It is therefore essential that a somewhat more rigorous approach is followed, so that a lexical analyzer can be designed in a more structured way. However, to do this, it is necessary to look first of all at the grammatical structure of the tokens and then at the techniques by which these structures can be translated into the backbone of a well-structured lexical analyzer.

5.2   Regular Grammars

In Chapter 4, the characteristics of Chomsky type 3 (finite-state or regular) grammars were described. These grammars have a special significance to lexical analysis.

Recall that a type 3 grammar has productions of the form:

$$A \rightarrow a \quad \text{or} \quad A \rightarrow aB$$

The structures defined by such grammars are syntactically quite simple. Alternation and repetition can be specified by these grammars, but more complex structures such as balanced parentheses cannot be handled. One of the strengths of these grammars lies in the fact that it is possible to construct simple and efficient parsers for them. In particular, if the lexical tokens of a programming language can be defined in terms of a type 3 grammar, then an efficient lexical analyzer for a compiler for that language can be constructed simply, derived directly from the set of production rules defining the tokens.

Before investigating the techniques whereby such analyzers can be constructed, a somewhat more compact notation for defining the syntax of these simple structures needs to be introduced. The notation of **regular expressions** can be used. A regular expression consists of symbols (in the alphabet of the language that is being defined) and a set of operators that allow:

- concatenation (units to be concatenated are adjacent),
- alternation (units are separated by |),
- repetition (units are followed by * specifying zero or more times).

Conventionally, * has the highest precedence, concatenation has the next highest precedence and | has the lowest precedence. Parentheses are introduced when other groupings are desired.

EXAMPLE

- *ab* denotes the set of strings {*ab*} – this set contains just one member
- *a*|*b* denotes {*a*, *b*}
- *a* * denotes {ε, *a*, *aa*, *aaa*, ...}
- *ab* * denotes {*a*, *ab*, *abb*, *abbb*, ...}
- (*a* | *b*) * denotes the set of strings made up of zero or more instances of an *a* or a *b*
- (*ab* | *c*) * *d* denotes the set of strings including {*d*, *abd*, *cd*, *abcd*, *ababcd*, ...}

Regular expressions have many features in common with conventional algebraic expressions. Consequently, it is quite easy to develop a set of rules indicating how regular expressions can be transformed into equivalent regular expressions. Regular expressions are said to be equivalent when they denote the same set of strings – that is, the same language. For example, the expressions *a*(*b* | *c*) and *ab* | *ac* are equivalent.

Regular grammars and regular expressions are equivalent notations. In other words, given a set of productions defining a regular grammar, it is possible to convert them to an equivalent regular expression by an algorithmic process. Similarly, a regular expression can be converted into an equivalent set of production rules; however, the formal proofs of this equivalence are beyond the scope of this book.

Regular expressions can be used to specify the syntax of the basic lexical tokens of programming languages in a clear and concise way. For example, the syntax of an integer constant could be specified as follows:

digit → 0 | 1 | 2 | 3 | 4 | 5 | 6 | 7 | 8 | 9
sign → + | − | ε
integerconstant → sign digit digit *

This definition implies that an integer constant consists of an optional sign followed by one or more digits. Similarly, an identifier consisting of an initial letter followed by a string of letters or digits could be specified as:

digit → 0 | 1 | 2 | 3 | 4 | 5 | 6 | 7 | 8 | 9
letter → a | b | c | ... | z | A | B | C | ... | Z
identifier → letter (letter | digit) *

These regular expressions can be represented diagrammatically. For example, the expression (ab | c) * d is shown in Figure 5.1. Using this directed structure, which is in effect a syntax diagram, it is easy to see how to generate strings of the language by following the arrows and outputting the symbols contained in the boxes encountered in the paths. Fortunately, since the reverse problem of parsing such strings is also of concern here, this diagram can be used as the basis for a recognizing algorithm [Thompson, 1968]. Two Boolean variables are associated with each box in the diagram: one called **flag** and the other called **marker**. The algorithm starts by setting the **flag** variable in all boxes that can be reached directly from the start point to **true** and all other **flag** variables to **false**. The algorithm continues by reading the characters to be parsed one at a time, as follows:

```
while there are characters left to be read do
begin
    set all marker variables to false

    read a character from the input

    set marker variables to true in all boxes that have a true flag and match
    the character variable – if no marker variables can be set, the parse fails

    set all flag variables to false

    set flag variables of boxes that can be reached directly from the boxes
    having a true marker

end
```

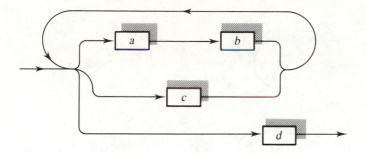

FIGURE 5.1

Representation of the regular expression $(ab \mid c) * d$.

Success of the parse is indicated by the algorithm following a pointer out of the diagram.

At first sight, it looks as though all the problems of lexical analysis have been solved, as long as the tokens can be expressed in terms of regular expressions. The parsing algorithm is simple to program, requires no backtracking and seems perfect for the job. Unfortunately, the algorithm proves to be too inefficient when presented with complex regular expressions involving large numbers of symbols, as would be found in the lexical analyzer for even the simplest of programming languages. So, a more efficient process is required.

5.3   Finite-State Automata

It is instructive at this point to look back at the diagrammatic representation of the regular expression $(ab \mid c) * d$ presented in Figure 5.1 and note why the associated parsing algorithm is not particularly efficient. The problem really arises from the fact that when each new character of the string to be parsed is read, the Boolean variables in *all* the boxes in the diagram have to be examined or altered several times. If the total number of boxes is large, then the algorithm will run very slowly. To improve the efficiency, the diagram somehow needs to be inverted so that the character read directly indicates how to proceed with the parse; that is, the characters should label transitions between boxes rather than the boxes themselves.

It is possible to represent a regular expression as a **transition diagram**; that is, a directed graph having labelled branches. For example, the regular expression $(ab \mid c) * d$ can be represented as shown in Figure 5.2(a). The nodes in a transition diagram are called **states** and the figure enclosed in a circle identifies the state number. States enclosed in a double circle are called **accepting states**, indicating a state reached if the expression to be parsed has been successfully recognized. One state is marked as being

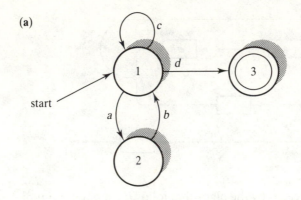

(a)

FIGURE 5.2

(a) Transition diagram
and (b) transition table
for the regular
expression $(ab \mid c) * d$.

(b)

	input symbol			
state	a	b	c	d
1	2	–	1	3
2	–	1	–	–
3		finished		

the start state. The arrowed lines connecting the states are called **edges** or
transitions. Each edge is labelled by the character required from the input
to cause the corresponding transition.

Using a transition diagram like this, parsing is extremely simple and
fast. For example, consider the parsing of the string *abcd*, as shown in
Figure 5.2(a). The action of the parser is as follows:

(1)   Starting in state 1.
(2)   Input *a*, transition to state 2.
(3)   Input *b*, transition to state 1.
(4)   Input *c*, transition to state 1.
(5)   Input *d*, transition to state 3, an accepting state.

Since the parse finishes in an accepting state, the parse succeeds.

Note also what happens when erroneous input is presented to the
parser. Consider the string *acd*:

(1)   Starting in state 1.
(2)   Input *a*, transition to state 2.

(3)   Input c: there are no edges labelled c from state 2 and hence this parse fails.

Since the parser knows that it is in state 2 when the parse fails, it can output the informative information that it was expecting the input of a b – the only edge emerging from state 2.

An alternative notation for representing the information contained in a transition diagram is the **transition table**. For example, the transition table for the regular expression (ab | c) * d is shown in Figure 5.2(b). An empty entry in the matrix, shown as – in the figure, indicates an illegal input symbol when in the specified state.

A transition diagram or a transition table describes a **finite-state automaton**. A finite-state automaton is a hypothetical machine that is characterized by a finite set of internal states together with rules indicating how the machine's state changes according to the symbols presented to it. Finite-state automata can be divided into two distinct categories: deterministic and non-deterministic. A **deterministic finite-state automaton (DFA)** has the characteristic that, for any state, there can only be one possible next state for any given input symbol. In other words, no two edges emerging from a state can be labelled by the same symbol. Furthermore, no transitions can be labelled with ε (the empty string) – all the edges have to be labelled with non-null symbols. The transition diagram shown in Figure 5.2 describes a DFA. However, if an input symbol can cause more than one next state, the machine is called a **non-deterministic finite-state automaton (NFA)**. Here, a state may have two or more edges emerging from it, labelled with the same input symbol.

EXAMPLE

Consider the transition diagram shown in Figure 5.3. As there are two edges labelled b coming from state 2, this diagram describes an NFA. Suppose that the automaton is in state 2 and b is received on the input. Under these circumstances, the machine goes to states 2 and 3 in parallel; that is, the machine replicates itself so that in one version of the machine the current state is still 2, while in the other the current state is 3. And, most important, the device accepts the input string if *any* of the parallel machine replications reach an accepting state. It can now be seen that the transition diagram describes an NFA that recognizes the regular expression a * bb * ba. The transition table for this NFA is also shown in Figure 5.3. The individual entries in the matrix are no longer single-state numbers as for the DFA. Sets of states have to be used.

(a)

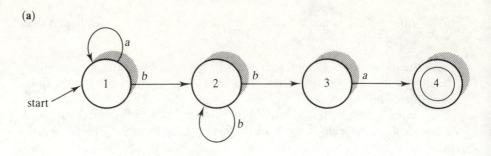

(b)

state	input symbol	
	a	b
1	{1}	{2}
2	–	{2, 3}
3	{4}	–
4	finished	

FIGURE 5.3

(a) Transition diagram and (b) transition table for an NFA recognizing the regular expression a * bb * ba.

To complicate matters further, an NFA can have multiple starting states. This inherent parallelism of an NFA can give rise to implementation headaches, especially on conventional single-processor serial machine architectures. Hence, some form of backtracking is required so that another edge, or path, can be followed when one has already failed.

It is clear from the foregoing description that an NFA is somewhat more difficult to implement on a conventional computer than a DFA. However, NFAs have the advantage that they generally require fewer states than an equivalent DFA. (Automata are said to be equivalent if they recognize strings described by the same regular expression.) Hence, the storage requirements of an NFA may be lower. Nevertheless, since implementations of DFAs are comparatively simple, it is important to be able to convert an NFA into an equivalent DFA. This process is described in Section 5.3.2.

For these automata to be of any practical use, there must be a method by which a regular expression can be transformed into a corresponding recognizing automaton. This automaton can then be expressed in terms of a programming language and hence a recognizer for the regular expression can be implemented.

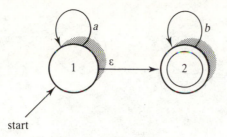

FIGURE 5.4

Transition diagram for an NFA recognizing the regular expression
$a * b *$.

5.3.1   Conversion of a regular expression to an NFA

The algorithm presented in this section generates NFAs as just described, but they can have transitions triggered by the empty string as input. These are called ε-**transitions**. For example, the regular expression $a * b *$ can be represented by the NFA shown in Figure 5.4. As soon as the string of *a*s has been recognized, the state changes from 1 to 2, with an empty string being implicitly input, and the following *b*s are recognized. These ε-transitions may appear confusing at first, but they simplify the task of converting a regular expression to an NFA. They can be removed at a later stage.

The algorithm to generate an NFA relies on the building up of the NFA from a set of simple NFAs, each corresponding to a basic syntactic structure in the original regular expression. Therefore, the first step is to define the NFAs corresponding to the whole set of basic syntactic structures used to build up a regular expression.

- The regular expression a (a single token) is represented by the NFA shown in Figure 5.5(a).
- The regular expression $R_1 R_2$ (the regular expression R_1 followed by the regular expression R_2) is represented by the diagram in Figure 5.5(b). Here, the box enclosing R_1 represents an NFA that recognizes the regular expression R_1. The finishing state in this composite NFA is the finishing (accepting) state of R_2.
- The regular expression $R_1 \mid R_2$ (alternation) is represented by the diagram in Figure 5.5(c).
- Finally, the regular expression $R*$ (zero or more repetitions of R) is represented by the diagram in Figure 5.5(d).

Bearing in mind the rules of precedence and any parentheses that may be present in the regular expression, it is now possible to build up a complete NFA. For example, consider the regular expression $(ab \mid c) * d$. This is made up of the regular expression $(ab \mid c) *$ followed by the regular expression d. The NFA is therefore as shown in Figure 5.6(a). Stage-by-stage conversion yields the NFAs shown in Figures 5.6(b) – (d).

At first sight, this 12-state NFA seems surprisingly complex in comparison with the original regular expression. Furthermore, when compared with the equivalent DFA derived for the same regular expression in

(a)

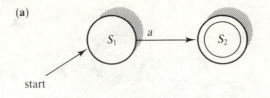

(b)

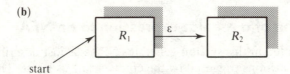

(c)

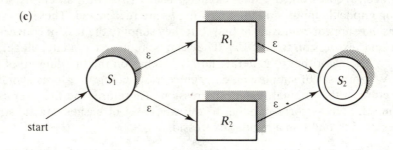

(d)

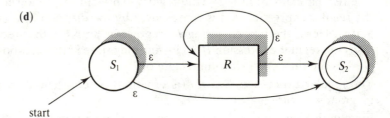

FIGURE 5.5

Conversion of regular
expressions to an NFA.

the previous section, it can be seen that many of these 12 states are
redundant. This simple example can in fact be greatly simplified by removing redundant ε-transitions, by simply looking at the diagram of the NFA.
However, for more complex examples, and when an automated process is
required, a formal algorithm must be developed. This simplification must
be performed before a real implementation via a programming language
can be contemplated. It can be carried out in two steps: the first step is to
convert the NFA into an equivalent DFA, while the second is to simplify
the DFA.

(a)

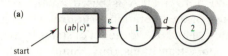

start

(b)

(c)

(d)

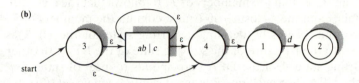
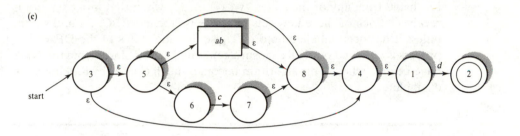
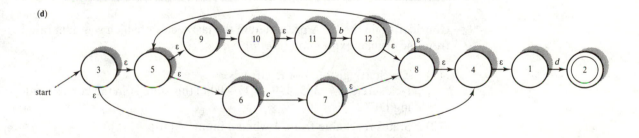

FIGURE 5.6

Conversion of the regular expression $(ab \mid c)*d$ to an NFA.

5.3.2   Conversion of an NFA to a DFA

As DFAs are much easier to implement directly than NFAs, it is important to be able to convert from an NFA to an equivalent DFA. The algorithm described here for converting an NFA to a DFA is based on the one presented in Aho [1979]. It makes use of the operation ε-**closure**, which is defined so that the ε-closure of a state s of an NFA is the set of states in that NFA that can be reached from s on ε-transitions only. Similarly, the ε-closure of a set of states T is the set of states that can be reached via ε-transitions from states that are members of T. It follows that the ε-closure of s must contain s and the ε-closure of T must contain the members of T.

The algorithm begins by defining a starting state for the DFA as being equivalent to the ε-closure of the starting state of the NFA. In other words, the starting state A of the DFA corresponds to a set of states $\{s_1, s_2, ..., s_n\}$ in the NFA. For each possible input symbol, a new set of states $\{t_1, t_2, ..., t_m\}$ of the NFA is calculated as the ε-closure of all the states reachable from any of the states $\{s_1, s_2, ..., s_n\}$ when that input symbol is received. Each of these new sets of states is labelled B, C, D, and so on, unless it has been labelled before. These become states of the DFA. The process is repeated until all ε-closure generated sets of states from the NFA have been labelled. This algorithm becomes much clearer by looking at an example.

EXAMPLE

Consider again the NFA presented in the last section, which was generated from the regular expression $(ab \mid c) * d$.

(1)   The starting state of the NFA is 3.
      ε-closure(3) = $\{3, 5, 4, 9, 6, 1\}$ – label this state A in the corresponding DFA.

(2)   States reachable from A when a input = $\{10\}$.
      ε-closure of this set of states = $\{10, 11\}$ – label this state B.

(3)   States reachable from A when b input = $\{\varnothing\}$ – these empty sets can be ignored.

(4)   States reachable from A when c input = $\{7\}$.
      ε-closure of this set of states = $\{7, 8, 5, 6, 9, 4, 1\}$ – label this state C.

(5)   States reachable from A when d input = $\{2\}$.
      ε-closure of this set of states = $\{2\}$ – label this state D, which is the final state of the DFA.

(6)   The process now starts again with state B.
      States reachable from B when a input = $\{\varnothing\}$.

(7)   States reachable from B when b input = $\{12\}$.
ε-closure of this set of states = $\{12, 8, 5, 9, 6, 4, 1\}$ – label this state E.

(8)   States reachable from B when c input = $\{\emptyset\}$.

(9)   States reachable from B when d input = $\{\emptyset\}$.

(10) For state C:
States reachable from C when a input = $\{10\}$.
ε-closure of this set of states = $\{10, 11\}$ – this has already been labelled as state B.

(11) States reachable from C when b input = $\{\emptyset\}$.

(12) States reachable from C when c input = $\{7\}$.
ε-closure of this set of states = $\{7, 8, 5, 6, 9, 4, 1\}$ – this has already been labelled as state C.

(13) States reachable from C when d input = $\{2\}$.
ε-closure of this set of states = $\{2\}$ – this has already been labelled as state D.

(14) For state D:
States reachable from D when a input = $\{\emptyset\}$.

(15) States reachable from D when b input = $\{\emptyset\}$.

(16) States reachable from D when c input = $\{\emptyset\}$.

(17) States reachable from D when d input = $\{\emptyset\}$.

(18) For state E:
States reachable from E when a input = $\{10\}$.
ε-closure of this set = B.

(19) States reachable from E when b input = $\{\emptyset\}$.

(20) States reachable from E when c input = $\{7\}$.
ε-closure of this set = C.

(21) States reachable from E when d input = $\{2\}$.
ε-closure of this set = D.

The algorithm terminates at this point. Information generated by the algorithm can now be extracted to construct a transition diagram or table for the DFA. These are shown in Figure 5.7.

The conversion algorithm presented here is very time consuming when executed by hand, even for simple examples. Computer implementations of this and related algorithms are essential for the rapid production of recognizing automata for complex regular expressions.

The DFA produced in the foregoing example is actually much simpler than the NFA from which it was constructed, but it is still much

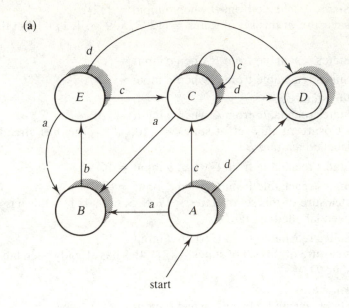

(a)

(b)

state	next state			
	a	b	c	d
A	B	–	C	D
B	–	E	–	–
C	B	–	C	D
D	–	–	–	–
E	B	–	C	D

FIGURE 5.7

(a) Transition diagram and (b) transition table for the regular expression $(ab \mid c) * d$.

more complicated than it needs to be. A further process of state minimization is required.

5.3.3 State minimization of a DFA

The larger the number of states of a DFA, the greater its storage requirements when run on a computer. It is therefore important, especially when there are many states, to ensure that the DFA is the simplest possible for a given regular expression.

The state minimization algorithm presented here is again based on that described in Aho [1979]. The essential part of the algorithm operates by repeatedly partitioning the set of states of the original machine. The first step is to partition the set of states so that the finishing state(s) are in one group and all the other states are in another group. Taking the DFA produced in the last section as an example, the original set of states (*ABCDE*) is partitioned as:

(*ABCE*) (*D*)

since *D* is the finishing state. The next step is to apply a partitioning procedure to each of these groups of states to produce a new partition. This partitioning is repeated until no new partitions are produced and the final partitioning defines the structure of the reduced machine.

The procedure performing the partitioning operates as follows. If a group of states consists of just one element, it cannot be subdivided further, so it is left unaffected. Each other group is taken in turn. Each group is partitioned into subgroups so that two states *s* and *t* are in the same subgroup if, and only if, for all possible input symbols, *s* and *t* both have transitions on each input symbol to states in the same group of the current partitioning. This process is difficult to describe but easy to perform as shown by the following example.

EXAMPLE

Consider the DFA described earlier. The current partitioning of states is:

(*ABCE*) (*D*)

Suppose these groups are called *P* and *Q*, respectively. The possible transitions from each state can be shown as follows:

$$
P = \begin{bmatrix} A & B & C & E \\ B\text{-}CD & \text{-}E\text{--} & B\text{-}CD & B\text{-}CD \end{bmatrix} \qquad Q = \begin{bmatrix} D \\ \text{----} \end{bmatrix}
$$

In this notation, the construct:

$$
\begin{bmatrix} A \\ B\text{-}CD \end{bmatrix}
$$

is taken to mean that the states reachable from a starting state of *A* on input of the symbols *a*, *b*, *c* and *d* are *B*, - (illegal input), *C* and *D*, respectively. The groups to which the destination states belong can be indicated as:

$$
\begin{bmatrix} A & B & C & E \\ P\text{-}PQ & \text{-}P\text{--} & P\text{-}PQ & P\text{-}PQ \end{bmatrix} \quad \begin{bmatrix} D \\ \text{----} \end{bmatrix}
$$

By matching patterns of destination groups, another partition is created:

$$
\begin{bmatrix} A & C & E \\ P\text{-}PQ & P\text{-}PQ & P\text{-}PQ \end{bmatrix} \quad \begin{bmatrix} B \\ \text{-}P\text{--} \end{bmatrix} \quad \begin{bmatrix} D \\ \text{----} \end{bmatrix}
$$

The groups can be labelled again:

$$
R = \begin{bmatrix} A & C & E \\ P\text{-}PQ & P\text{-}PQ & P\text{-}PQ \end{bmatrix} \quad S = \begin{bmatrix} B \\ \text{-}P\text{--} \end{bmatrix} \quad T = \begin{bmatrix} D \\ \text{----} \end{bmatrix}
$$

The partitioning procedure is reapplied:

$$
\begin{bmatrix} A & C & E \\ S\text{-}RT & S\text{-}RT & S\text{-}RT \end{bmatrix} \quad \begin{bmatrix} B \\ \text{-}R\text{--} \end{bmatrix} \quad \begin{bmatrix} D \\ \text{----} \end{bmatrix}
$$

yielding the same partition as before, so the process halts here. This means that states A, C and E of the original machine can be grouped together as a single state in the new machine while states B and D must remain. If the states in the new machine are labelled R, S and T, corresponding to states (A, C, E), B and D respectively in the old machine, the state-transition table for the new machine is then:

state	next state			
	a	b	c	d
R	S	–	R	T
S	–	R	–	–
T	–	–	–	–

So the five states in the original machine have been reduced to three states in the new minimal machine.

5.3.4 Implementation considerations

Lexical analysis can be a very time-consuming phase of the compilation process. It is therefore important that the technique used for implementing the lexical analyzer be chosen with care to ensure run-time efficiency. A DFA can often be used in the implementation of a lexical analyzer, since regular expressions are a convenient and suitable notation for expressing the syntax of lexical constructs. Therefore, the state-transition table for the DFA must be coded so as to maximize the speed at which the DFA runs and recognizes these lexical constructs.

An obvious representation of the state-transition table is a two-dimensional array, with rows representing states and columns representing input characters. For the examples presented in the preceding sections, this is a perfectly feasible and recommended approach. But the DFA for a real language will have an enormous transition table, with many states and as many possible input characters as there are in the character set of the computer. Hence, a straightforward implementation using a two-dimensional array is not possible, due to the memory requirements, and alternative representations have to be sought. Inspection of one of these transition tables reveals that the vast majority of entries denote an error due to an unacceptable input. When the DFA is in any particular state, there are usually comparatively few characters that can be accepted and that cause a transition to another state. Even in the simple example presented in the last section, two-thirds of the entries in the state-transition table represent error conditions. The presence of many common entries in the table suggests that techniques for sparse matrix storage may be appropriate to this problem. Structures involving pointers and linked lists are therefore often used and, although there may be a small time penalty, the benefits in terms of saving of storage are very great.

5.4 Implementing a Lexical Analyzer

The descriptions of various types of automata presented in the preceding sections may appear to have little immediate relevance to the practical problem of implementing a lexical analyzer for a language such as Pascal. Although lexical analyzers often contain implementations of finite-state automata, it is important to consider the overall structure of a lexical analyzer and to determine how it interfaces with the rest of the compiler.

The remainder of this chapter concentrates on the problems of writing a lexical analyzer for Pascal. Fortunately, the techniques presented here are relevant to a wide range of other languages. Obviously, details will be different, but the same overall structure and philosophy can be applied widely.

The task of the lexical analyzer is to recognize basic tokens in its input and to return some encoded representation of these tokens to the next part of the compiler. One of the first steps in the implementation process is to decide on the precise set of tokens the lexical analyzer should recognize and on the notation to be used to specify the syntax of these tokens, preferably in some formal notation. Such a choice may be quite simple for some languages, but in others it may involve making a decision as to whether a construct should be recognized by the lexical analyzer or by the syntax analyzer.

The method by which the lexical analyzer codes the identity and, possibly, the value of the token for passing to the syntax analyzer is not critically important, but usually depends to some extent on the facilities offered by the language in which the compiler is being written. Typically, each token is identified by an integer value or equivalent, such as by the use of an enumerated type in Pascal, and the syntax analyzer uses these values to identify tokens in the parsing process. A convenient way of implementing the lexical analyzer is as a procedure or function called by the syntax analyzer. Values could be returned by the lexical analyzer through the function name or rather more conveniently via global variables. It may be appropriate to use a record structure designed to contain all the characteristics of any possible token. It is also useful for the syntax analyzer to have access to the source program line number at which the lexical analyzer is currently reading. This information may help the syntax analyzer provide more informative error messages. Whenever the syntax analyzer requires the next token from the input, it calls the lexical analyzer, which then reads an appropriate number of characters from the source program making up the next token. Using this general structure, a lexical analyzer for a language such as Pascal could be written in Pascal, including lines of the form:

type *lextoken* = (*beginsym, endsym, ifsym, dosym, whilesym, periodsym, commasym, semicolonsym, ...*);

var *token* : *lextoken*;
  (* *the lexical analyzer updates this variable each time it is called* *)

procedure *NextToken*;
  .
  .
  .

Here, the lexical analyzer is implemented by the *NextToken* procedure.

NextToken has to read characters from the compiler's input and return the identity of a single lexical token in the global variable *token* each time it is called. The methods by which the tokens are recognized depends to a large extent on the syntax of the tokens, but it is instructive to examine in a little detail some of the methods that can be used to recognize some of the lexical tokens of Pascal.

It is possible to construct a regular grammar for all the symbols the lexical analyzer is to recognize. A vast DFA could then be produced and a table-driven recognizer written. However, such an approach is not recommended for a handwritten lexical analyzer, since it would result in a huge, complex and unreadable program. A better approach is to use a rather more informal technique at the top level and to resort to the use of an implementation of an automaton when recognizing the more complex individual tokens.

As stated earlier, the first step in the implementation is to decide on the set of tokens the lexical analyzer is to recognize. The Pascal report [Jensen, 1985] defines 21 special symbols, 35 word symbols or reserved words, one directive and a few alternative representations. In addition to these symbols, the lexical analyzer must also be able to handle tokens such as identifiers and numerical and character constants. It should also be able to skip comments and non-significant spaces, tabs and newlines. Another important aspect of the lexical analyzer is that it should be able to handle erroneous input and issue informative error messages.

Given this specification, it is possible to start designing and coding a lexical analyzer, implemented as a procedure to be called by the syntax analyzer. The coding of the lexical analyzer is made much simpler if it is assumed that there is a single-character lookahead on the input; in other words, each time the lexical analyzer is entered, the next input character to be analyzed has already been read (into a global variable, called *ch*). Suppose that the procedure *NextCh* reads the next character from the input and places it into *ch*. Therefore, *NextCh* has to be called once – for example, in the main program of the compiler – before the first call of *NextToken*.

5.4.1 Special symbols

Each time *NextToken* is entered, the next character of the input already stored in the variable *ch* is examined. Fortunately, many of the lexical tokens of Pascal consist of a single character and so the value of *ch* may uniquely and immediately identify the token. The action of *NextToken* in such cases is almost complete – all that remains to be done is to update the global variable *token* to indicate the nature of the single-character token and then to read the next character of the input, to maintain the single-character lookahead. When *ch* is recognized as not starting a single-character token, further characters have to be read, with the precise action of *NextToken* depending on the initial and perhaps subsequent values of *ch*. A convenient method for implementing the top-level control structure of *NextToken* in Pascal is to use the **case** statement. The body of *NextToken* therefore starts as follows:

```
while (ch = spacechar) or (ch = tabchar) do NextCh;
   (* skip white space *)
case ch of
   '+' : begin token := plussym; NextCh end;
   '−' : begin token := minussym; NextCh end;
   (* and so on for all the other single-character tokens *)
```

Since there is a fairly large number of single-character tokens in Pascal, it may be more efficient to use some form of array or table lookup to return the corresponding *lextoken* value in *token*. This then enables all such tokens to be handled within the same **case** alternative and hence removes the necessity for all the separate calls to *NextCh*. Retaining the **case** statement for these symbols, as in the example, does, however, promote readability.

Other special symbols have to be handled a little more carefully. For example, the character < can introduce the tokens <, <= or <>. *NextToken* could contain code of the form:

```
'<':
begin
   NextCh;
   if ch = '=' then
   begin
      token := lesseqsym;
      NextCh
   end
   else
   if ch = '>' then
   begin
      token := noteqsym;
      NextCh
   end
   else sym := lesssym   (* one-character lookahead already performed *)
end;
```

In this example, the advantage of adopting a one-character lookahead policy is clear. All the special symbols in Pascal can be recognized in this general way.

5.4.2 Comments

Comments in Pascal are introduced by the symbols { or (* and terminated by } or *). When *NextToken* encounters a { or a (* symbol, it must call *NextCh* repeatedly until } or *) is found. It may be tempting to insert the code to remove comments within *NextCh* so that comments need not be handled at all by *NextToken*. Although this is possible, it has to be done with some care. The danger with this approach is illustrated by a statement of the form:

> *count{this is a comment}er* := 0;

If comments were removed completely by *NextCh*, then this statement would be equivalent to:

> *counter* := 0;

which is valid Pascal. However, the Pascal report states that the meaning of a program is unaltered if a comment is replaced by a space. So, in this case, the original statement should be flagged as an error as spaces are not allowed within identifiers. Perhaps the easiest way of handling this requirement is to implement a low-level character-reading routine within the lexical analyzer, which returns a single-space character to the caller on encountering a comment construct in the input text.

5.4.3 Numerical constants

The *NextToken* procedure should read and evaluate numerical constants. The code to handle both integer and floating-point constants as well as the different meanings of the . symbol, as in 0..9, is surprisingly complex.

If only integer constants were allowed, then the code to handle numerical constants in *NextToken* could be based on the following:

```
'0': '1': '2': '3': '4':
'5': '6': '7': '8': '9':
begin
  intval := 0;
  while ch in ['0'..'9'] do
  begin   (* accumulate decimal value *)
    intval := intval * 10 + ord(ch) − ord('0');
    NextCh
  end;
  token := integersym
end;   (* value of constant returned in intval *)
```

The variable *intval* presumably would be declared as a global so that the syntax analyzer could access the numerical value of the constant.

The inclusion of floating-point constants adds greatly to the complexity of this code. As many different forms of numerical constant are allowed by Pascal, the various valid possibilities should be listed before any recognizing code is written. This will help a great deal in planning the numerical constant code in *NextToken*.

Table 5.1 Actions taken on reading a full stop in a numerical constant.

Character after full stop	Action	Example
digit	Return floating-point constant	$x := 3.5$
.	Return integer, then double-stop symbol	**var** a : **array** $[1..5]$ **of** *real*
)	Return integer, then] symbol	$a(.2.) := x$

NextToken should start by assuming that the constant has type *integer*. It should then proceed to read the digits one by one, accumulating the constant's value, until a non-digit character is read. The next action depends on the nature of this character.

- If the character is a full stop, then a further character has to be read to determine exactly how to continue processing the constant. If the further character is a digit, then the constant is assumed to be floating point and fractional part is processed. If the further character is another full stop, then an integer followed by a double full stop symbol have been read, as in **array** $[1..10]$ **of** *real*, and a flag has to be set within the lexical analyzer to indicate that the next time it is called it should return the double full stop symbol. A similar problem occurs with the symbol .), which is an alternative representation for the character symbol]. These actions are summarized in Table 5.1.

- If the character following the first sequence of digits is E or e, then an integer exponent is expected. The value of the floating-point constant accumulated so far is then adjusted accordingly. Similarly, an exponent can follow a constant with a fractional part – for example, $1.23e4$.

- If the following character is a letter other than E or e, then the lexical analyzer should issue an error, since the Pascal report states that there must be at least one symbol separator (space, newline or comment) between a number and an identifier, directive or word symbol.

- Finally, if the following character does not fall into any of these cases, then the processing of the numerical constant is complete and the character is taken as the first character of the next lexical token.

To add further to the difficulties in writing this code, a special check has to be made to prevent numerical overflow. Suppose that the lexical analyzer reads the string of digits 123456789123456. In the example program presented, where the value of *intval* is increased each time a numerical character is read, a run-time error may be generated during the execution of *NextToken* as a result of integer overflow in the statement:

$$intval := intval * 10 + ord(ch) - ord('0')$$

In some Pascal implementations, this overflow may not be detected and a wildly incorrect value may be returned instead. There are many ways of avoiding this situation, including counting digits and only allowing integer constants with fewer than a certain maximum number of digits. Machine- and implementation-dependent facilities may also be of help here.

The comparative complexity of the syntax of numerical constants suggests that a DFA-based recognizer may be appropriate here. Actions such as the accumulation of the value of the constant and checking for overflow could be added by hand.

5.4.4 Character and string constants

Character and string constants in Pascal are enclosed by apostrophes. A character constant is a string constant having just one element – for example, 'a'. At first sight, the recognition of these tokens seems trivial: after the first apostrophe, continue reading characters, storing them in some appropriate place, until the closing apostrophe is found. Unfortunately, there are a few complications in Pascal to trap the unwary:

- Two adjacent apostrophes can be used within a string to denote a single apostrophe character. This has to be handled specially. If an apostrophe is found while reading a string, an additional character must be read. If that additional character is another apostrophe, a single apostrophe character is stored in the string, otherwise the string is terminated.

- A string cannot continue over more than one line. So, if a newline is reached before a string has been terminated, the lexical analyzer should signal an error and recover by automatically closing the string at the end of the line. This requirement implies that *NextCh* should be capable of indicating when it has reached the end of an input line or, alternatively, that the code to read a string bypasses *NextCh* and performs the input directly. A similar consideration applies to end of file being detected before the string has been terminated.

If the string is found to contain just one character, the token returned is a character constant; if the length is greater than one, a string constant is returned. Null strings are not permitted and should be flagged as an error.

As it is being read, the string has to be stored somewhere. One obvious possibility is to pass the string back to the syntax analyzer in an array. Alternatively, all the strings could be saved in a single data structure managed by the lexical analyzer with pointers to the strings being returned to the syntax analyzer. Both of these approaches offer advantages. For example, the first approach offers a simple and clean interface between the lexical and syntax analyzers, while the second approach may help to reduce the need for frequent string-copying operations.

5.4.5   Identifiers and reserved words

When *NextToken* encounters an upper- or lower-case alphabetic character, it assumes that this signals the start of an identifier or reserved word. Although these tokens have to start with a letter, the following characters can be letters or digits. Once the initial letter has been read, the basic algorithm for handling these tokens is therefore to continue reading characters, saving them in some appropriate place, until a character that is neither a letter nor a digit is read. This saved sequence of characters is then checked against a list of all reserved words and if a match is found, the corresponding token is passed back to the syntax analyzer; for example, the token *beginsym* is passed back if the reserved word **begin** is identified. If no match is found, the token *identifiersym* is passed back to the syntax analyzer together with the characters making up the identifier.

Implementation of this algorithm poses no major difficulties. The use of set operations in the implementation language can help in the construction of a simple and readable lexical analyzer. For example, the main loop to read an identifier or reserved word could start with a statement of the form:

> **while** *ch* **in** *valididentifierchars* **do**

Here, *valididentifierchars* is a set of characters initialized to contain the characters that may be found within an identifier. An important detail to consider here concerns the handling of the case of letters input to the lexical analyzer. As Standard Pascal enforces equivalence of lower- and upper-case letters, it is appropriate for *NextToken* to convert all letters to a single case, except within character strings, so that all identifiers and reserved words are stored internally in this case. Then, subsequent actions of the compiler need not be concerned with case conversion.

Identifiers in Pascal can be of any length, while fitting on a single input line. Consequently, the data structure used for storing identifiers must be chosen with some care to ensure compact storage and fast processing. Welsh [1986] describes an attractive method for handling identifiers of arbitrary length by using a linked structure. The first 12 characters of the identifier are placed in the head node and any remaining characters are placed in chained nodes in four character groups. The particular advantage of this structure becomes evident when it is realized that, in most Pascal programs, very few of the identifiers are longer than 12 characters. Furthermore, even fewer distinct identifiers start with the same 12 characters. Therefore, manipulation of identifiers usually involves just the head nodes, with nodes chained from the head rarely being needed.

Checking for reserved words has to be done efficiently. As there are 35 reserved words in Standard Pascal, the use of a linear search each time a word symbol is read is probably not sufficiently fast. Binary chop or hash tables are often used.

Identifiers, like character strings, usually consist of more than one character, and so the question arises as to whether *NextToken* should store the identifiers within a data structure that it manages itself and pass pointers to the representation of the identifiers to the syntax analyzer or, alternatively, pass back the identifier itself. Whatever happens, the syntax analyzer, and possibly other parts of the compiler, need to manage a symbol table containing information not directly available to the lexical analyzer. Therefore, it may be more appropriate to pass the identifier back to the syntax analyzer for further analysis.

At this point, it is worth stressing again the importance of the single-character lookahead performed by the lexical analyzer, as described in Section 5.4.

EXAMPLE

Consider the character string *abc<def* input to *NextToken*. The letter *a* guides *NextToken* into the routine to read an identifier; thus, the characters are read one by one until the < character is encountered. This character is retained as the first character to be analyzed when *NextToken* is next called – there is no need to backspace on the input stream. This situation where a single character causes the termination of one token and starts another is very common and is handled naturally by the single-character lookahead.

5.4.6 Errors

Several errors detected by the lexical analyzer have already been noted. These include *a letter not allowed to terminate a number*, *numerical overflow*, *end of line before end of string* and *null string detected*. *NextToken* should also issue an error when it encounters a character that is not a member of the character set of Pascal. For example, an exclamation mark (outside a character string or comment) should be reported as an error.

Care has to be taken when writing a lexical analyzer in Pascal to avoid run-time errors when an illegal character is encountered. As has been seen, it is appropriate to structure the *NextToken* procedure around a large **case** statement, with a whole set of alternatives introduced by different characters returned by *NextCh*. All characters that can start valid tokens appear in the **case** alternatives, but it would be extremely convenient if Pascal, used as an implementation language, supported an 'otherwise' alternative in the **case** statement to cater for all the remaining illegal characters. Some compilers support this extension to Pascal.

Error recovery is an important concern in compiler design. Fortunately, error recovery in the lexical analyzer is comparatively simple. For example, illegal characters cause an error message to be output and a reasonable approach would be for *NextToken* to simply skip over them. If the end of a source line is detected while processing a character string, the string should be closed immediately. In general, the lexical analyzer should avoid skipping over valid tokens in an attempt to perform error recovery. This task is better performed by the syntax analyzer.

The skipping of input characters until a valid token is found is called **panic-mode** error recovery and it is of course very simple to implement. However, if the illegal character is a mistyping of a valid character, rather than an extraneous character in the source, this panic-mode error recovery can result in one or more tokens being missed. Under these circumstances, it may be possible for the syntax analyzer to keep the lexical analyzer informed of the current set of valid expected tokens. In this way, and perhaps by using an approximate pattern-matching routine, the lexical analyzer may be able to guess what the user meant to type. For example, if **begin** was a member of the set of valid expected tokens and *beggin* was read, it would be reasonable to assume that **begin** had been mistyped.

5.5   Automating the Production of Lexical Analyzers

Writing a lexical analyzer completely from scratch is a fairly demanding task, but it can of course be made much easier by modifying an existing lexical analyzer for a similar language. Although some of the programming may be simple and even repetitive, other aspects may be extremely taxing – for example, the goals of correctness and efficiency may be very hard to achieve. But, to a large extent, given the syntax specification of the lexical tokens, the coding of the lexical analyzer should be mechanical. Fortunately, software tools that can automate the production of lexical analyzers are now available. Perhaps the most famous of these tools is Lex, one of the many utilities available with the UNIX operating system. Lex requires that the syntax of each lexical token be defined in terms of a regular expression. Associated with each regular expression is a fragment of code that defines the action to be taken when that expression is recognized. From this specification, Lex generates a recognizer program – the lexical analyzer.

Given a set of regular expressions, Lex can transform them to an equivalent deterministic finite-state automaton. Lex also provides code to read in the source characters and to act on them according to the rules encoded in the automaton.

The advantages of this approach are clear. Lexical analyzers that are reliable and efficient can be produced very rapidly, while the control file for Lex provides clear and accurate documentation. Lex is described further in Chapter 9 and an example of its use is given in the appendix.

SUMMARY

- The role of the lexical analyzer is to read characters from its input and group them together into tokens according to the lexical structure of the language.

- The syntax of these simple tokens can often be conveniently specified in terms of regular grammars or regular expressions.

- These regular expressions can be transformed via non-deterministic finite-state automata to deterministic finite-state automata, which can be implemented in software simply and efficiently.

- Practical lexical analyzers tend to use a combination of formal approaches and more *ad hoc* methods. Great care has to be taken when coding a lexical analyzer to ensure that all tokens and special cases have been handled.

- Error handling and recovery in a lexical analyzer is comparatively straightforward. Panic-mode error recovery may be acceptable for most errors.

- Automated tools are available to help with the construction of lexical analyzers.

EXERCISES

5.1 Explain the relevance of regular grammars to lexical analysis.

5.2 Design a finite-state automaton that recognizes a Pascal comment introduced by the character pair (* and terminated by the pair *).

5.3 Implement Thompson's recognizing algorithm presented in Section 5.2. Make some sort of assessment of its efficiency.

5.4 In Section 5.1.1, a piece of code is presented to recognize an unsigned integer constant. It makes use of a procedure called *NextCh*. Write this procedure.

5.5 Do the I/O facilities supplied by Standard Pascal support the straightforward input of characters for a lexical analyzer? If not, suggest an alternative view of character input which could be supported in Pascal by writing new input routines, effectively hiding the original routines.

5.6 Devise techniques for avoiding numerical overflow in a lexical analyzer (see Section 5.4.3).

5.7 Look at the specification of several languages and determine the precise rules governing the handling of:

(a) blanks, tabs and newlines,

(b) comments, and

(c) upper-case versus lower-case letters.

5.8 Look at the specification of several languages and rate them in order of the ease of writing their lexical analyzers.

5.9 Devise a regular grammar to describe the syntax of a conventional representation of floating-point numbers in a programming language. Derive from this a non-deterministic finite-state automaton, convert this into a deterministic finite-state automaton, minimize the number of states in the automaton thus produced and implement the automaton as a piece of software.

5.10 Write some software tools to help with the general problems encountered in Exercise 5.9.

5.11 Write a complete lexical analyzer for Pascal. Or, at the very least, look carefully at some of the references in the bibliography for other programmers' efforts.

5.12 Write a lexical analyzer for FORTRAN. Before embarking on this project, it would be worth consulting the more specialized literature on the subject.

CHAPTER 6

Syntax and Semantic Analysis

The syntax analyzer forms the backbone of a compiler. It receives sequences of tokens from the lexical analyzer and attempts to group these tokens to form syntactic structures, as defined by the grammar of the language. The data structure constructed by the syntax analyzer to represent its analysis of the source program can then be used by subsequent phases of the compiler, ultimately to generate low-level object code. In some of the simpler compilers, this data structure is not constructed explicitly; rather, the code generator is built into the syntax analyzer so that the appropriate code is output as soon as each syntactic structure has been recognized. But, often, the code generator is quite distinct from the syntax analyzer, perhaps separated by a clearly identifiable semantic analysis phase. It is the role of the semantic analyzer to check the semantic aspects of the program. For example, it performs any type checking and type conversions required by the rules of the language. In this case, the task of the syntax and semantic analyzers becomes one of producing a representation of the source program in a form suitable for the code generator, such as a linear sequence of fairly low-level operations.

This chapter investigates various techniques by which this transformation can be achieved. As the choice of parsing technique depends on the form of the grammar of the programming language being compiled, the chapter starts with a description of another method for grammar classification.

6.1 A Classification for Grammars and Parsers

The Chomsky hierarchy, as described in Chapter 4, offers a simple method for classifying grammars. The complexity ranges from the virtually unrestricted type 0 grammar to the type 3 finite-state grammar, which is too restrictive for a general-purpose programming language but very relevant to the description of lexical tokens. For the grammars of most interest here – that is, the type 2 or context-free grammars – the Chomsky classification offers little further help. What is needed is a method for characterizing the grammars that are useful for describing programming languages, so that the choice of a parsing technique becomes easier.

6.1.1 LL(k) grammars

A grammar is said to be **LL(k)** if a top-down parser can be written for that grammar which can make a decision as to which production to apply at any stage by simply examining at most the next k symbols of the input. The term LL is derived from the fact that the input is read from *Left* to right and the parser constructs the *Leftmost* derivation of the sentence in reverse. Derivations are described in Section 4.5.3.

The LL(1) grammars are a simple but important group in this category. Parsers for these languages need only examine the next symbol of the input to determine which production to apply at any stage. In other words, one-symbol lookahead is required. Given an arbitrary grammar, it may be quite difficult to determine whether it is LL(1) or LL(k), although automated techniques are now available to help make this decision.

Productions of the form:

$$A \rightarrow aB \mid bC$$

can be handled by an LL(1) parser. If the parser is given the task of recognizing A, it will examine the next symbol of the input. If that symbol is a, the parser will apply the production $A \rightarrow aB$; if the symbol is b, it will apply the production $A \rightarrow bC$.

The introduction of extra non-terminals and productions in the grammar, as in:

$$A \rightarrow X \mid Y$$
$$X \rightarrow aB$$
$$Y \rightarrow bC$$

has no effect on the grammar's classification – an LL(1) parser is still appropriate. However, productions of the form:

$A \rightarrow aB \mid aC$

immediately cause problems for an LL(1) parser because it is unable to determine which alternative to follow, given that the next symbol of the input is an *a*. There are other simple-looking productions that cannot be handled by a straightforward LL(1) parser, such as the left-recursive productions described in Section 6.2.1. Fortunately, techniques have been developed to transform some of these specific types of productions to make them comply with the rules of an LL(1) grammar. In fact, this simple example can be dealt with very easily using a technique known as **factoring**, which is described later in the chapter. Such transformations effectively extend the class of grammars that can be handled by an LL(1) parser.

There is a great benefit in designing a programming language to have an LL(1) grammar. Efficient parsers, operating in a top-down manner, can be written for these languages very easily indeed, either by hand or by automated parser-generating tools. Furthermore, such parsers do not have to perform any backtracking, since at any stage the next production to be applied can be determined uniquely. Hence, the parser can be written so that it requires just a single pass through the source text.

6.1.2   LR(k) grammars

A grammar is said to be **LR(k)** if a bottom-up parser can be written for that grammar which makes a single left-to-right pass over the input while examining at most the next *k* symbols of the input. The term LR is derived from the fact that the input is read from *Left* to right and the parser constructs the *Rightmost* derivation of the sentence in reverse.

LR(k) parsing is a bottom-up technique. The parser reads symbols from the sentence from left to right and uses up to *k* symbols of lookahead to determine the productions to be applied, which will ultimately reduce the sentence to the grammar's starting symbol. Determining whether a given grammar can be parsed by an LR(k) parser is not trivial. The most straightforward method is to attempt to construct the parser using a standard technique; if the attempt fails, the grammar is not LR(k). This technique will be illustrated later in the chapter.

Just as with LL(k) parsers, LR(k) parsers require no backtracking and they operate efficiently. Unlike LL(k) parsers, LR(k) parsers are rarely written by hand; automated techniques are now normally used. As LR(k) grammars seem to be a natural and convenient notation for defining the syntax of a wide range of programming language constructs, production compilers often make use of LR(k) parsing techniques.

A theoretical result with some practical consequence is that if a grammar is LL(k), it is also LR(k). Hence, the set of LR(k) grammars is larger than the set of LL(k) grammars. Furthermore, it should be noted that all LR(k) grammars can be transformed to equivalent LR(1) grammars.

6.2 Top-Down Parsing

The basic concepts of top-down parsing were introduced in Chapter 4. To summarize briefly, a top-down parser starts by trying to recognize the starting symbol of the grammar. This goal is then successively broken down into simpler subgoals, according to the production rules defining the grammar, until the parser reaches the level where it matches the terminal symbols in the productions with the terminal symbols in the sentence being analyzed. This approach to parsing generates the leftmost derivation of the input sentence.

Not all grammars are suited to top-down parsing. Some grammars can be transformed by simple mechanisms so that they are expressed in a form from which a top-down parser can be generated easily. Other grammars may need completely redesigning and rewriting. The efficiency of the parser may also depend to a great extent on the way in which the grammar is expressed. In particular, if the parser has to resort to backtracking, then efficiency may suffer. Because of this inefficiency, backtracking top-down parsers are in general never used. But given a suitable grammar, it is possible to write an efficient top-down parser comparatively easily.

6.2.1 A general approach

Suppose the grammar for which a parser is to be written starts with the productions:

$$S \rightarrow AB$$
$$A \rightarrow C \mid D$$
$$B \rightarrow aD \mid CD$$

A top-down parser will operate as follows. In attempting to accomplish its goal of recognizing S (the start symbol), it will restate that goal as first recognizing A in the input sentence and then recognizing B in the remainder of the input sentence. In attempting to recognize A, it will use the second production to realize that if it recognizes C or D it will have achieved its goal of recognizing A. Similarly, the goal of recognizing B will be satisfied if the parser matches aD or CD with the appropriate part of the input string. Obviously, character matching with the input string can only occur when the right-hand side of the production in use contains one or more terminal symbols. So, if the parser is trying to match aD with an input string, that input string must start with an a. The parser can then remove that first a from the input string and the next goal is to match the remainder of the input string with D.

Probably the easiest and most popular method for implementing such a parser is to associate a procedure with each non-terminal symbol. The task of this procedure is to recognize the characters making up the non-terminal symbol and to call procedures for other non-terminals, if necessary. Therefore, in the parser for the language illustrated, a call to procedure S would run the parser. The procedure S would simply be made up of a call to procedure A followed by a call to procedure B. Other procedures would be constructed in a similar fashion. Obviously, in a real parser, rather than just a recognizer for well-formed sentences, there would have to be code in these procedures to handle errors and to construct some form of parse tree to indicate the structure of the input sentence.

This approach sounds very hopeful, as the recognizing procedures can be coded directly from the productions. Whenever a non-terminal appears on the right-hand side of a production, the corresponding procedure is called. Whenever a terminal symbol appears, it is matched with the next symbol in the input string. It also looks as though there is no inherent problem with recursive or mutually recursive calls of these non-terminal recognizing procedures. But, as might be expected, the actual implementation of top-down parsing is not quite so straightforward. To illustrate this, consider the coding of recognizing procedures for a few specific productions.

As already indicated, writing a procedure for A defined as $A \rightarrow BC$ is easy. It will have the form:

```
procedure A;
begin
  B;
  C
end;
```

Now consider the production $A \rightarrow B \mid C$. This cannot be coded in such a simple manner because the decision as to whether C should be called may depend on whether B succeeds in matching the appropriate input. At first sight, it may seem that a simple method involving the propagation of flags indicating success or failure in recognition could be used. B could be called and, only if it failed, would C be called.

The consequences of writing such a simple piece of code are not quite as straightforward as might first appear. The first problem is one of backtracking.

EXAMPLE

Suppose that the routine to recognize A is presented with the input string $s_1s_2s_3...s_n$. The function first attempts to match B with this input string. If this match succeeds, then symbols $s_1s_2s_3...s_i$ will have been consumed during the recognition of B, leaving symbols $s_{i+1}s_{i+2}...s_n$ to be matched by routines called after A returns. In this case, there are apparently no practical difficulties. But consider what happens if the attempt to match B fails. In this abortive attempt, some of the input symbols, say $s_1s_2s_3...s_j$, will have been consumed. Routine B returns to A with a result of false and so routine C is called. In a careless attempt at implementing the parser, C will then start processing on the input string $s_{j+1}s_{j+2}...s_n$ instead of $s_1s_2s_3...s_n$. To avoid this problem, the parser must backtrack before calling C, so that C can operate on the correct input string. This backtracking has to be achieved by backspacing on the parser's input.

There is a related problem with this implementation of function A, also concerned with backtracking. Given the production $A \rightarrow B \mid C$, the implementation will always select the B alternative, if it succeeds in matching the input. But the situation where both B *and* C succeed in matching (possibly different) input strings must also be considered.

EXAMPLE

If the input string $s_1s_2s_3...s_n$ is presented to A, then symbols $s_1s_2s_3...s_k$ could be successfully matched by a call to B and symbols $s_1s_2s_3...s_l$ could be successfully matched by a call to C. This means that the string remaining to be matched by the caller or callers of A is $s_{k+1}s_{k+2}...s_n$ if the B alternative had been chosen and $s_{l+1}s_{l+2}...s_n$ if the C alternative had been chosen.

It is therefore essential in this type of parser that the function or procedure A tries *both* alternatives, irrespective of the success or failure of the first. Managing this exhaustive checking and associated backtracking demands careful programming. The necessity for backtracking makes the parser inefficient and either necessitates many passes over the input data, using file rewind or backspace operations, or the storage of the complete input data in primary memory. If at all possible, backtracking parsers should be avoided.

Chapter 4 showed how it is often convenient to use recursion in a BNF production. For example, when specifying the syntax of an expression, a production of the form:

$$E \rightarrow E + T \mid T$$

may be used. But if the approach already described is adopted, a problem occurs because the first action of the procedure or function E is to call itself recursively, without consuming any characters of the input. The parser will therefore recurse for ever and fail. Productions of this form are called **left-recursive** and obviously they must be avoided when using a conventional top-down parser.

Detecting left recursion in this production is very easy – the non-terminal on the left-hand side appears as the first symbol on the right-hand side. In other cases, left recursion may not be quite so obvious.

EXAMPLE

$$A \rightarrow Ba \mid a$$
$$B \rightarrow AB \mid b$$

shows how left recursion involving more than one production can occur. Procedure A starts by calling procedure B. Procedure B then starts by calling procedure A.

Fortunately, a grammar can always be rewritten to eliminate left recursion. Given a small and reasonable set of restrictions on the grammar, a fairly simple algorithm can be used – for example, see Aho [1986]. Left recursion disappears at the cost of an increase in complexity of the grammar, but also with the risk that the underlying semantic meaning given to the grammar, such as operator precedence or associativity, may disappear. For example, the pair of productions:

$$E \rightarrow E + T \mid T$$

can be transformed to eliminate the left recursion in the first production by rewriting them as:

$$E \rightarrow T \, Z$$
$$Z \rightarrow + T \, Z \mid \varepsilon$$

But it may be possible in some simple cases to avoid the application of this formal algorithm and instead transform the offending productions by hand. For example, the same pair of productions may be rewritten as:

$$E \rightarrow T \, \{ + T \}$$

This expresses the production in EBNF, where the curly brackets specify zero or more repetitions. Productions of this form can be transformed into code for a top-down parser very easily, with the recursion in the parser, and in the rule, being replaced by repetition. Unfortunately, the associativity conferred to + by the original productions has been lost in this transformation.

There is yet another characteristic of productions that causes problems when implementing a top-down parser. If the grammar contains a production with alternatives of the general form:

$$A \rightarrow \alpha\beta \mid \alpha\gamma \qquad \text{where } \alpha \text{ is not null}$$

then the parser will have to be capable of backtracking if these productions are implemented in this form. Backtracking is necessary because the parser cannot decide, without perhaps considerable lookahead, which of the alternatives to choose, since they both start with the string α. However, this rule can be rewritten as:

$$A \rightarrow \alpha A_1$$
$$A_1 \rightarrow \beta \mid \gamma$$

and now the parser may not need to backtrack, depending of course on the precise forms of β and γ. This technique is called **left factoring** and it can help a great deal in simplifying the parser for some grammars.

Ideally, grammars should not be ambiguous or, at the very least, if there are ambiguities in the grammar, then there should be semantic rules to resolve the ambiguity. An ambiguous grammar results in more than one parse tree for a given sentence. One of the most famous examples of ambiguity is the **if**...**then**...**else** construct of programming languages, including Pascal. This is known as the 'dangling **else** problem'. For example, a problem can occur in the parse of a statement of the form:

if $C1$ **then if** $C2$ **then** $S1$ **else** $S2$

as there is a nested **if** statement. If the productions defining a <statement> include the alternatives:

<statement> → **if** <condition> **then** <statement>
            | **if** <condition> **then** <statement> **else** <statement>
            | ...

then the parser has no way of deciding whether the statement *S2* forms the **else** part of the first **if** or the second **if**. Some languages impose the convention that *S2* should be matched with the second **if**, but this is not imposed by this grammar. The neatest solution in these cases of ambiguity may be to rewrite the offending section of the grammar to remove the ambiguity. An alternative is to introduce *ad hoc* rules into the parser to cope with these special problems. Having briefly touched on the topic of ambiguity, it is worth noting that the grammars of many modern programming languages have aspects that are ambiguous.

Assuming that the context-free grammar has been transformed to remove any ambiguity and left-recursive productions, it is usually possible to write a top-down backtracking parser for the grammar. Maintaining the state of the parse, together with the management of the backtracking, is however not trivial. A parsing algorithm is given in Tremblay [1985].

Top-down parsing with backtracking is not a very popular technique. Implementations tend to be complex as well as inefficient, since the management of a potentially very large number of recursive procedure calls requires much time and stack space. It is very difficult to achieve good error reporting and error recovery because errors will only be detected when all alternatives have been explored. But by this time, it is virtually impossible to indicate the particular symbol in the input string that actually caused the error. It is also very difficult indeed to include semantic actions within the parser, such as direct output of target machine code. This difficulty arises because the parser may follow one path, outputting code as it goes, and then it discovers that that particular path was incorrect and has to backtrack. It is very awkward to retract the code that has already been generated.

6.2.2   Predictive parsing

To make top-down parsing a more attractive proposition, it is essential to be able to construct parsers that do not require backtracking. To do this, the parser must always be able to determine which of the alternative productions to choose by knowing the identity of just the current input symbol. In other words, the parser must be made deterministic. A

predictive parser (or **recursive descent parser**) uses recursive procedures or functions to recognize the input string and, because it can determine the correct production to apply at each stage, it requires no backtracking. As was described earlier, the predictive parser will include one procedure or function for each non-terminal symbol in the grammar.

Implementation of predictive parsers is very easy. The production rules can be transformed into the code for the parser by a process that is simple to follow and easily automated.

EXAMPLE

Consider the following grammar that defines the syntax of an <assignment>:

<assignment> → <identifier> = <expression> ;
<expression> → <expression> + <term> | <term>
<term> → <identifier> | (<expression>)
<identifier> → x | y | z

Because the second production is left-recursive, it has to be transformed. In this case, the simplest approach is to rewrite it as:

<expression> → <term> { + <term> }

Now, a recursive descent parser can be written for this grammar, but some care has to be taken in choosing the nesting and the order in which the procedures are defined because of the scope rules of Pascal.

```
var token : char;

procedure assignment;

  procedure expression; forward;

  procedure identifier;
  begin
    if token in ['x', 'y', 'z'] then NextToken
    else error('Identifier expected')
  end;
```

```
procedure term;
begin
  if token = '(' then
  begin
    NextToken;
    expression;
    if token <> ')' then
      error(') expected')
    else NextToken
  end
  else identifier
end;

procedure expression;
begin
  term;
  while token = '+' do
  begin
    NextToken;
    term
  end
end;

begin   (* body of assignment *)
  identifier;
  if token <> '=' then error('= expected')
  else
  begin
    NextToken;
    expression;
    if token <> ';' then error ('; expected')
    else NextToken
  end
end;
```

Several points should be noted about this predictive parser. It assumes the existence of two procedures: *NextToken* and *error*. *NextToken* implements the lexical analyzer: every time it is called, it reads the next character token from the input and places it in the global variable *token*. For the same reasons as described for lexical analyzers in the last chapter, the parser makes use of one-character lookahead; hence, all the recognizing procedures are written so that when they exit, the input symbol immediately following the string they have just recognized is already placed in *token*. The procedure *error* outputs its argument as an error message. Note that explicit error messages can be output precisely at the site of the error. As no attempt has been made in this simple example to implement any effective form of error recovery, it would be appropriate for *error* to output the message and then halt the parser. The subject of error recovery will be discussed later.

The coding of the individual recognizing procedures is obtained directly from the productions. Note particularly how the EBNF production for an <expression> is naturally translated using a **while** loop. This example does not include any procedures to output target machine code or to construct structures such as parse trees for subsequent phases of the compiler. In its present form, this parser can only give an indication of whether an input string is a well-formed assignment; the extra code to make this parser usable can be added later.

Predictive parsing is a very popular technique, far more important than the general backtracking top-down parser. Predictive parsers are easy to write, they perform fairly efficiently, assuming that the implementation language supports efficient recursive procedure calls, and they are capable of good error reporting and recovery. Because the parser is deterministic, it is easy to add semantic routines – for example, for code generation. Unfortunately, predictive parsing is not appropriate for all context-free grammars, for the reasons presented in the last section. Comparatively few grammars can be translated directly into the code for such a parser. However, many more grammars can be transformed easily into a form suitable for predictive parsing, by using techniques of factoring, eliminating left recursion and so on. Many programming languages have been designed so that predictive parsers can be used in their compilers; for example, writing a predictive parser for Pascal is a comparatively straightforward task. Various aspects of such a parser will be examined in a later section.

A rather informal approach has been taken in this section to the construction of a predictive parser. It is possible to take a more formal approach to the design of a predictive parser by considering lookahead sets and the construction of predictive parsing tables. This technique is described in the next section.

6.2.3   LL(k) parsing

To avoid backtracking in a top-down parser, it must be possible to select the correct production, so that the current input symbol can be applied at each step of the parse. This requirement relates to the structure of a grammar and its productions in the following way:

- If there are no alternative productions for any of the non-terminal symbols, then predictive parsing is of course possible. But such grammars are not particularly useful and they certainly cannot cope with the syntax definition of even the simplest of programming languages.

- If alternative productions do exist but each alternative starts with a different terminal symbol, predictive parsing is still possible. The parser compares the initial terminal symbols with the current input symbol and selects the alternative for which the symbols match. If there are no matching symbols, then the parser reports an error. These grammars are sometimes called **S-grammars** and they occur quite often in the design of programming languages.

But these are not all the grammars that can be handled by a recursive descent parser. It is quite possible for alternatives not to start with different terminal symbols and recursive descent can still be applied. Formally, for a grammar to be suitable for recursive descent parsing, it has to be shown to be an LL(k) grammar. Because LL(k) ($k > 1$) parsers are difficult to implement, and hence are comparatively rare, the discussion here will be confined to LL(1) grammars.

To determine whether a particular grammar is LL(1), a **parsing table** has to be constructed. This is an error-prone and tedious process for large grammars and so is best left for automated tools. However, for simple grammars, the process can be carried out fairly painlessly by hand. The techniques presented here are taken from Aho [1979].

The first step in this process is to determine the FIRST and the FOLLOW sets of each of the symbols defined or used in the grammar. Informally, FIRST(α) is defined to be the set of terminal symbols that can appear on the left-hand side of strings derived from α. If α is non-terminal and the empty string ε can be derived from α, then ε must be included in the set FIRST(α). Similarly, FOLLOW(α) is the set of terminal symbols that can appear immediately to the right of α in a sentential form. If α appears on the extreme right-hand side of any sentential form, then a special symbol indicating the end of the symbol to be parsed – here, represented as $ – is added to the set FOLLOW(α).

The actual calculation of these sets is fairly straightforward. Calculating the FIRST(α) sets first involves checking whether α is a terminal. If so, then FIRST(α) = $\{\alpha\}$. If α is non-terminal, then the productions defining α have to be examined. If there is a production $\alpha \to \varepsilon$, then ε is added to FIRST(α). If there is a production of the form:

$$\alpha \to \beta_1\beta_2\beta_3\ldots\beta_n$$

then FIRST(α) should include β_1 if β_1 is a terminal symbol. If β_1 is non-terminal, then all the non-ε symbols in FIRST(β_1) should be added to FIRST(α). If FIRST(β_1) contains ε, then all the non-ε symbols of FIRST(β_2) should be added to FIRST(α), and so on. If FIRST(β_1), FIRST(β_2), …, FIRST(β_n) all contain ε, then ε should be added to FIRST(α).

FIRST can also be applied to any string. $\text{FIRST}(\gamma_1\gamma_2\ldots\gamma_n)$ is calculated as $\text{FIRST}(\alpha)$ by assuming the existence of the extra production $\alpha \rightarrow \gamma_1\gamma_2\ldots\gamma_n$.

The calculation of $\text{FOLLOW}(\alpha)$ is based on the same method as used for the FIRST sets. FOLLOW is only defined for non-terminal symbols and so α cannot be a terminal symbol here. If α is the starting symbol of the grammar, then \$ is placed in $\text{FOLLOW}(\alpha)$. If there is a production of the form $A \rightarrow \alpha\beta$, then all the non-$\varepsilon$ symbols in $\text{FIRST}(\beta)$ are placed in $\text{FOLLOW}(\alpha)$. If there are productions of the form $A \rightarrow \beta\alpha$ or $A \rightarrow \beta\alpha\gamma$, where $\text{FIRST}(\gamma)$ contains ε, then everything in $\text{FOLLOW}(A)$ is in $\text{FOLLOW}(\alpha)$. Consider now a simple example.

EXAMPLE

The FIRST and FOLLOW sets of the following grammar are required:

$$S \rightarrow (A)$$
$$A \rightarrow CB$$
$$B \rightarrow ;A \mid \varepsilon$$
$$C \rightarrow x \mid S$$

Then:

$$\text{FIRST}(S) = \{\ (\ \}$$
$$\text{FIRST}(A) = \{\ x\ (\ \}$$
$$\text{FIRST}(B) = \{\ ;\varepsilon\ \}$$
$$\text{FIRST}(C) = \{\ x\ (\ \}$$

and:

$$\text{FOLLOW}(S) = \{\ \$\ ;\ )\ \}$$
$$\text{FOLLOW}(A) = \{\ )\ \}$$
$$\text{FOLLOW}(B) = \{\ )\ \}$$
$$\text{FOLLOW}(C) = \{\ ;\ )\ \}$$

The calculation of the FIRST sets is comparatively easy. The FOLLOW sets, on the other hand, are slightly harder. The easiest method of calculating the latter is to repeatedly apply the rules presented until the sets grow no larger.

Given these FIRST and FOLLOW sets, the next step is to construct the actual parsing table. The parsing table is a matrix where each entry is either empty or contains a production rule from the grammar. There is one row in the matrix for each non-terminal symbol of the grammar and one column for each terminal symbol. There is an extra column for the end of the string symbol ($). The symbols labelling the columns form the set of symbols that can be read from the input to the parser.

Entries in the table are completed by examining all the productions of the grammar, one at a time. Given a production $A \rightarrow \alpha$, then the set FIRST(α) is examined. For each non-ε symbol a in FIRST(α), the production $A \rightarrow \alpha$ is placed in the table entry identified by row A, column a. If FIRST(α) contains ε, then the production $A \rightarrow \alpha$ is placed in the table entries row A, column b for all symbols b in FOLLOW(A) – b can be $ here.

Using this algorithm, the parsing table for the simple grammar presented can be constructed. The table should have four rows, one for each of the non-terminals, and five columns, one for each of the four terminals and $.

	(	)	;	x	$
S	$S \rightarrow (A)$				
A	$A \rightarrow CB$			$A \rightarrow CB$	
B		$B \rightarrow \varepsilon$	$B \rightarrow ;A$		
C	$C \rightarrow S$			$C \rightarrow x$	

The parsing table can be used to construct an efficient top-down parser. This parser maintains a stack of symbols, which is initialized to contain the special symbol $ at the bottom and S (the starting symbol) at the top. The parser reads symbols from the input, one at a time, and the end of the input string is indicated by the special symbol $. The parser's actions are governed by the current input symbol a and the symbol α at the top of the stack. The parser recognizes four possibilities.

(1)   If $\alpha = a$ and $a \neq $, an input symbol has been recognized and α is popped off the stack.

(2)   If $\alpha = a = $, then the parser has accepted the input string and it has completed its task.

If α is a non-terminal symbol, then the parser consults row α, column a in the parsing table.

(3)   If the entry contains a production, then α on the stack is replaced by the symbols on the right-hand side of the production, the symbols

being pushed onto the stack in reverse order, so that the leftmost symbol of the production ends up at the top of the stack.

(4)   If the entry is empty, the parser flags an error indicating that the input string does not conform to the grammar.

EXAMPLE

As an example of this parsing algorithm, consider the parsing of the string $(x; (x))$. The steps below show the state of the stack (with the top of the stack to the right), the symbols left to be read from the input string and any production extracted from the parsing table.

Stack	Input	Production used
$S	(x;(x))$	$S \rightarrow (A)$
$)A(	(x;(x))$	
$)A	x;(x))$	$A \rightarrow CB$
$)BC	x;(x))$	$C \rightarrow x$
$)Bx	x;(x))$	
$)B	;(x))$	$B \rightarrow ;A$
$)A;	;(x))$	
$)A	(x))$	$A \rightarrow CB$
$)BC	(x))$	$C \rightarrow S$
$)BS	(x))$	$S \rightarrow (A)$
$)B)A(	(x))$	
$)B)A	x))$	$A \rightarrow CB$
$)B)BC	x))$	$C \rightarrow x$
$)B)Bx	x))$	
$)B)B	))$	$B \rightarrow \varepsilon$
$)B)	))$	
$)B	)$	$B \rightarrow \varepsilon$
$)	)$	
$	$	

In this case, the parse succeeds.

Returning to the explicit discussion of LL(1) grammars, it can now be stated that a grammar is LL(1) if it is possible to construct a parsing table that has no entries containing more than one production; in other words, there is never any doubt as to which production to apply at any stage of the parse. If the construction of the parsing table succeeds and a grammar is therefore deduced to be LL(1), then it is automatically known that the grammar is neither left-recursive nor ambiguous.

Writing an LL(1) parser according to the algorithm given here is comparatively simple. Nevertheless, some thought has to be directed towards the representation of the parsing table so that it provides both compact storage and sufficiently fast access. The stack maintained by the parser is essentially equivalent to the stack produced as a result of the recursive procedure calls of the recursive descent parser. The LL(1) parser itself is non-recursive (it does not need to make use of recursive routines). This parser is also efficient and there are a few programming tricks that can be used to make further small efficiency gains. Unfortunately, it may be very difficult or impossible to massage some grammars into an LL(1) form; so, this parsing technique cannot have universal applicability.

6.2.4 Error recovery

It is a sad and inevitable fact that few programmers always write syntactically correct programs. It is therefore essential that any practical parsing technique should be able to detect errors in the input, producing informative error messages. In addition, it should be able to recover gracefully from the errors, without skipping too much input or producing extra spurious error messages. There is no correct way of doing this. There are of course some general guidelines, but experience of compiler writing and a knowledge of the more common syntactic errors are also very important.

Error detection in a recursive descent parser is naturally included within the parsing code. It is easy to detect when an unexpected symbol has been read and an informative error message can be generated. Error recovery, on the other hand, is much more difficult. A simple policy of ignoring the offending symbol will work well when the programmer has inserted an extra incorrect symbol into the source program, but such a policy would be much less satisfactory when the programmer accidentally omits a symbol from the source program. For example, the omission of a semicolon from a Pascal program, which is an extremely common error, would most probably result in a large number of error messages being output after an initial 'semicolon missing' message and it could take a long time for the parser to become synchronized with the source program again.

As error recovery is not very easy to implement, it may be tempting to code the error routine so that it prints out the error message and then causes the compiler to stop. But such an approach is not acceptable, since most programmers prefer *all* the syntactic errors in their programs to be reported by a single compilation attempt. Therefore, once the error has been detected, the parser must continue as best it can and search for any further errors. Note that the primary aim of error recovery is not to attempt to deduce what the programmer *meant* to write; rather, the parser should give clear and concise error information so that the programmer can correct the errors. One general approach that can be adopted for error recovery is to provide a whole set of recovery actions, which are selected according to the particular error detected. For example, if a semicolon is found to be missing, then a reasonable action might be to automatically introduce an extra semicolon and continue with the parse. In this way, the compiler writer can anticipate the more common errors and so provide customized code to deal with them in an appropriate and graceful way. Unfortunately, more obscure and unanticipated errors may cause the parser to recover poorly.

A more structured approach can be adopted by some parsers. For example, it is possible to implement a simple yet adequate error-recovery mechanism in a recursive descent parser. The general policy is to attempt to ensure that the parser is synchronized with its input at the beginning and the end of each of the recognizing procedures. A commonly used technique for implementing this is to pass each recognizing procedure a set of symbols that the caller of the procedure feels should terminate the construct being recognized by the procedure. This set is made up of the symbols that can legitimately follow the construct being recognized – that is, the FOLLOW set – together with the symbols that do not normally follow the construct, but for which the caller of the procedure will perform some error-reporting action. The recognizing procedure must be designed so that when it terminates, the current symbol is guaranteed to be a member of the set of symbols passed to the procedure as an argument.

When a recognizing procedure is entered, it must first check that the current symbol is a valid FIRST symbol for the construct being recognized. If this symbol is invalid, the procedure reports an error and skips symbols until it finds a symbol that is either a member of the FIRST set or of the terminating set passed to the procedure. Assuming that the symbol is now a member of the FIRST set, the procedure attempts to recognize the construct. At the end of the procedure, a check is made to ensure that the current symbol is a member of the terminating set. If not, an error is reported and symbols are skipped until a member of that set is found. This technique of skipping symbols is sometimes called **panic-mode** error recovery.

This method of error reporting and recovery has been used in many compilers. A complete parser using this technique is described in Welsh [1986]. A similar technique can be used in the table-driven LL(1) parser described earlier. Using such a method, the parser should report an error when an addressed table entry is found to be empty or when the current input symbol does not match the terminal symbol at the top of the stack.

Another approach to error recovery using this table-driven parser is to insert pointers to appropriate error routines in all the empty entries in the table. Actions precisely geared towards the particular error can then be specified. A related approach adds productions to the grammar, corresponding to common errors. Should the syntax analyzer follow one of these productions while parsing the user's input, then an accurate error message can be output and an error-specific recovery can be initiated. This approach can also be adopted in bottom-up table-driven parsers where again the empty entries in the table indicate error states.

It is also possible for the syntax analyzer to adopt the strategy of attempting to correct the error and then to continue. For example, if the error message stated that a semicolon was expected, then the syntax analyzer could insert a semicolon and continue with the parse. Similarly, extraneous input symbols could be modified or deleted. There are practical implementation difficulties with such an approach, but it can allow the compiler to repair some errors automatically.

6.2.5   A top-down parser for Pascal

This section illustrates the use of top-down parsing techniques by writing small sections of a parser for Pascal. The aim is to recognize rather than to produce a representation of the parsed program.

Consider the coding of just one of the many procedures required for a recursive descent parser for Pascal. The construct *SimpleExpression* is defined in EBNF in the Pascal report [Jensen, 1985] as:

SimpleExpression = [*Sign*] *Term* {*AddingOperator Term*}

A basic recognizer can be written directly from this definition:

```
procedure SimpleExpression;
begin
  if token in [plussym, minussym] then    (* sign either + or − *)
    NextToken;   (* skip optional preceding sign *)
  Term;

  while token in [plussym, minussym, orsym] do
    (* AddingOperator is either +, − or 'or' *)
  begin
    NextToken;   (* skip AddingOperator *)
    Term
  end
end;
```

This recognizer simply reflects the structure of the EBNF production and does nothing apart from reading the input in a structured fashion. Two important additions have to be made to this procedure. Firstly, error detection and recovery have to be included, since in its present form the procedure makes no checks on the syntactic validity of the input. Secondly, some form of parse tree or other representation of the structure of the program has to be generated for the purposes of code generation. It may be possible to arrange for the syntax analyzer to output some form of target machine code directly.

Consider first error detection and recovery for this procedure. *SimpleExpression* should be passed a set of tokens by its caller indicating that *SimpleExpression* should not skip over any of these tokens during error recovery. Error recovery adopted here involves the synchronization at both the beginning and the end of the procedure. Synchronization at the beginning of the procedure involves searching for a token that is a member of one or more of the following sets:

- the set of tokens passed to *SimpleExpression* by its caller;
- the tokens that can legitimately start a *Sign* (+, −);
- the tokens that can legitimately start a *Term*;
- the tokens that can legitimately start an *AddingOperator* (+, −, 'or').

This last set is included to prevent the error recovery from skipping too far under some circumstances. The code in *SimpleExpression* can resynchronize itself comparatively easily if, for example, the initial *Term* is omitted and the *SimpleExpression* starts with an *AddingOperator*.

Synchronization at the end of the procedure is performed within the **while** loop. Before each call to *Term*, the parser expects that the current token is one that can legitimately start a *Term*.

Error detection and recovery can now be introduced into *SimpleExpression* to give the following procedure:

```
procedure SimpleExpression(stoptokens : tokenset);
var signtokens, addingoptokens : tokenset;
begin
    signtokens := [plussym, minussym];
    addingoptokens := [plussym, minussym, orsym];

    checkfor(stoptokens + signtokens + termtokens + addingoptokens);

    if token in signtokens then
    begin
        NextToken;
        checkfor(stoptokens + termtokens + addingoptokens);
        Term(stoptokens + addingoptokens)
    end
    else Term(stoptokens + addingoptokens);
```

```
    while token in addingoptokens do
    begin
        NextToken;
        checkfor(stoptokens + termtokens + addingoptokens);
        Term(stoptokens + addingoptokens)
    end
end;
```

As the complexity of this procedure has now increased, this new code needs a little extra explanation. The argument *stoptokens* passed to the procedure is a set of tokens that should be used for synchronization at the end of the procedure. When *SimpleExpression* terminates, the current token must be a member of *stoptokens*. The variables *signtokens* and *addingoptokens* are declared and initialized locally, but in a real parser these variables would have a more global scope, since they would be of use in other procedures. The variable *termtoken* is assumed to be declared and initialized outside this procedure. It contains the tokens that can legitimately start a *Term*.

The procedure *checkfor* determines whether the current token is a member of its set argument. If it is a member, then *checkfor* returns immediately. If not, then *checkfor* outputs a syntax error message and repeatedly calls the lexical analyzer to skip tokens until the current token is a member of the set. It then returns.

If the first token to be found in *SimpleExpression* is a *signtoken*, it is skipped, and before *Term* is called, *checkfor* is entered to skip any extraneous tokens. The argument passed to *Term* signifies that it should terminate, so that the current token is either a member of *stoptokens* or a member of *addingoptokens*.

The remainder of the procedure is comparatively straightforward. However, before leaving the procedure, a check must be made to ensure that the terminating condition is satisfied; in other words, the current token should be a member of *stoptokens*. This can be justified as follows. The last action of *SimpleExpression* is to call *Term* with the argument *stoptokens* + *addingoptokens*. Hence, after the call, token must be a member of *stoptokens* + *addingoptokens*. But the terminating condition of the **while** loop is that *token* is not a member of *addingoptokens*. Hence, when *SimpleExpression* terminates, *token* must be a member of *stoptokens*, thereby satisfying the requirement.

Adding code to this procedure to generate a parse tree or other representation is not particularly difficult. This topic will be covered later.

There are now many textbooks describing the construction of compilers for Pascal or subsets of Pascal. Readers requiring a much more complete and detailed coverage of syntax analysis and error recovery should see, for example, Brinch Hansen [1985], Welsh [1986], Rees [1987], Pemberton [1982] and Berry [1981].

6.3   Bottom-Up Parsing

Bottom-up parsers operate by starting with the tokens in the input string, rather than the starting symbol of the grammar. The parser then proceeds to match input strings with strings on the right-hand sides of production rules and performs the indicated substitutions. This process is repeated until, hopefully, the input string is replaced by the starting symbol. As described in Section 4.5.3, the major problem with bottom-up parsing is the identification of the handle; that is, the substring to be matched with the right-hand side of a production and reduced to the contents of the left-hand side. The choice of production to use for the reduction may also lead to problems if two or more productions have identical right-hand sides. But, as might be expected, the principal aim is to develop bottom-up parsers that do not require backtracking.

This section presents several techniques for bottom-up parsing. Although there are many differences in detail between these techniques, they all fall into the category of **shift-reduce parsers**. Note that the parse of *a * b + c* presented in Section 4.5.3 was performed using an informal shift-reduce method. Such parsers implement two main operations:

(1)   The shift operation reads and stores an input symbol.

(2)   The reduce operation matches a group of adjacent stored symbols with the right-hand side of a production and replaces the stored group with the left-hand side of the production.

One of the simplest methods for managing a shift-reduce parser involves the use of a stack. Here, the shift operation pushes a symbol on to the stack while the reduce operation replaces a group of symbols forming the topmost symbols on the stack.

EXAMPLE

Consider again the parse of *a * b + c* using the grammar:

<expression> → <term> | <expression> + <term>
<term> → <primary> | <term> * <primary>
<primary> → *a* | *b* | *c*

The stack starts off empty, then is modified as follows:

Stack	Input	Action
	$a * b + c$	shift a
a	$* b + c$	reduce using $<\text{primary}> \rightarrow a$
<primary>	$* b + c$	reduce using $<\text{term}> \rightarrow <\text{primary}>$
<term>	$* b + c$	shift $*$
<term> *	$b + c$	shift b
<term> * b	$+ c$	reduce using $<\text{primary}> \rightarrow b$
<term> * <primary>	$+ c$	reduce using $<\text{term}> \rightarrow$ $<\text{term}> * <\text{primary}>$
<term>	$+ c$	reduce using $<\text{expression}> \rightarrow$ $<\text{term}>$
<expression>	$+ c$	shift $+$
<expression> +	c	shift c
<expression> + c		reduce using $<\text{primary}> \rightarrow c$
<expression> + <primary>		reduce using $<\text{term}> \rightarrow <\text{primary}>$
<expression> + <term>		reduce using $<\text{expression}> \rightarrow$ $<\text{expression}> + <\text{term}>$
<expression>		

Because the stack now contains just the starting symbol <expression> and there is no pending input, the parse succeeds.

The parser must have general rules indicating when to shift and when to reduce, and, if reducing, which production is to be used. The different methods of bottom-up parsing use different rules.

Shift-reduce parsing does not work smoothly in all cases. The particular combination of symbols on the stack may allow several different reduce operations to be performed, only one of which may be correct. Also, it may not be clear whether a shift or a reduce should be performed at some point. Typically, an ambiguous grammar will fall into this category. In theory, shift-reduce parsing cannot be used for such grammars, but in practice it may be possible to include *ad hoc* rules within the parser to select a route out of this ambiguity, as in the case of top-down parsers.

6.3.1 Simple precedence parsing

Writing a bottom-up parser by hand for a general context-free grammar is no easy task. However, there is a class of grammars called **simple precedence grammars** for which the writing of a parser is an easy proposition.

Recall that the primary aim of the bottom-up parsing technique is to identify the handle of a sentential form, as this forms the substring to be reduced next. In a left-to-right scan of the sentential form, pairs of adjacent symbols must be inspected, moving on one symbol at a time, until the **tail** (that is, the end) of the handle is reached. The first symbol of the pair will be the last symbol of the handle and the second symbol will not be part of the handle at all. Once the tail has been identified, the **head** (that is, the start) of the handle can be found in a similar manner by proceeding backwards from right to left along the sentential form. The head and tail thus identify the handle, and hence in this type of grammar, indicate the reduction to be performed.

The method uses precedence relations between symbols to determine the positions of the head and tail. For example, consider the sentential form:

$...RS...$

where the pair of symbols RS may be preceded and followed by a possibly empty sequence of symbols. There are three viable possibilities concerning the positioning of the handle within this sentential form. At some point during the parse, either R or S or both will be part of the handle:

(1) R is part of the handle and S is not. R forms the tail of the handle. In this case, R is said to have greater precedence than S or precedence over S. R has to be reduced before S, which is written as $R \gtrdot S$. Because R marks the end of the handle, it must be the last symbol on the right-hand side of some production rule.

(2) Both R and S are in the handle. Here, R and S are said to have the same precedence and they must be reduced together. This is indicated as $R \doteq S$.

(3) S is part of the handle and R is not. S forms the head of the handle. Here, R has lower precedence than S; that is, $R \lessdot S$.

In the first case, where $R \gtrdot S$, R must be the last symbol on the right-hand side of some production rule, since it marks the end of the handle. Similarly, in the last case, S must be the first symbol on the right-hand side of some production. In the second case, there must be a production of the form $T \rightarrow ...RS...$ in the grammar. Note that these three precedence relations are *not* commutative or symmetrical (see Section 2.3.3). For example, $R \doteq S$ does not imply $S \doteq R$ and $R \lessdot S$ does not imply $S \gtrdot R$.

Given a grammar, there must be a method for defining the precedence relations between all the valid pairs of symbols that can appear adjacent in a sentential form. Assuming that these relations are known, finding the handle and thus developing a parsing algorithm is straightforward. These precedence relations are most conveniently represented in the form of a **precedence matrix**. A formal technique for completing the entries in the matrix can be developed using the following methods.

The precedence relations can be formally defined thus:

- $A \doteq B$ if there exists a production $P \rightarrow \alpha A B \beta$ (α, β can be null).
- $A \lessdot B$ if there exists a production $P \rightarrow \alpha X \beta$ and X derives $B\pi$ for some string π. In other words, there has to be a sequence of productions $X \rightarrow X_1...; X_1 \rightarrow X_2...; X_n \rightarrow B... $.
- $A \gtrdot B$ if there exists a production $P \rightarrow \alpha X Y \beta$ such that X derives γA for some string γ and Y is the symbol B, or Y derives $B\delta$ for some string δ.

A compact notation is sometimes used to indicate the derivations:

- $\alpha => \beta$ signifies that α derives β in one step – that is, by using a single production.
- $\alpha \overset{*}{=}> \beta$ signifies that α derives β in zero or more steps.
- $\alpha \overset{+}{=}> \beta$ signifies that α derives β in one or more steps.

Hence, the second rule above can be rewritten as:

$A \lessdot B$ if there exists a production $P \rightarrow \alpha A X \beta$ and $X \overset{+}{=}> B\pi$

The precedence matrix can now be completed using the rules just defined together with the productions for the language. But the process can be simplified in the following way by making explicit a step performed in the application of these rules. LEFT(P) is defined to be the set of symbols that can occur on the left-hand side of any string derived from P. Similarly, RIGHT(P) is defined to be the set of symbols that can occur on the right-hand side of any string derived from P. Hence, the rules presented can be rewritten as:

- $A \doteq B$ if there exists a production $P \rightarrow \alpha A B \beta$.
- $A \lessdot B$ if there exists a production $P \rightarrow \alpha A X \beta$ and $B \in$ LEFT(X).
- $A \gtrdot B$ if there exists a production $P \rightarrow \alpha X Y \beta$ and either $Y = B$ and $A \in$ RIGHT(X) or $A \in$ RIGHT(X) and $B \in$ LEFT(Y).

EXAMPLE

Now consider a simple example. The aim is to examine the grammar and produce the precedence matrix. If no clashes of precedence are found – that is, at most one of the three precedence relations is placed in each cell of the matrix – then the grammar is a precedence grammar.

$$S \to [E]$$
$$E \to T$$
$$T \to T + F \mid F$$
$$F \to P$$
$$P \to P * x \mid x$$

The first step is to construct the LEFT and RIGHT sets of all the non-terminal symbols:

$$\text{LEFT}(S) = \{\,[\,\} \qquad \text{RIGHT}(S) = \{\,]\,\}$$
$$\text{LEFT}(E) = \{\,T\,F\,P\,x\,\} \qquad \text{RIGHT}(E) = \{\,T\,F\,P\,x\,\}$$
$$\text{LEFT}(T) = \{\,T\,F\,P\,x\,\} \qquad \text{RIGHT}(T) = \{\,F\,P\,x\,\}$$
$$\text{LEFT}(F) = \{\,P\,x\,\} \qquad \text{RIGHT}(F) = \{\,P\,x\,\}$$
$$\text{LEFT}(P) = \{\,P\,x\,\} \qquad \text{RIGHT}(P) = \{\,x\,\}$$

Now the precedence matrix can be constructed. It is a good idea to start with the $\doteq$ relationships, since they are the easiest to determine; a quick glance at the productions gives all the information that is required.

	S	E	T	F	P	[	]	+	*	x
S										
E							$\doteq$			
T							$>$	$\doteq$		
F							$>$	$>$		
P							$>$	$>$	$\doteq$	
[		$\doteq$	$<$	$<$	$<$					$<$
]										
+				$\doteq$	$<$					$<$
*										$\doteq$
x							$>$	$>$	$>$	

The entry in each cell shows how the symbol identifying the row is related to the symbol defining the column. For example, the table shows that $+ \doteq F$, and not $F \doteq +$.

This grammar is a precedence grammar because there are no clashes of precedence; each entry in the table contains at most one precedence relation.

Having obtained the precedence matrix, parsing is simple. The general method is to proceed from left to right along the sentential form to find the tail of the handle and then return from right to left to find the head of the handle. The identity of the handle determines which production rule should be used to perform the reduction. The process is then repeated until an error is detected or until the starting symbol is obtained.

A convenient method for implementing such a parser is to use a stack, as in the shift-reduce parser presented in Section 6.3. Symbols are read from the input and are pushed one by one on to a stack until there is a $>$ relation between the symbol at the top of the stack and the next input symbol. The symbols forming the handle must then all be on the stack. Symbols are then taken off the stack until there is a $<$ relation between the symbol at the top of the stack and the symbol just removed. The symbols that have been removed constitute the handle and the left-hand side of the corresponding production is pushed on to the stack. The process is now repeated by examining the next character of the input. Successful parsing is indicated by the end of the input string being encountered with the stack containing the starting symbol.

EXAMPLE

Consider the parsing of $[x + x * x * x]$.

Stack	Input	Relation	Handle
	$[x + x * x * x]$		
$[$	$x + x * x * x]$	$<$	
$[x$	$+ x * x * x]$	$>$	x
$[P$	$+ x * x * x]$	$>$	P
$[F$	$+ x * x * x]$	$>$	F
$[T$	$+ x * x * x]$	$\doteq$	
$[T +$	$x * x * x]$	$<$	
$[T + x$	$* x * x]$	$>$	x
$[T + P$	$* x * x]$	$\doteq$	
$[T + P *$	$x * x]$	$\doteq$	

$[T + P * x$	$* x]$	$>$	$P * x$
$[T + P$	$* x]$	$\doteq$	
$[T + P *$	$x]$	$\doteq$	
$[T + P * x$	$]$	$>$	$P * x$
$[T + P$	$]$	$>$	P
$[T + F$	$]$	$>$	$T + F$
$[T$	$]$	$>$	T
$[E$	$]$	$\doteq$	
$[E]$	empty		S
S	empty		

One of the more obvious drawbacks of this method of parsing concerns the storage of the precedence matrix. In the simple example presented here, there are only 10 symbols in the grammar, and so the matrix must have space for 100 entries. But in grammars for real programming languages, there may be hundreds of symbols; hence, the precedence matrix may become too large for storage using a conventional representation. Some compression may be achieved by using just two bits per cell, but even this may result in excessive storage demands. One way of reducing the storage requirements is to employ techniques for sparse matrix representation – precedence matrices are usually very sparsely filled with precedence relations. Some form of linked structure can also be used, assuming that lookup is fast.

An alternative approach, which yields the precedence relations very quickly, makes use of **precedence functions**. Two numerical values are assigned to each symbol and the precedence relation is obtained by comparing these two numerical values. Two functions $f(X)$ and $g(X)$ are defined such that:

- If $A > B$, then $f(A) > g(B)$.
- If $A \doteq B$, then $f(A) = g(B)$.
- If $A < B$, then $f(A) < g(B)$.

Conventionally, f and g are defined by two arrays of n integers, where there are n symbols in the grammar. Hence, the storage requirements for the precedence information have dropped from n^2 to $2n$ elements. Unfortunately, it is not possible to define such functions for all precedence matrices, so this method does not have universal applicability. Algorithms for deriving these functions are presented in Gries [1971] and Floyd [1963].

The f and g functions for the grammar described here are:

	S	E	T	F	P	[	]	+	*	x
f	1	1	2	3	3	1	1	2	3	4
g	1	1	2	2	3	1	1	2	3	3

It is easy to verify that these functions satisfy the requirements. Note that these functions are not unique; for example, adding one to each value produces a new and valid pair of functions.

In the cases where it is possible to obtain the functions f and g, this approach for representing the precedence information seems very convenient. But this compacted representation loses valuable information present in the precedence matrix, which is useful for error detection. If the precedence parser encounters a pair of symbols, one at the top of the stack and the other being the next in the input string, for which no precedence relation exists, then a syntax error has been detected. But if the parser is just using the f and g functions to perform precedence comparisons, then this error cannot be detected directly. The f and g functions effectively define a precedence relation between all pairs of symbols, and illegal symbol pairs cannot be detected by this means. Hence, important information has been lost in moving from the storage of a full precedence matrix to the storage of just the f and g functions.

The parser should also report an error when it detects a handle that does not match the right-hand side of any of the productions. Both of these types of error are easy for the parser to detect, but recovery from the error is not quite so simple.

Simple precedence is a very efficient parsing technique. The heart of the parser is very easy to write and only small amounts of working storage are required. It is also reassuring to know that a precedence grammar can be shown to be unambiguous. But this technique is of limited application, since grammars of practical use are unlikely to be precedence grammars. Although transformations can be applied to a grammar to make it conform to the precedence constraints, the grammar may become very much more complicated and opaque in the process, possibly requiring the introduction of extra symbols. For example, in the grammar described here, the two seemingly unnecessary productions $E \rightarrow T$ and $F \rightarrow P$ had to be added to make the grammar a precedence grammar.

A simple precedence parser never examines more than a pair of symbols at a time. However, it is possible to construct parsers that can cope with precedence conflicts appearing in a simple precedence matrix by examining more than two symbols at a time. These are the **extended precedence parsers** and they are described in Tremblay [1985].

6.3.2   Operator precedence parsing

In simple precedence grammars, precedence relations can be defined between all pairs of symbols. It is possible, however, just to describe the relations between terminal symbols.

An **operator grammar** is one in which there are no productions with right-hand sides containing two adjacent non-terminal symbols. In other words, there must be a terminal symbol, called an **operator**, separating each non-terminal.

An **operator precedence grammar** is an operator grammar in which there is at most one precedence relation between pairs of terminal symbols. Given these precedence relations, it is easy to write a parser for the grammar.

The definition of the precedence relations and the method for constructing the precedence matrix are very similar to those for simple precedence grammars. The precedence relations between pairs of terminal symbols are defined as follows:

- $a \doteq b$ if there exists a production $P \to \alpha a b \beta$ or $P \to \alpha a A b \beta$ (A non-terminal and α, β can be null).

- $a \lessdot b$ if there exists a production $P \to \alpha A X \beta$ and X derives $b\pi$ or $Bb\pi$ (B non-terminal) for some string π.

- $a \gtrdot b$ if there exists a production $P \to \alpha X b \beta$ such that X derives πa or $\pi a B$ (B non-terminal) for some string π.

The left and right sets can also be defined in a similar way. LEFT(P) is the set of terminals that appear as the leftmost terminal, which is not necessarily the symbol at the leftmost end, in any string derived from P. Similarly, RIGHT(P) is the set of terminals that appear as the rightmost terminal in any string derived from P. So, the rules presented above are equivalent to:

- $a \doteq b$ if there exists a production $P \to \alpha a b \beta$ or $P \to \alpha a A b \beta$.

- $a \lessdot b$ if there exists a production $P \to \alpha a X \beta$ and $b \in$ LEFT(X).

- $a \gtrdot b$ if there exists a production $P \to \alpha X b \beta$ and $a \in$ RIGHT(X).

Now consider a traditional example:

$$S \to [E]$$
$$E \to E + T \mid T$$
$$T \to T * F \mid F$$
$$F \to (E) \mid x$$

The LEFT and RIGHT sets for all the non-terminal symbols are:

LEFT(S) = { [}   RIGHT(S) = {] }
LEFT(E) = { + * (x }   RIGHT(E) = { + *) x }
LEFT(T) = { * (x }   RIGHT(T) = { *) x }
LEFT(F) = { (x }   RIGHT(F) = {) x }

The precedence matrix can now be constructed:

	[	]	+	*	(	)	x
[		$\doteq$	$\lessdot$	$\lessdot$	$\lessdot$		$\lessdot$
]							
+		$\gtrdot$	$\gtrdot$	$\lessdot$	$\lessdot$	$\gtrdot$	$\lessdot$
*		$\gtrdot$	$\gtrdot$	$\gtrdot$	$\lessdot$	$\gtrdot$	$\lessdot$
(			$\lessdot$	$\lessdot$	$\lessdot$	$\doteq$	$\lessdot$
)		$\gtrdot$	$\gtrdot$	$\gtrdot$		$\gtrdot$	
x		$\gtrdot$	$\gtrdot$	$\gtrdot$		$\gtrdot$	

This grammar is an operator precedence grammar because there are no adjacent non-terminals in any of the productions (hence an operator grammar) and there are no clashes of precedence.

Parsing can be carried out in the same way as before except that non-terminals are not directly involved in the parsing process. Therefore, there is no need to distinguish between the non-terminals being pushed on to the stack, since they are transparent to the precedence relations.

EXAMPLE

Consider the parsing of the string [x * (x + x * x)]. The symbol A is used to indicate an arbitrary non-terminal on the stack.

Stack	Input	Relation	Handle
	[x * (x + x * x)]		
[	x * (x + x * x)]	$\lessdot$	
[x	* (x + x * x)]	$\gtrdot$	x
[A	* (x + x * x)]	$\lessdot$	
[A *	(x + x * x)]	$\lessdot$	
[A * (	x + x * x)]	$\lessdot$	
[A * (x	+ x * x)]	$\gtrdot$	x

$[A * (A$	$+ x * x)]$	$<$	
$[A * (A +$	$x * x)]$	$<$	
$[A * (A + x$	$* x)]$	$>$	x
$[A * (A + A$	$* x)]$	$<$	
$[A * (A + A *$	$x)]$	$<$	
$[A * (A + A * x$	$)]$	$>$	x
$[A * (A + A * A$	$)]$	$>$	$A * A$
$[A * (A + A$	$)]$	$>$	$A + A$
$[A * (A$	$)]$	$\doteq$	
$(A * (A)$	$]$	$>$	(A)
$[A * A$	$]$	$>$	$A * A$
$[A$	$]$	$\doteq$	
$[A]$			
A			

Note that in the expression $x + x * x$, the * operator is reduced before the + operator: * has higher precedence than +.

As might be expected, it is of course possible to calculate f and g functions to represent the precedence relations between the terminals. However, as the precedence matrix in this case is much smaller than that for the simple precedence parser, it may be possible to store the precedence matrix directly. Another simplification arises from the fact that since the parser is only really considering the terminal symbols, it is not concerned with making reductions like $E \rightarrow T$. The nature of the non-terminal on the stack is unimportant. But analysis of these operands has to be performed somewhere, which puts a burden on later stages of the syntax analyzer or translator. On the other hand, simple precedence does carry out this operand analysis automatically.

Operator precedence grammars are often useful when writing parsers for real high-level languages. Making use of just an operator precedence parser and no other technique is almost certainly out of the question, largely because the class of operator precedence grammars is not large enough to encompass the set of useful high-level language grammars. However, it is possible to use an operator precedence parser for a small part of the language, such as for the parsing of expressions. Some other technique, such as top-down parsing, can be used for the rest of the language. This is a powerful technique and it is often used. An operator precedence grammar is certainly powerful enough to specify associativity as well as precedence.

One of the major problems with operator precedence parsing is that good error detection and recovery is hard to achieve. In particular, errors can be detected a long way from the site of the actual error – for example, consider parsing $[x + {}^* (x + x {}^* x)]$). However, some solutions to these difficulties do exist [Aho, 1986].

6.3.3 LR(k) parsing

All the parsers examined so far seem to be rather restrictive in the set of grammars they will accept. In particular, massaging the grammar of a real high-level language so that it becomes a precedence grammar seems hardly worth attempting. Even top-down parsers have their problems: left recursion has to be removed and further restrictions have to be imposed to ensure a deterministic and efficient parser. Fortunately, a parsing technique for LR(k) grammars has been developed that overcomes many of the disadvantages of other less powerful parsing techniques. This method was first described by Knuth [1965] and has since been widely used and much developed. The theory of this method is comparatively complex and implementations are difficult and time consuming to produce by hand. But, fortunately, LR(k) parser-generating programs that are very easy to use are now available, and so this parsing technique has become very popular.

LR parsers have several overwhelming advantages. Perhaps the most important advantage is that it is possible to write an LR parser for most context-free grammars – there is in general no need to apply any transformations to alter the grammar. In particular, LR parsers can cope with the important programming constructs. Error detection can be effective and the parsers can operate efficiently without backtracking.

LR(k) grammars were introduced in Section 6.1.2. A sentence of an LR(k) grammar can be parsed from left to right using up to k symbols of lookahead. The handle to be reduced must be identifiable by all the symbols making up its left context, the handle itself and the k symbols to the right of the handle. So, a construct is recognized – that is, a handle is identified – after it, as well as k symbols after the handle, have been completely read. This contrasts with the top-down LL(k) parsers which determine which reduction to apply on the basis of the starting symbols of the construct. Hence, it can be seen that all LL(k) grammars are also LR(k). Because of efficiency reasons and practical implementation considerations, LR(0) and LR(1) parsers are most frequently used. This section concentrates on LR(1) parsers.

The method of operation of an LR(1) parser is quite simple. Just as with the other bottom-up parsers described, the LR parser reads the input symbol by symbol from left to right and maintains a stack. Unlike the other parsers, however, the LR parser's stack does not contain symbols; instead, it contains states, coded, for example, as integers. The function of a state is to provide a coded indication of all the information contained in the stack below it. It effectively indicates the current left context. The LR parser also makes use of a parsing table which contains an array of **actions**. This table is indexed by the current input symbol and the state number at the top of the stack to yield the next action the parser should perform. All the information defining the grammar and the actions to be taken by the parser are contained in this parsing table – the actual parsing program is independent of the grammar being used. Thus, the task of constructing an LR parser becomes one of constructing the appropriate parsing table.

The LR parsing program itself is not very complicated, since there is a very restricted set of actions that can be specified in the parsing table. Suppose that the current symbol is x and the state at the top of the stack is s. The parser consults entry (s, x) in the parsing table. Each entry can have one of four types of value:

(1)   Shift: The current input symbol is discarded and the state number specified in the current table entry is pushed on to the stack.

(2)   Reduce: The table entry identifies one of the productions of the grammar to be used to perform a reduction. The number of symbols on the right-hand side of this production is determined and an equal number of states is popped off the stack. The current input symbol is then set to be the symbol appearing on the left-hand side of the production.

(3)   Accept: The parsing has been completed successfully.

(4)   Error: A syntax error has been detected.

So, the action of the parsing program is to read a symbol from the input, consult the entry in the parsing table selected by this symbol and the state at the top of the stack, and then to perform the action specified in the table entry. If a reduce action is specified, the next input symbol to be read should come from the left-hand side of the specified production, rather than from the input string.

The coding of the table entries is important, since there may be many symbols and states. The obvious, although not very compact, method of doing this is to use a simple two-dimensional matrix with entries of the form $s3$ (meaning shift and push state number 3 on to the stack), $r6$ (reduce using production number 6), a (accept) or blank (error).

The process of constructing a parsing table is complex, especially for large grammars. Fortunately, several programs are now available that will take a grammar and produce a corresponding parsing table. Perhaps the most famous and widely used of these programs is Yacc, which is described in Chapter 9. It is rarely essential for the users of these programs to be aware of the algorithms by which the parsing table is being constructed. Three methods, in order of increasing power, are **SLR (simple LR)**, **LALR (lookahead LR)** and **canonical LR**. SLR and LALR reduce the size of the parsing table, but they cannot handle all the grammars that can be parsed by the canonical LR method. The SLR(1) parser is based on an LR(0) parsing table, but one-symbol lookahead is added after the table has been built. The method by which an SLR parsing table can be built is described in the next section.

The machine-generated LR parser is often a very attractive solution to the parsing problem. It can be applied to a wide range of grammars, it is easy to implement and it runs efficiently. Good error detection and error recovery can also be included comparatively easily. Furthermore, even if the initial grammar is ambiguous, it may well be possible to construct an LR parser for it, despite the fact that it can be shown that an ambiguous grammar cannot be an LR grammar. The parser-generating process should detect action conflicts in the parser arising from the ambiguity and it may be possible to resolve these conflicts by supplying further information. For example, information on precedence and/or associativity may have the effect of removing the ambiguity.

Construction of an SLR parsing table

The method used for the construction of an SLR parsing table is moderately straightforward, but can easily become unwieldy if performed by hand for grammars with more than a few productions. In this section, the method is demonstrated using the familiar set of productions:

$$E \rightarrow E + T \mid T$$
$$T \rightarrow (E) \mid x$$

An **item** of a grammar is a production that contains a full stop (a marker character) at some position on its right-hand side. For example, an item of the grammar above is $E \rightarrow E. + T$. Such an item can show how far a parse has progressed, with the symbols to the left of the full stop already having been recognized and the symbols to the right hopefully still waiting to be read.

The central problem of shift-reduce parsers is knowing when to shift and when to reduce. Or, restated another way, it is knowing the parser's particular stack contents which indicates that a certain production may be used in a reduce step. The symbols at the top of the stack must correspond to the right-hand side of the production. The symbols below these on the stack are called the **prefix** of the symbol on the left-hand side of the production. So, for example, if the grammar contains the production $P \rightarrow \alpha$, the prefix of P is the string of symbols that can appear below α on the stack when the production $P \rightarrow \alpha$ can be applied in a reduce step. A **viable prefix** of a right sentential form is any prefix that does not extend beyond the handle of that sentential form. Hence, by adding terminal symbols to the right-hand side of a viable prefix, a right sentential form can be produced. The crucial characteristic of viable prefixes is that they form a regular language; therefore, a deterministic finite-state automaton can be constructed to recognize these viable prefixes. This automaton forms the basis for the construction of the parsing table.

The first step in the production of an SLR parsing table is to produce the **augmented grammar**, by adding a new start symbol S' and the production $S' \rightarrow S$, where S is the starting symbol of the original grammar. Therefore, the grammar can be rewritten as:

$$S' \rightarrow E$$
$$E \rightarrow E + T \mid T$$
$$T \rightarrow (E) \mid x$$

When the parser attempts to reduce using the production $S' \rightarrow S$ (or $S' \rightarrow E$), it is known that the parse has succeeded.

Two operations now need to be defined. The **closure operation** is defined on a set I of items such that:

closure(I) contains I together with the items defined as follows.
If the item $X \rightarrow \alpha.A\beta$ is in closure(I) and there is a production $A \rightarrow \gamma$, then add the item $A \rightarrow .\gamma$ to I if it is not already present. This rule is applied repeatedly until closure(I) grows no more.

EXAMPLE

If I is the set of items consisting of the single item $S' \rightarrow .E$, then closure(I) contains:

$$S' \rightarrow .E$$
$$E \rightarrow .E + T$$
$$E \rightarrow .T$$
$$T \rightarrow .(E)$$
$$T \rightarrow .x$$

The second operation is the **goto operation**. This is defined on a set of items and a grammar symbol such that:

goto(I, Z) is the closure of the set of all items of the form $X \rightarrow \alpha Z.\beta$ where the item $X \rightarrow \alpha.Z\beta$ is in I.

The set goto(I, Z) is called the **successor** of I under the symbol Z.

EXAMPLE

If I contains the single item $E \rightarrow E. + T$, then goto(I, +) is the closure of the set containing the single item $E \rightarrow E + .T$. Therefore, goto(I, +) contains:

$E \rightarrow E + .T$

$T \rightarrow .(E)$

$T \rightarrow .x$

Items can now be grouped into sets that represent states of the deterministic automaton recognizing viable prefixes. Firstly, consider a set of sets called C, which initially contains the closure of the single item $S' \rightarrow .S$. This set is called I_0. The algorithm to construct C continues by repeatedly examining each set I of items in C. For each grammar symbol Z such that goto(I, Z) is non-empty and not already in C, goto(I, Z) is added to C. This process continues until no more sets can be added to C.

EXAMPLE

In the case of the grammar under question, C will start off with the set I_0 containing:

$S' \rightarrow .E$

$E \rightarrow .E + T$

$E \rightarrow .T$

$T \rightarrow .(E)$

$T \rightarrow .x$

Then, evaluating goto(I_0, Z) for set Z to each of the symbols of the grammar in turn, the non-empty sets are goto(I_0, E), goto(I_0, T), goto(I_0, () and goto(I_0, x). These yield in turn:

I_1: $S' \rightarrow E.$

     $E \rightarrow E. + T$

I_2: $E \rightarrow T.$

I_3: $T \to (.E)$

$E \to .E + T$

$E \to .T$

$T \to .(E)$

$T \to .x$

I_4: $T \to x.$

Repeated application of the algorithm yields the remaining sets in C:

I_5: $E \to E + .T$

$T \to .(E)$

$T \to .x$

I_6: $T \to (E.)$

$E \to E. + T$

I_7: $E \to E + T.$

I_8: $T \to (E).$

The transition diagram of the deterministic finite-state automaton representing the goto function can now be constructed. This is shown in Figure 6.1(a).

Finally, the parsing table can be constructed. This algorithm makes use of the FOLLOW function defined in Section 6.2.3. Each state corresponds to one of the sets I_n in the automaton above.

- For state i, if the item $A \to \alpha.a\beta$ (a terminal) is in I_i and goto(I_i, a) = I_j, then table[i, a] is set to 'shift j'.

- If the item $A \to \alpha.$ is in I_i, then set table[i, a] to 'reduce using $A \to \alpha$' for all the terminal symbols $a \in$ FOLLOW(A), $A \ne S'$.

- Finally, if the item $S' \to S.$ is in I_i, then table[i, \$] is set to 'accept' where \$ is the end-of-input symbol.

At last, the parsing table can be completed, as shown in Figure 6.1(b). This parsing table is divided into two: the main part ('table') is constructed as specified above; the 'goto' part is constructed directly from the deterministic automaton developed earlier. Entries that are blank indicate error conditions. Parsing using this table is simple – the method is as described earlier in this section.

(a)

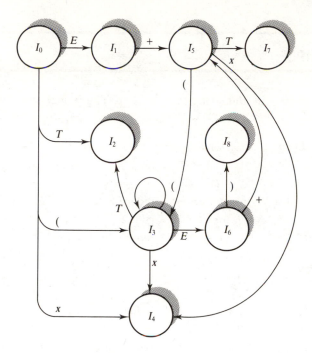

(b)

state	table					goto	
	+	(	)	x	$	E	T
0	–	s3	–	s4	–	1	2
1	s5	–	–	–	accept	–	–
2	reduce $E \rightarrow T$	–	reduce $E \rightarrow T$	reduce $E \rightarrow T$	reduce $E \rightarrow T$	–	–
3	–	s3	–	s4	–	6	2
4	reduce $T \rightarrow x$	–	reduce $T \rightarrow x$	reduce $T \rightarrow x$	reduce $T \rightarrow x$	–	–
5	–	s3	–	s4	–	–	7
6	s5	–	s8	–	–	–	–
7	reduce $E \rightarrow E + T$	–	reduce $E \rightarrow E + T$	reduce $E \rightarrow E + T$	reduce $E \rightarrow E + T$	–	–
8	reduce $T \rightarrow (E)$	–	reduce $T \rightarrow (E)$	reduce $T \rightarrow (E)$	reduce $T \rightarrow (E)$	–	–

FIGURE 6.1

(a) Transition diagram and (b) parsing table for DFA representing the goto function.

EXAMPLE

Consider parsing the string $(x + x) + x$. The parser starts with state 0 on the stack.

Stack	Input	Action
0	$(x + x) + x\$$	$s3$
0 3	$x + x) + x\$$	$s4$
0 3 4	$+ x) + x\$$	reduce by $T \rightarrow x$
0 3	$T + x) + x\$$	goto 2
0 3 2	$+ x) + x\$$	reduce by $E \rightarrow T$
0 3	$E + x) + x\$$	goto 6
0 3 6	$+ x) + x\$$	$s5$
0 3 6 5	$x) + x\$$	$s4$
0 3 6 5 4	$) + x\$$	reduce by $T \rightarrow x$
0 3 6 5	$T) + x\$$	goto 7
0 3 6 5 7	$) + x\$$	reduce by $E \rightarrow E + T$
0 3	$E) + x\$$	goto 6
0 3 6	$) + x\$$	$s8$
0 3 6 8	$+ x\$$	reduce by $T \rightarrow (E)$
0	$T + x\$$	goto 2
0 2	$+ x\$$	reduce by $E \rightarrow T$
0	$E + x\$$	goto 1
0 1	$+ x\$$	$s5$
0 1 5	$x\$$	$s4$
0 1 5 4	$\$$	reduce by $T \rightarrow x$
0 1 5	$T\$$	goto 7
0 1 5 7	$\$$	reduce by $E \rightarrow E + T$
0	$E\$$	goto 1
0 1	$\$$	accept

The parse has succeeded!

6.3.4   Other parsing methods

Many other bottom-up parsing methods have been developed but they are not used nearly as often as the methods already described. For example, Gries [1971] describes the **bounded-context parser**, which extends the ideas of the simple precedence parser to allow limited context information on either side of the handle to assist in determining which production to use in performing the reduction. This extension allows the grammar to contain production rules with identical right-hand sides. Aho [1986] mentions some other developments from simple precedence parsing, but these methods are now looking a little dated in comparison with the more recent developments of LR parsing.

Finally, brief mention should be made of a parsing method developed by Earley [1970]. This method works on any context-free grammar and, although efficient, it is not nearly as efficient as the less general methods already presented. This and other general parsing methods are described in Aho [1972].

For most of the widely used parsing methods, running time is more or less proportional to the length of the string to be parsed. General parsers, however, tend not to perform so well; for example, the running time of Earley's method can be proportional to as much as the square of the length of the input string when parsing using unambiguous grammars. A performance comparison of several important parsing techniques appears in Tremblay [1985].

6.4 Semantic Analysis

The lexical and syntax analyzers are not concerned with the meaning or semantics of the programs they process. Once the analysis of a source program is complete, the synthesis of the object program can start, and this is where considerations of semantics become important. The role of the semantic analyzer is to derive methods by which the structures constructed by the syntax analyzer may be evaluated or executed. For example, the semantic analyzer in a Pascal compiler must be able to define an evaluation procedure for expressions by determining the type attributes of the components, selecting appropriate forms of the operators, issuing error messages if the operands are incompatible and so on. For languages that are analyzed using a context-free syntax analyzer, it is the role of the semantic analyzer to ensure that all the context-sensitive rules of the language are upheld. A compiler will maintain a symbol table containing information on the symbols used in the program being compiled and many of these rules may be applied as the symbol table is used, such as the check that a name has been declared before it is used. The symbol table can be thought of as 'belonging' to the semantic analyzer, although it may be used by other parts of the compiler.

There are two common and essentially equivalent ways in which the semantic analyzer can build on the work performed by the syntax analyzer.

If the syntax analyzer constructs a parse tree, then the semantic analyzer 'flattens' this tree, producing some form of intermediate language as it goes. This intermediate language can then be passed on to the code generator for the production of code for the target hardware. An alternative approach, which avoids the explicit construction of a parse tree, is to embed the actions of the semantic analyzer within the syntax analyzer; hence, semantic actions can be associated with the recognition of each grammar rule. This technique is known as **syntax-driven translation** because the syntax rules direct the translation into object code, as well as directing the operations of the syntax analyzer. These two approaches for the semantic analyzer are equivalent, since the parser will normally create a new node in the parse tree each time a production rule is applied.

To illustrate some of the actions of a semantic analyzer, it is instructive to consider the problem of the translation of arithmetic expressions from a parse tree into an intermediate code. The semantic analyzer has to perform two distinguishable processes:

(1)   It has to flatten the tree, since the aim of this stage of compilation is the production of a linear sequence of instructions in some intermediate code.

(2)   It has to cope with type information.

To simplify matters, only expressions involving real and integer data will be considered, but even in this simple case the semantic analyzer has to propagate type attributes through the parse tree.

Consider the expression $i + j - k * r$ in a language such as Pascal, where i, j and k have type *integer* and r has type *real*. The syntax analyzer produces a parse tree of the form shown in Figure 6.2(a).

One of the tasks of the semantic analyzer is to perform type checking within this expression. By consulting the symbol table, the types of all the variables can be inserted into the tree as shown in Figure 6.2(b).

The semantic analyzer can determine the types of the intermediate results and thus propagate the type attributes through the tree, checking for compatibility as it goes. In this case, the semantic analyzer first considers the result of $k * r$ – since the Pascal semantic rules state that *integer* * *real* $\rightarrow$ *real*, the * node can be labelled as *real*. This is shown in Figure 6.2(c). In this case, the semantic analyzer discovers no type conflicts. But if the expression had read i **div** $(j - k * r)$, a type conflict would have been detected since **div** cannot handle an *integer* and a *real* argument.

This process of type propagation allows the semantic analyzer to determine when type coercions are required and which forms of the operators should be selected. In the tree of Figure 6.2(c), the subtree for $k * r$ shows that the * operator produces a *real* result; in other words, the floating-point (rather than integer) multiplication operator is required here. This determines the type of machine instruction selected by the code

(a)

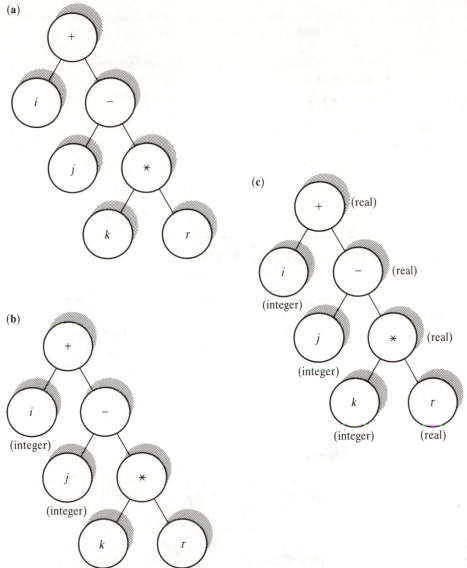

(c)

(b)

FIGURE 6.2

Translation of an
arithmetic expression.

generator. Furthermore, since the floating-point multiplication operator
will presumably require both its operands in floating-point form, the
semantic analyzer must specify that a type coercion operation from *integer*
to *real* is required before *k* is used in this calculation.

Attribute grammars (see Section 4.3.3) can help rationalize the
actions of a semantic analyzer. Semantic attributes are stored with each
symbol in the tree. The attribute grammar associates a set of semantic

functions with the conventional context-free productions of the grammar and these semantic functions indicate how the semantic attributes are to be manipulated.

Compilers vary widely in the role taken by the semantic analyzer. In some simpler compilers, there is no easily identifiable semantic analysis phase; the syntax analyzer contains semantic operations and outputs intermediate code or object code directly. In other compilers, the semantic analyzer or translator takes a complete syntax tree produced by the syntax analyzer and generates intermediate code from the tree. Intermediate codes are described in Section 6.6, while the methods by which intermediate code (or target machine code) can be generated from the syntax tree are described in Chapter 7.

6.5   The Symbol Table

One of the most important central data structures of a compiler is the **symbol table**. This is the table in which symbols such as identifiers are stored and associated with other information such as their type, location, scope and so on. Because a typical high-level language program contains many references to these symbols, fast access to the symbol table is of utmost importance to maintain efficient compilation. If an inappropriate symbol table structure is chosen, then compilation time may easily become unacceptable.

6.5.1   Data structures

A data structure has to be defined that can be accessed using a name as the key. To devise an appropriate structure, as much information as possible is needed about the structure of names – for example, the characters that can be used to make up a name, the permitted length of a name. Syntactic issues such as these are comparatively easy to resolve, since they are normally handled within the syntax specification of the language. But there are other issues concerning the structure of names that may affect the form of the symbol table. For example, there may be conventions or habits that affect the choice or length of names in a typical program. It would be quite wrong to use a symbol table structure that relied on a balanced distribution of initial letters of the names used in a program for efficient operation, since in practice it is often found that programs contain groups of similar identifiers, sharing the same starting characters – for example, *totalpay*, *totaltax*, *totalins*.

The use of a simple linear-search algorithm to access the symbol table is inadequate. Lookup times of $O(\log n)$ or better are required.

Techniques frequently used are hash tables, binary chop and binary trees. Details of these methods appear in most texts on data structures – for example, see Aho [1983]. Whichever data structure is chosen, it must be capable of being dynamically extended, since the compiler cannot predict in advance, without an extra pass through the source program, how many names will be defined in a program.

Special care must also be given to the methods used for storing the name itself. In languages where identifiers are limited in length or when only the first few characters of the identifier are significant (the remainder being discarded), it may be possible to use a fixed length field for the storage of names. Using such a scheme, short names can be padded out with blanks. The overhead incurred in storing these padding characters is traded against the speed and simplicity of the algorithms used for name manipulation, particularly name comparison.

More often, names have to be stored as variable length strings. Many techniques have been developed over the years to maintain rapid comparison, even for variable length strings. For example, it may be possible to compare name lengths before the actual characters of the names; if the lengths are not equal, there is no point in checking the names themselves. The technique for name storage used in Welsh [1986] for a Pascal compiler is a good example of the optimizations that may be achieved.

6.5.2 Symbol table contents

The symbol table must be able to associate various attributes for each name it contains. The precise nature of the data stored will of course depend on the design of the language being compiled as well as, to a slightly lesser extent, on the design of the compiler. However, there is certain information that should be associated with identifiers in a wide range of programming languages.

Firstly, some form of type information should be stored with the name. For example, in Pascal, a name may refer to a constant, a variable, a type, a procedure or a function. If the name refers to a variable, the variable's type must be included in the symbol table; if the name refers to a constant, the value of the constant and its type must be stored.

If the name refers to an object that can exist at run time, such as a variable, then some means of identifying a name's run-time location must be included. In only the simplest of systems can this be an absolute address. A location specified as an offset in a certain stack frame is more common. If the name refers to a subprogram, then some means of identifying the starting address of the subprogram must be included.

There are circumstances when it would be useful to store the source line numbers of name declarations and their use. This enables the compiler to produce name cross-reference listings and to issue rather more informative error messages when, for example, the use of a variable clashes with its type at its declaration.

Languages that are strongly typed need detailed and extensive information in the symbol table, and the structures required to store this information can become quite complex. For example, creating a symbol table entry for the name *flags* in the Pascal declaration:

type *flags* = **packed array** ['*a*'..'*z*', 3..7] **of** −1..2;

requires considerably more than just storing the text string *flags*. Similarly, the storage of Pascal record type definitions poses particular problems. The parameter lists for procedures and functions also have to be stored so that argument checking, perhaps at run time as well as at compile time, may be carried out. It can be seen that viewing the symbol table as a simple two-dimensional table is quite inappropriate, as the 'table' has become a complex linked structure.

For languages that are not quite so strongly typed, the problems of symbol table structure are eased. For example, the language BCPL manipulates untyped values; that is, the compiler need make no distinction between names referring to integers, floating-point numbers, functions, vectors and so on. The BCPL symbol table can therefore be made a comparatively simple data structure.

6.5.3 Scope rules

In the description of the symbol table just presented, it was implicitly assumed that the key used for symbol table lookup was the identifier. However, in block-structured languages such as Pascal, ALGOL 60 and PL/I, the same name can be used to refer to more than one object within the same program. For example, consider the following Pascal program:

```
program scope(output);
var i, j : integer;   (* declaration 1 *)
  .
  .
  .


procedure pscope;
var i, k : integer;   (* declaration 2 *)
begin
  .
  .
  .
end;
```

begin   (* *main program* *)
.
.
.
end.

The name *i* is used to refer to two distinct variables in this program. Fortunately, the scope rules of Pascal prevent any confusion between these two variables. When the name *i* is used in the main program, the corresponding declaration is declaration 1; when *i* is used within the procedure *pscope*, declaration 1 is hidden and the local declaration 2 is used instead. Similar rules permit variable *j* to be used throughout the procedure *pscope*, as well as in the main program as *j* has global scope, and variable *k* to be used only within the procedure *pscope*.

Therefore, scope information has to be included in the symbol table for these block-structured languages. Many ways have been suggested for representing this information, but the method chosen depends to a large extent on the structure of the rest of the symbol table. One method that is quite simple to implement requires the compiler to keep a running count of block numbers. Each time a new block that can contain declarations is encountered, this block number is incremented. Whenever a name is declared, it is stored in the symbol table with its block number. Associated with the symbol table is a separate data structure that defines the block numbers currently in scope, together with nesting information. So, whenever a symbol table lookup is required, this separate data structure is examined to obtain the block number of the current local block. The name having this block number is then searched for in the symbol table. If the search fails, then the name has not been declared locally, and the search is performed again with the block number of the next enclosing block. This process continues until the name/block number pair is found or until the outermost block is reached and the name has not been found there.

Another approach for these block-structured languages is to structure the symbol table as a stack. Whenever a new block is entered, the names declared in that block are stored at the top of the stack. Correct name lookup is achieved if the search starts at the top of the stack and moves down towards entries defined in enclosing blocks. When the compiler finishes the compilation of a block, the declarations for that block are popped off the stack and are discarded. It may not be very easy to maintain rapid name lookup in a symbol table organized as a stack, but Tremblay [1985] offers some suggestions.

6.5.4   Use of the symbol table by the compiler

Names are inserted into the symbol table by either the lexical analyzer or the syntax analyzer. Initially, it seems preferable to perform this task in the lexical analyzer, but in a block-structured language, the lexical analyzer may not maintain the necessary scope information. The information contained in the symbol table is of particular relevance in the later stages of compilation. For most context-free languages, the syntax analyzer has no real use for the symbol table, since successful syntax analysis does not depend on names having to be declared, type compatibility between operators and operands, and so on. This checking is performed in the semantic analysis phase, when the information in the symbol table is used heavily. The code generator may also require access to the symbol table, depending on the extent of translation already performed by the semantic analyzer.

In some languages, names have to be declared before they are used. Such declarations result in the names being inserted in the symbol table and use of the name causes a lookup. Pascal is an example of a language that falls in this category with one exception: a type identifier may appear in the definition of a pointer type before its own declaration. In languages where declarations are not required, a name is inserted in the symbol table when it is encountered for the first time. Some languages permit the declaration of a name after its use. In this case, a tentative entry can be made in the symbol table when the name is first used. The entry is then checked and confirmed when the declaration is encountered. Even in languages where names have to be declared before they are used, it is advisable to make special entries in the symbol table for undeclared names as they are used. This avoids repeated error messages when, for example, a name is incorrectly spelled in the declaration – a single error message should appear when the name is first used.

The symbol table may form a convenient depository for all the reserved words of a language. For example, the lexical analyzer of a Pascal compiler may include code in its initialization to insert all the reserved words of Pascal into the symbol table. Whenever the lexical analyzer encounters a word in the source text, it looks it up in the symbol table to determine whether it is a reserved word and, if it is, it extracts its representation for passing to the syntax analyzer.

6.5.5 Symbols and separate compilation

It is appropriate to make a brief mention here of the problems of separate compilation. It is now an accepted practice that large programs should be ideally constructed as a set of separately compiled modules. Different programming languages vary greatly in the support that they offer for separate compilation. For example, Standard Pascal offers little support, but most implementations support some form of reference to procedures and functions defined in other modules. More recent (and much larger) languages such as Ada support much more comprehensive facilities.

The implementation of compile-time communication between modules is a language-specific issue. The problem is really one of producing a file of environment information during compilation. This file can be read at an appropriate point during the compilation of another module, thereby enabling the module to have access to the variables and procedures defined in the first module. A good starting point in designing a technique for the implementation of separate compilation is to consider saving the contents of the symbol table in a file. Language facilities supporting controlled sharing of names or objects may result in only a subset of the symbol table being shared.

Some form of linker has to be used to combine all the separately compiled modules into a single executable unit. This linker must also perform some checking to ensure that modules have not been compiled with out-of-date environment information from other modules. For example, module 1 is compiled, producing an environment file for the compilation of module 2. Before linking module 1 and module 2, module 1 is changed and recompiled. The linker should notice this discrepancy. Machine and operating system dependencies now begin to cloud the issue.

6.6   Intermediate Codes

In many compilers, the interface between the analysis phase and the synthesis phase – or, more precisely, between the syntax/semantic analyzers and the code generator – is via a representation of the source program in an intermediate code. This intermediate code can be regarded as the machine code for an abstract machine.

Making use of an explicit intermediate code in this way has many attractions:

- The problems arising from the characteristics and idiosyncrasies of the target hardware can be confined to the code generator.

- The intermediate code should have been designed so that it can be generated easily from the parse tree or from within the syntax analyzer.

- Portability is improved, since the front end of the compiler can be used for a whole set of different code generators for different machines.

- It may be possible to implement a simple interpreter rather than a code generator for the intermediate code, allowing rapid implementation of a language on new hardware.

On the other hand, the generation of highly optimized machine code from intermediate code may be somewhat harder than generating code directly from the parse tree. This seems to be a comparatively minor disadvantage in practice and, indeed, there are some optimizations that are more easily performed via an intermediate code representation.

Intermediate codes are usually designed with one particular source language in mind. The basic operations supported by the intermediate code then mirror the constructs, data types and operators provided by the source language. Perhaps the most famous intermediate code in this category is **P-code**, running on the P-code abstract machine, designed for Pascal compilers [Nori, 1981]. The P-machine is a hypothetical stack-based machine with a very simple structure, containing many instructions that correspond closely with constructs in the Pascal language. Several Pascal front ends, producing P-code or a slight variant thereof, are now available and code generators for a large variety of machines have been written. P-code interpreters are also available. Welsh [1986] describes a complete P-code system.

Intermediate codes specifically designed for other languages are widespread. These intermediate codes are designed so that translation into them and code generation from them are both feasible tasks. For most intermediate codes, code generators have been written for different target machine types. The related problem of designing an intermediate code for use with several different source languages is a much harder task. As different programming languages have widely differing characteristics, defining a common intermediate code that is sufficiently simple and regular is an extremely difficult project. However, some progress has been made in this direction. This topic will be examined in detail in Chapter 8.

Obviously, these 'flat', linear intermediate codes are not the only method by which the analysis phase of a compiler can communicate with the code generator. In some cases, it may be convenient to maintain the interface via the parse tree, but this may involve the code generator in a great deal of work, converting from a fairly high-level structure to low-level machine instructions. A popular form of this type is **three-address code**. This is a simple intermediate code that is based on instructions with the general form:

$$result := arg1 \text{ } \textbf{op} \text{ } arg2$$

This simple code has many attractions and it is possible to generate high-quality target machine code from such a representation.

SUMMARY

- LL(k) grammars are those for which a parser can be written which can make a decision as to which production to apply at any stage by simply examining at most the next *k* symbols of the input.

- LR(k) grammars are those for which a parser can be written which makes a single left-to-right pass over the input while examining at most the next *k* symbols of the input.

- Top-down parsing is a simple technique to implement, assuming that backtracking is not required. It may be possible to transform productions of a grammar to make it more suitable for a top-down technique.

- A predictive parser always knows which production to apply next, by knowing the identity of the current input symbol.

- A more general approach for LL(1) grammars involves the use of a table-driven parser.

- Error recovery is an important aspect of syntax analyzer design and has to be considered at an early stage in the design of a parser. Panic-mode error recovery is easy to implement, but does not always yield the best results. In some circumstances, automatic error repair may be possible.

- The bottom-up parsers presented in this chapter fall into the category of shift-reduce parsers. The shift operation pushes an input symbol on to a stack, while the reduce operation replaces a group of stored symbols by the symbol appearing on the left-hand side of the production.

- Precedence parsing involves the construction of a precedence matrix. The relations between adjacent symbols in a sentential form determine the handle.

- LR(k) parsers offer a powerful solution for the parsing of many grammars. Automated techniques are now available for the production of such parsers.

- A semantic analysis phase may appear between syntax analysis and code generation. This phase is responsible for determining methods by which the structure produced by the syntax analyzer may be evaluated.

- The symbol table is a central data structure for the compiler. Fast compilation relies on efficient access to the data in the symbol table.

- The interface between the analysis phase of the compiler and the code generator is often via some form of linear intermediate code. This intermediate language has to be designed carefully so that (a) it can be produced without too much difficulty by the syntax analyzer and (b) it forms a suitable structure from which efficient code can be generated.

EXERCISES

6.1 Distinguish carefully between LL(k) and LR(k) grammars.

6.2 Explain why LL(1) grammars are not ambiguous.

6.3 What properties of a grammar prevent the writing of a predictive parser from being straightforward? Construct the procedures for a predictive parser for the grammar:

<value> → **if** <expr> **then** <expr> **else** <expr>
| **if** <expr> **then** <expr>
| <expr>

<expr> → <expr> + <term> | <term>

<term> → x | y | z

6.4 Produce the precedence matrix for the following grammar:

$P \rightarrow P(F) \mid P() \mid F$
$F \rightarrow C$
$C \rightarrow a\%C.a \mid a$

Is it a precedence grammar?

6.5 Consult the references for techniques for calculating the precedence functions and implement a program to read a precedence matrix and output, if possible, an appropriate set of precedence functions.

6.6 Use the precedence matrix developed in Section 6.3.1 to parse the strings $[x + x + x * x]$ and $[x + x * + x]$.

6.7 Use the precedence matrix developed in Section 6.3.2 to parse the strings $[x + x + x * x]$ and $[x + x * + x]$.

6.8 Use the SLR parsing table developed in Section 6.3.3 to parse the strings $x + (x + x)$ and $x +) x ($.

6.9 Consider the difficulties in writing an incremental parser for Pascal. As statements are typed into the system, they are checked for syntactic correctness and some form of parse tree or intermediate code is generated incrementally.

6.10 Write predictive parsing routines for some of the constructs of Pascal. These routines can be used as the basis of a prettyprinter for Pascal programs – syntactic constructs have to be recognized before layout can be adjusted automatically.

6.11 Devise a grammar for a simple desk calculator language and write a corresponding predictive parser. Then embed appropriate actions in the recognizing procedures to make the parser execute the commands as they are recognized. This programming exercise can of course be based on the grammar developed in Exercise 4.10. Ensure that proper care is taken with error reporting and recovery.

6.12 Extend this desk calculator language to become similar to interactive mode BASIC, where variables, repetition and so on are permitted.

6.13 Implement an efficient name storage and retrieval system suitable for implementing as part of the symbol table handling code of a Pascal compiler. How do the definitions of identifiers in other languages simplify the management of the strings representing the identifiers?

CHAPTER 7

Code Generation

The final major phase of the compiler is the code generator. The code generator takes as input the intermediate representation of the program produced by the syntax analyzer. This representation may be in the form of a parse tree or perhaps a linear sequence of intermediate code instructions, and the code generator has to translate this input into an equivalent sequence of instructions for execution by the target hardware.

A good code generator is not an easy program to write. Although standard techniques can be applied to the writing of lexical and syntax analyzers, code generators tend to be written on a much more ad hoc basis as their design is dependent on both the form of the input and the design of the instruction set of the target machine. However, some techniques are presented in this chapter that can assist in the coding of certain aspects of almost any code generator, particularly those concerned with code optimization.

7.1 Interfaces

The writer of a code generator must start with a precise specification of the output of the analysis phase of the compiler. A syntax tree and/or intermediate code representation may also be available. This representation should explicitly include all operations, such as type conversion, that may have been implicitly included in the source program. Furthermore, the task of the code generator is eased if it can be assumed that the input is syntactically correct. The code generator has to output correct and preferably efficient code capable of being executed on the target hardware. To achieve this aim, the designer of the code generator must pay careful attention to the methods by which space is allocated and variables are accessed at run time. This obviously has a bearing on the implementation of the scope rules of the language. The designer must also have a detailed and thorough knowledge of the hardware organization of the target machine, as well as of its instruction set. This detailed knowledge is invaluable when the code generator has to produce high-quality code, since this involves the careful selection of addressing modes and instruction sequences. The code generator should also be concerned with optimization at a slightly higher level by adopting policies such as storing data, which is frequently used in fast machine registers.

The writer of a code generator will also want to know the format in which the target code is to be output. For example, some compilers output the translated source program in the form of symbolic assembly language which has to be passed through the system's assembler to produce a machine language or object code program. Other compilers produce object code directly. In some cases, this object code can be executed directly, but it is more likely for it to have to be passed through the system's loader or linkage editor to produce an executable program. The task of the code generator is slightly simplified if it has to produce assembly language rather than object modules or executable code directly. For example, some of the problems of forward references can be left to the assembler to resolve. Furthermore, having a human-readable assembly language output makes the compiler somewhat easier to debug, and there may be occasions when the ability to post-process the assembly language may be an advantage. But the extra overhead in invoking the assembler after the compiler may prove to be excessive, and so compilers producing object code directly may be preferred.

7.2 Run-Time Storage Allocation and Access

Whenever a new name is declared in the source program, the corresponding information is stored in the compiler's symbol table (see Section 6.5). Whenever that name is used again in the program, a search is made for the name in the symbol table. For names referring to objects such as variables, the code generator is normally completely unconcerned with the textual representation of the name; so, these names can be represented by a much more compact notation in the input to the code generator. The representation in this notation for any particular variable is of course obtained from the symbol table. But it must be possible for the code generator to transform these representations into machine address references with minimal effort. And to do this, the placing of variable storage at run time and also its organization must be considered with great care.

7.2.1 Simple variable access

Primary memory space has to be set aside for the storage of variables. In a simple non-block-structured language such as BASIC where all the variables have global scope, a reasonable approach to the management of variable storage is to maintain a single contiguous storage area and a pointer to indicate the next free location in that block. Each time a new variable is encountered, space is set aside for it in this storage area. The current value of the next free pointer is stored with that name in the symbol table and the next free pointer is incremented by the size of that variable.

Using this general technique, the code generator can produce code to access particular variables very easily. The input to the code generator refers to variables by their offsets in the variable storage area. The code generator then produces one or more machine instructions referring to the variable's address. This can be done by either adding the absolute address of the start of the variable storage area to the offset or, more likely, by always keeping the start address of the storage area in a register and using indexed addressing or an equivalent to include the offset value. The code generator does not have to be informed explicitly of the length or type of the variable, since this will have been resolved by the semantic analyzer. The form of the instructions in the intermediate code or parse tree implicitly gives this information.

The methods for variable storage and access for block-structured languages have to be somewhat more complex to handle the dynamic nature of storage allocation. This topic is tackled in the next section where mechanisms for procedure call are described. But the underlying technique is still more or less the same as the simple approach just described.

Variables are identified by their offsets in variable storage areas, but instead of there being just one variable storage area per program, several distinct areas may be in use simultaneously, with areas being dynamically created and destroyed. These variable storage areas are normally implemented as stacks.

7.2.2   Array access

Most high-level languages support the array. In some languages, the maximum number of dimensions is limited to one, while in others there is no enforced limit. The simplest way of implementing an array is to reserve a contiguous area of storage sufficiently large to hold all the elements of the array and to associate the array name with the starting address of this storage area. But the code generator will require more information about the array to enable it to generate instructions referring to particular elements. The compiler's symbol table must store at least the following items of information about an array:

- the name of the array,
- the type (and hence size) of each element,
- the number of dimensions,
- the range of each subscript.

Obviously, in some languages where the array structure is limited in complexity, it may be possible to omit and assume some of this information, such as the number of dimensions.

When the code generator has to access an element of an array, it receives the identification of the array, together with the values or expressions making up the array subscripts. It then has several distinct tasks to perform:

- It must generate code to evaluate the subscripts.
- It must generate code to calculate the address of the requested element, given the values of the subscripts and the address of the first element of the array.
- Finally, it must generate the code to perform the type of access required.

The evaluation of the subscripts is covered in Section 7.3.2 where techniques for the code generation of arithmetic expressions are described. This section is primarily concerned with the method for transforming the subscript values to obtain an offset within the array. In the case of vectors (single-dimensional arrays), access is comparatively simple. The address of element i of array $a[0..max]$ is given by:

address of first element of $a + i *$ size of each element

If the size of each element is equal to the unit of addressing, such as a byte or a word, then no multiplication need take place. If the hardware supports indexed addressing, which allows an argument address to be specified as a base address added to the contents of an index register, and the result of the subscript calculation is left in an index register, then the access can be achieved in a single instruction. If the size of each element is not one, but instead is a larger power of two, then the multiplication required in the access can usually be achieved by using a bit-shifting instruction. On most processors, this instruction executes much more rapidly than a normal multiplication. Furthermore, this is a situation that occurs very frequently in practice: integer and real numbers are both often implemented using four or eight bytes on a byte-addressed machine. If the size of each element is not a power of two, then there may be no alternative to the use of a costly multiplication. If the size of each element is less than one – that is, in each unit of addressing, several array elements are stored – special techniques may have to be used, and if the machine supports bit indexing, the problem may be eased.

If the array is defined so that the first element does not have subscript zero, then no significant complication is introduced. If the array were defined in Pascal as $a[p..q]$ with p and q defined as constants, then the address of element i would be given by:

address of first element of $a + (i - p) *$ size of each element

Since p is a constant, known to the code generator, the code generated for this case should be identical in form to that generated for the array starting at element zero.

For multi-dimensional arrays, access is somewhat more complicated. Consider the Pascal array $a[0..m1, 0..m2]$. This array needs $(m1 + 1) * (m2 + 1) *$ (size of each element) units of storage. Suppose that the elements are stored with the second subscript varying the most rapidly; that is, in the order $a[0, 0], a[0, 1], ..., a[0, m2], a[1, 1], ...$. The address of element $a[i, j]$ is therefore:

address of first element of $a + (i * (m2 + 1) + j) *$ size of each element

At least one multiplication seems inevitable in this case. Similarly, for three-dimensional arrays, at least two multiplications will be required for each array access, and so on. Access to individual elements of multi-dimensional arrays can be quite costly. For the general array $a[p1..q1, p2..q2, ..., pj..qj]$, a similar accessing scheme can be used, but the calculations are simplified if the code generator maintains a record of the address of element $a[0, 0, ..., 0]$ of the array, even though this particular element may not exist. If this is done, then the subtraction of each pi bound from the corresponding index need not be performed.

On machines where multiplication is extremely slow, or where it has to be avoided for other reasons, it is possible to perform multi-dimensional array access without multiplication. When the array is declared, the compiler can set up, or the code generator can generate code to set up, a set of vectors allowing indirect access to the array. For example, in the case of the two-dimensional array $a[0..m1, 0..m2]$, a separate vector $p[0..m1]$ could be calculated so that $p[i]$ contains the address of element $a[i, 0]$. Then the code generator obtains the address of element $a[i, j]$ as:

$p[i] + j *$ size of each element

Hence, the multiplication has been removed at the cost of additional storage. These vectors are sometimes called **Illiffe vectors**, but their use is not very popular now because of the space they require, especially for arrays of many dimensions, and also because of the effort required for their initialization.

Array bound checking is appropriate and useful in the implementation of most of the popular high-level languages. Code generators should include a facility for generating additional code to check that the index values are in permissible ranges each time an array access is performed. The checking code can be very compact and fast, especially if the hardware supports a set of instructions specifically tailored for the purpose. But for tested applications that are trying to squeeze the last drop of performance from the hardware, it may be advantageous to use an object program that has been generated without the array bound checking code. Such instances, however, should be very rare since the benefits of array bound checking are considerable. Users of programs based on intensive array access may of course disagree with this statement!

7.2.3   Record structure access

Many modern programming languages provide some form of record data structure. The contents of the record are defined in terms of a set of named fields, each capable of holding values of specified types. Records can be accessed as a single unit or by referencing the individual fields. For example, Pascal allows the definition of a record type and variables of that type as follows:

```
type person = record
        name : packed array [1..20] of char;
        age : 0..100;
        married : Boolean;
        sex : (male, female)
    end;


    var staff1, staff2 : person;
```

Variables of a record type can be represented in a fixed number of contiguous storage locations. Access to an entire variable of type *person* is simple. For example, in the execution of the assignment *staff*1 := *staff*2, the run-time locations of the variables *staff*1 and *staff*2 have to be obtained, while the symbol table will specify the total size of a variable of type *person*. This size will determine the choice of target machine instructions used to copy the contents of *staff*2 into *staff*1. Therefore, there is no real difference between accessing an entire record variable and accessing a simple variable, except that a simple variable may occupy less storage and hence access to the variable may be slightly simpler or faster.

Access to the individual fields of a record variable – for example, *staff*1.*age* := 30 – requires information on how and where the individual fields are stored within the record. Therefore, the symbol table should store an offset value and a type specification for each field within the record. For the example above, the field *age* may be specified in the symbol table as starting at offset 20 in the record *person*, its length being one byte. Given the assignment *staff*1.*age* := 30, the code generator can output an instruction or instructions to store the value 30, expressed as a single byte, at offset 20 from the starting address of the variable *staff*1.

No significant complexities in access are introduced when Pascal's variant records (or equivalents in other languages) are allowed. As long as an offset and a type can be associated with each field name, the code generator should have no difficulties.

7.2.4 Storage management and the stack

The mechanism by which objects are associated with run-time addresses is of fundamental concern to the code generator. For some languages, it may be possible to use some form of **static allocation** scheme for objects. The symbol table will contain a run-time address (in an absolute or relative form) for each named object. This scheme will only work if the compiler can determine the number and types, and hence sizes, of all the objects that can be referenced. In particular, it is important that only a single run-time occurrence is allowed for each object, thus denying the possibility of recursive procedure calls. Similarly, static allocation is not possible when the language allows arrays with non-constant bounds, since the compiler cannot predict the size of storage required by the arrays.

To handle recursive procedures and arrays with calculated bounds, some form of **dynamic allocation** scheme is required. Most of the more modern programming languages allow recursive calls and hence require dynamic storage allocation. Fortunately, a very simple implementation technique based on a stack is applicable to such languages.

At run time, an area of memory is set aside for a stack. The size of this stack depends on many factors, including the language, its implementation and the depth of procedure nesting at run time. Typically, a language implementation allocates most or all of the storage space left over when all other requirements, such as storage of program code and other fixed areas, have been fulfilled. The stack is used for the storage of variables, as well as information to manage the procedure call/return mechanism. Whenever a new block or procedure is entered, space is reserved at the top of the stack for the locally defined variables; on leaving the block or procedure, this space is relinquished. The philosophy of the stack accurately reflects the semantics of the procedure call/return mechanism and also the scope rules of the languages of the Pascal and ALGOL families.

Dynamic allocation on a stack

Given a Pascal program of the form:

```
program stackdemo(output);
var j, k : integer;

procedure p1;
var i, j : integer;
begin
   .
   .
   .
   p1;
   .
   .
   .
end;
```

```
procedure p2;
var a, b, c : integer;
begin
    .
    .
    .
    p1;
    .
    .
    .

end;

begin    (* main program *)
    .
    .
    .
    p2;
    .
    .
    .
end.
```

consider how a stack can be used in a slightly simplified implementation of
this program. On entry to the main program, the stack will contain just two
entries: the space required for the storage of the two global variables j and
k. This is shown in Figure 7.1(a).

The implementation is made convenient if a hardware register of the
target machine, called sp here, points to the base of the current **stack
frame**; that is, the starting location of the first variable declared in the
current block or procedure. Assuming that the target hardware supports
some form of indexed addressing, the main program can access variables j
and k via constant offsets from register sp. Assuming that the unit of
addressing on the target hardware is the space required by an integer
value, and adopting a widespread assembly language notation, the code
generator could refer to j and k as 0(sp) and 1(sp), respectively. As will be
seen later in this section, there are good practical reasons for setting aside a
few locations at the start of a stack frame to store various items of
additional data. Therefore, j and k will be referenced as $k(sp)$ and $k +
1(sp)$, where k is the (constant) length of this additional data.

When $p2$ is entered due to the call from the main program, space has
to be reserved for a, b and c. The stack can also be used for the storage of
linkage information, including a **return address**, to allow $p2$ to return to the
correct location in its caller. The precise nature of this linkage information
is described later. So, just after $p2$ has been entered, the stack has the form
shown in Figure 7.1(b), where L denotes the linkage information. Variables a, b and c are referred to in the code generated for $p2$ as $k(sp)$,
$k + 1(sp)$ and $k + 2(sp)$, respectively, where k is the length of the linkage

(a)

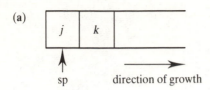

(b)

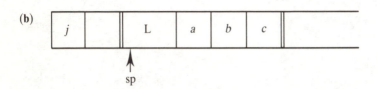

(c)

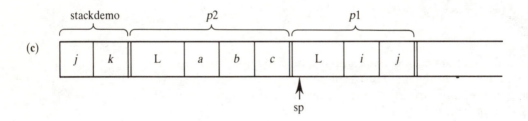

(d)

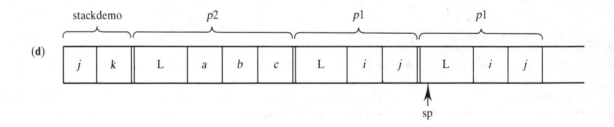

FIGURE 7.1

Use of a stack for storage management.

information. Similarly, when $p2$ has just called $p1$, the stack has the form depicted in Figure 7.1(c). Variables i and j in $p1$ are referred to as $k(sp)$ and $k + 1(sp)$, respectively.

Now suppose that $p1$ calls itself recursively. Immediately after the first recursive call, the stack has the form shown in Figure 7.1(d). The crucial point here is that by referring to the variables i and j in $p1$ as $k(sp)$ and $k + 1(sp)$, the correct – that is, the most recently defined – set of variables is accessed, irrespective of the depth of recursion. A new set of local variables is created on each entry to the procedure.

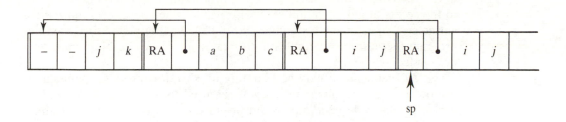

FIGURE 7.2

The dynamic chain.

The contents of the linkage information field requires careful consideration. This field has to contain sufficient information for the structure of the stack, and hence the execution environment, to be restored to what it was immediately before the call to the current procedure. Clearly, the procedure's return address has to be stored so that an instruction(s) produced by the code generator can load this address from the stack and transfer control to the referenced location. But to complete the restoration of the environment, the stack pointer has to be reset to its old value. Therefore, the linkage information should contain an old stack pointer value. The return address and old stack pointer must therefore be saved on a procedure call. Strictly speaking, it is possible for the compiler to generate code to restore the stack pointer without having to store the value of the old stack pointer, since it knows the size of the stack frame currently being left. But, in practice, it is much more convenient to store this value on the stack.

A slightly more detailed picture of the contents of the stack after the first recursive call of $p1$ is shown in Figure 7.2, where RA denotes the return address. Two extra locations at the base of the stack are shown in the diagram. These do not contain any useful information, but are present to ensure that the format of the first stack frame is identical to all the others. The chain of old stack pointer values is called the **dynamic chain**, since it reflects the dynamic structure of the procedure calls of the program.

Access to non-local variables

So far, the discussion has only considered references to variables declared locally. But in the example just presented, the globally declared variables j and k are accessible within $p2$. Also, globally declared k is accessible within $p1$ – the global declaration of j is hidden by the local declaration. These global variables are not stored in the current stack frame, and so they are not directly accessible via an offset on the current stack frame pointer. Furthermore, the code generator cannot produce code referring to these variables via some negative offset of the stack pointer because the compiler has no way of knowing how deep the run-time stack is going to be at any time; for example, the offset within the first recursive invocation of $p1$ is different to that within the second invocation. This problem is not confined to the access of global variables. It also occurs when access is required to variables defined in any textually enclosing block, although in this example program there are no variables in this category, since the blocks are not nested deeply enough.

At first sight, it may be tempting to solve this problem by making use of the dynamic chain. If access is required to, say, one of the global variables, the code generator could produce code to follow the dynamic chain down the stack until the stack frame corresponding to the outermost level is reached. This could produce an address that would allow subsequent instructions to have access to the global variable locations. But if the dynamic chain is long, there will be an appreciable overhead in each access of a non-local variable, with global variable access being the slowest of all. Long dynamic chains can occur very easily when recursive procedures are used. Recursion depths of several thousand chains are by no means uncommon and access to global variables in such cases is prohibitively slow. Therefore, this method has no practical use.

There are in fact several solutions to the problem of access to non-local variables. As has already been seen, it is clear that the use of the dynamic chain for this purpose is inappropriate, since it is not a data structure that reflects the static scope structure of a program. However, another chain can be specifically set up, using a field in the linkage area in each stack frame, to reflect the program's block nesting and hence scope structure. This additional data structure is called the **static chain**. The static chain pointer in any stack frame points back down the stack to the frame corresponding to the latest invocation of the next textually enclosing block or procedure. In other words, by following the static chain down the stack, the stack frames of all blocks or procedures containing variables in scope are identified, unless they are hidden by more recent declarations of the same name.

EXAMPLE

Consider a Pascal program of the form:

```
program static(output);
var i, j : integer;

procedure p1;
var a, b : integer;

    procedure p1a;
    var c, d : integer;
    begin ...; p1a; ... end;
```

dynamic chain

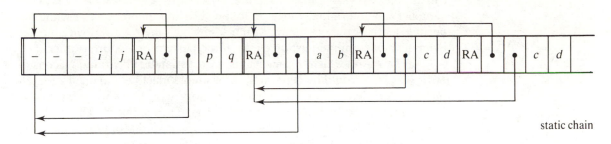

static chain

begin ...; $p1a$; ... **end**;

procedure $p2$;
var p, q : *integer*;
   begin ...; $p1$; ... **end**;

begin   (* *main program* *)
   .
   .

   .
   $p2$;
   .
   .

   .
end.

FIGURE 7.3
The static chain.

If the stack now incorporates the static chain, then three locations have to be set aside in each frame for linkage information. Immediately after $p1a$ has called itself recursively for the first time – that is, there has been two activations of $p1a$ – the stack has the form shown in Figure 7.3.

By examining the static chain from the latest invocation of $p1a$, it can be seen that the variables defined in the enclosing procedure $p1$ and in the main program can be accessed by following the static chain back down the stack. Note that in following this particular chain, the variables for $p2$ are bypassed, since they are not in scope within $p1a$.

Given the existence of a static chain, it is comparatively easy for the code generator to produce code to access any of the variables in scope. Access to local variables is simply via an offset of the current stack pointer, just as before. Access to non-local variables is slightly more complex, involving following the static chain through an appropriate number of links until the correct stack frame has been found. Then, the required variable can be accessed via an offset from the base address of that stack frame. The compiler can determine how far to follow the static chain by subtracting the nesting depth of the procedure or block in which the required variable has been defined from the nesting depth of the current procedure or block.

The way in which this mechanism works can be illustrated by considering how code could be generated for a simple machine having a general-purpose MOVE instruction for loading memory to a register, passing data from one register to another or storing a register to memory. This machine also has a set of general registers (R1, R2, ...) and a register containing the stack pointer (SP). Various other simple instructions are available, such as addition to a register (ADD), subroutine call (CALL) and subroutine return (RET). CALL takes two arguments: a register in which to store the procedure's return address (the address of the instruction following the CALL) and the entry address of the procedure. RET simply transfers control to the specified address – it is just a jump instruction. Code clarity and efficiency is enhanced if one more register is devoted to a specific function. A register called S contains the current static chain pointer. The target machine also supports the use of any of the registers as index registers and instructions can specify addresses as offsets off index registers.

Consider the code that might be produced by a code generator on the call of $p1a$ from $p1$. The new pointer to the head of the static chain will point to $p1$'s stack frame, since $p1$ is $p1a$'s textually enclosing procedure. Therefore, the code for the call is:

```
MOVE SP, S       ;update static chain pointer
CALL R1, p1a     ;save return address in R1 and jump to p1a
```

On entry to $p1a$, various stack housekeeping operations must be done to create and initialize the new stack frame:

```
p1a:   MOVE SP, R2       ;temporarily save the old stack pointer
       ADD <stack frame size for p1>, SP
       MOVE R1, 0(SP)    ;save return address
       MOVE R2, 1(SP)    ;save old stack pointer
       MOVE S, 2(SP)     ;save static chain pointer
```

Within $p1a$, the local variables c and d can be accessed via the stack pointer:

```
MOVE 3(SP), R1    ;load c
MOVE 4(SP), R2    ;load d
```

Access is possible to the variables defined within $p1$. Since the difference in nesting levels is one, code has to be generated to follow the static chain pointer down by one link each time such a non-local access is required.

This code takes the form:

```
MOVE 2(SP), S      ;S points to p1's stack frame
MOVE 3(S), R1      ;load a
MOVE 4(S), R2      ;load b
```

Similarly, if access to the global variables is required, the static chain has to be followed down through two links:

```
MOVE 2(SP), S      ;S points to p1's stack frame
MOVE 2(S), S       ;S points to the outermost stack frame
MOVE 3(S), R1      ;load i
MOVE 4(S), R2      ;load j
```

This general method can be applied to access variables in scope in any of the enclosing procedures.

Once $p1a$ has completed its work, it returns control to $p1$. The stack and hence the addressing environment now has to be restored to the state it was in just before the call to $p1a$. But to restore the state of the stack, all that needs to be done is to reinstate the old stack pointer. The code to implement the procedure return is therefore:

```
MOVE 0(SP), R1     ;temporarily save return address
MOVE 1(SP), SP     ;restore old stack pointer
RET R1             ;return to the address in R1
```

Note that there is no need to reinstate the static chain pointer register S immediately if the code generator follows the convention of always loading it before any non-local variable access, as shown above.

This example describes an implementation technique for procedure call/return and for variable access that can be applied generally. The only difference between this example and the call of $p1$ from $p2$, for example, is in the loading of S immediately before the call. When $p1$ is being called from $p2$, S has to be loaded to point to the outermost stack frame – that is, the one for $p1$'s textually enclosing procedure. Hence, the call has the form:

```
MOVE 2(SP), S
CALL R1, p1
```

The method for obtaining a value to be placed in S is determined uniquely by the difference in textual levels between the calling and called procedures. The mechanism corresponds directly to that used for accessing non-local variables.

Before making any sort of assessment of this technique, it must be pointed out that no provision has yet been made for the passing of parameters to procedures. However, in practice, this does not add significantly to the complexity. The subject of argument passing is discussed in the next section. Another point that should be recognized is that the use of a simple storage allocation and freeing method based on a stack does impose some restrictions on the use of the programming language. The language should not allow the programmer to create references to objects whose values are stored in a stack frame nearer the top of the stack; in other words, the language should forbid the existence of pointers pointing to stack frames further up the stack. If such pointers were allowed, it would not be possible to free the storage in the target stack frame until the stack frame containing the pointer had been disposed of. Languages such as Pascal are careful to avoid this situation, but other languages do allow the careless programmer to leave these dangling references. For example, in BCPL and C, an operator is available that yields the address of its variable argument. If a variable is defined locally within a routine and this variable is of a type such that it is stored on the stack, then problems may occur when the address of this variable is saved in a global variable. When the routine has returned to its caller, the location pointed to by the global variable will no longer be allocated to the original variable and unpredictable values may be obtained via that pointer.

Performance issues

This technique involving both a static and a dynamic chain seems to solve the problems of variable access while at the same time being straightforward to implement. However, there are several aspects in which improvements may be possible. It is easy to see that there may be an overhead of several instructions in the call and return sequences. These instructions perform various stack housekeeping operations and do not contribute directly to the operation of the calling or called procedures. However, although not much can be done to remove this overhead – it is the price that has to be paid for the benefits offered by the static and dynamic chains – it can be reduced to some extent by hardware and/or microprogram support of 'fancy' subroutine call and return instructions. These instructions incorporate logic to help maintain the static and dynamic chains, as well as the stack pointer and the program counter. Many processors now support such instructions and there are clear benefits in code size and efficiency. The topic of hardware support for high-level languages is covered in Section 8.2. It is also worth noting that the implementation presented here makes extensive use of (presumably fast) machine registers. Procedure call and return become much slower and more complex if the hardware severely limits the number of index registers.

An analysis of most programs written in a block-structured programming language shows that most variable accesses are either to locally defined variables or to globally defined variables. Variables defined in the intervening blocks or procedures are accessed comparatively rarely. The mechanism for variable access presented here is efficient for local variables, but if the textual nesting is deep, the efficiency of global variable access leaves something to be desired, since the static chain has to be followed along several links to obtain the global stack frame. It is true that the code generator may be able to perform some degree of optimization by, for example, not repeatedly loading S if accesses to several global variables are required in quick succession, but even so, the overhead may prove to be unacceptable. Perhaps the simplest solution to this efficiency problem is to dedicate another register to the function always pointing to the base of the stack. Global variables can then be referenced via offsets of this register. Although this is a common solution in practice, in some implementations it may be possible instead to use some form of absolute addressing for global variables or perhaps to use relative addresses to be resolved by a linker or loader.

A simple extension of this approach is to use one machine register for each nesting level, thereby providing access to all the variables in scope, no matter where they are defined, without the associated overhead. It is a very easy task for the code generator to produce instructions to maintain the contents of such registers. Furthermore, the availability of such registers means that there is no longer any need for the static chain on the stack. To implement this scheme, some restriction will have to be placed on the maximum nesting level, since the number of registers available for this purpose will almost certainly be limited. A hybrid scheme, combining the use of several registers with the static chain, could also be used.

A more general but equivalent solution makes use of a data structure called a **display**. The display is simply a table of pointers to all the stack frames containing accessible variables – that is, all the stack frames that would have been connected by the static chain. In this scheme, access to non-local variables is via an indirection through the display. It is virtually essential to dedicate one register to point to the display. It is possible to store the display on the stack, with a new display being created each time a new stack frame is entered. However, as this may prove to be rather wasteful of storage, the maintenance of a single copy of the display is often preferred.

Before deciding on a method for implementing the environment at run time, a careful assessment of relative efficiencies must be made. The simple static chain turns out to be surprisingly efficient in practice, especially if there is a fast and compact method for accessing the global variables, such as via a register pointing to the base of the stack. Probably the best method of all, assuming that there are enough registers available, is to store the entire display vector in registers. Using main storage for the display adds a memory access to each non-local memory access, which may prove to be an unacceptable overhead, and the necessity of reconstructing the display at each procedure entry may add to the attraction of the static chain. A detailed knowledge of the target hardware is required to resolve these issues.

Start-of-block declarations

In this section, the descriptions of the techniques have been tailored towards languages such as Pascal, where declarations can only occur at the start of the main program or the procedures (and functions). In contrast, in languages such as ALGOL 68, declarations can occur at the start of any block. For example, a procedure could be defined as follows:

```
proc p1 = void;
begin
   int a, b;
   .
   .
   .
   begin
      int p, q, r;
      .
      .
      .
      begin
         int s, t;
         .
         .
         .
      end;
      .
      .
      .
   end;
   .
   .
   .
end
```

It is perfectly possible to implement this type of language in the same general way, creating a new stack frame each time a new block is entered, even despite the fact that no transfer of control is required on block entry, and hence there is no need for link information to be stored. But with this type of block structure, access to non-local variables is very common. As it is easy for the nesting to become very deep, the overheads of accessing distant non-local variables may therefore be enormous. Furthermore, few machines have enough registers to support a display vector completely in registers. Another constraint is that it is important to keep block entry and exit as efficient as possible, otherwise the programmer will be discouraged from using this valuable structuring technique.

A simple and often used solution to the problem of variable access in these languages is to allocate space on the stack for all the variables a, b, p, q, r, s and t when $p1$ is entered. In this way, there is only one stack frame for the procedure and all its blocks, and there is no overhead on entering or leaving a block. Using this technique, less stack space is used for linkage information, but *all* the space required by all the blocks of the procedure is claimed as soon as the procedure is entered. Although this may cause problems in some rare cases, it does not outweigh the advantages that this method offers. A slight complication is introduced when space for dynamic arrays is required. In this case, stack offsets may not be known at compile time. It may be worth maintaining a 'top-of-stack' pointer in a register to indicate the next free location for dynamic variable allocation, together with locations on the stack to point to the start of each dynamic array.

7.2.5 Argument passing

In the last section, no provision was made for passing arguments to and from procedures. Few of the widely used programming languages rely solely on the updating of shared variables to communicate with procedures, and so the efficient implementation of an argument-passing mechanism is an important aspect of the design of a code generator.

Various methods of argument passing were described in Chapter 2. Of these, passing parameters by value is the most straightforward technique. The fact that the value of the actual parameter is assigned to the formal parameter on the procedure call gives a clue as to how to manage its implementation. That is, the formal parameters can be handled as local variables of the procedure, with space being reserved for them on the stack. Then, on procedure entry, the values of the actual parameters can be placed in these locations. For example, after entry to the procedure $p1$, defined as:

```
procedure p1(x, y : integer);
var a, b : integer;
begin
    .
    .
    .
```

the stack could have the form shown in Figure 7.4. The actual implementation of this type of scheme poses no particular problems. The body of $p1$ can reference the names x and y and these references are translated to the appropriate stack offsets. The procedure $p1$ can also update x and y, just like any other local variables, and doing this can have no direct effect on any of the caller's variables.

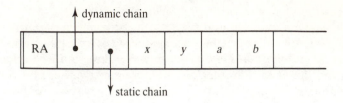

FIGURE 7.4

Argument passing on
the stack.

In the case of argument passing by reference, the addresses rather than the values of the actual parameters are passed to the called procedure. Call by reference in Pascal is specified by the use of **var** parameters and, again, the implementation poses no real difficulties. For example, if the procedure $p1$ had been defined with the heading:

> **procedure** $p1(\textbf{var}\ x, y : integer)$;

then the stack on procedure entry would look just the same. The difference would come when x or y were accessed, since the locations reserved on the stack now contain the addresses of x and y rather than the actual values of x and y. Therefore, to obtain the values of x and y at run time, an extra indirection is required. Similarly, when values are to be stored in x and y, the code generator has to be aware of the fact that the values should be stored in the locations *pointed to* by x and y. Incidentally, it should be noted that there are restrictions on the forms of the actual parameters when call by reference is used; typically, the actual parameters have to be variables.

This implementation of call by reference requires an additional storage access each time an argument is referenced within the procedure. Some machines provide efficient instructions to perform such indirect addressing and this helps a great deal in reducing the overhead. But if the arguments are referenced many times during the execution of the procedure, the following more efficient implementation may be possible. On procedure entry, code within the procedure makes a local copy of the arguments being called by reference. All references to the arguments within the procedure are diverted to the local copies. On procedure exit, the values of the local copies are copied back into the locations specified at the procedure call. This implements a mechanism sometimes known as call by value-result or call by copy-restore. The overheads imposed by this implementation technique are small when the arguments have simple types; that is, when the cost of making copies is small. When larger data types such as arrays are being passed as arguments, then the double copying may take an excessive time to perform and there may be insufficient space available to allow local copies of the arguments. In these cases, passing the address of the argument is usually preferred. Indeed, some languages restrict the form of a result argument to be a simple type.

Furthermore, access to these more complex structures is usually via an address; for example, array access requires the starting address of the array, and so passing an address to a procedure is precisely what is required. A similar consideration applies to the passing of large arguments in Pascal. For example, if a procedure is required to output the largest element in a single-dimensional array of type *vector*, the procedure heading:

    procedure *maxelement*(**var** *a* : *vector*);

may be preferred to:

    procedure *maxelement*(*a* : *vector*);

The first heading defines an argument to be called by reference: the address of *a* is passed to *maxelement*. In the second heading, *a* is passed by value, implying an automatic copy of the entire array. Since the procedure should not update the array *a*, call by value is preferred in theory, although run-time costs favour call by reference.

The language definition must be carefully examined before implementation techniques for argument passing can be selected. The differences between call by reference and call by value-result often cause confusion, and languages should prescribe which technique is to be used. Aho [1986] gives a clear example of a procedure that yields different results depending on whether the argument passing is by reference or by value-result.

Implementation of parameters passed by name is not so straightforward. Call by name is in effect a textual substitution of the actual parameters for the occurrences of the formal parameters in the procedure body. One implementation technique is to treat the procedure as a **macro** so that whenever the procedure is called, the compiler performs an automatic inline expansion of the procedure, substituting for the parameters called by name and ensuring that the names in the called procedure are kept distinct and hence do not clash with the names in the calling procedure. Such inline expansion is impractical if there are several calls to the procedure in the program and if the procedure is long.

An alternative approach is for the compiler to generate special additional procedures, invisible to the programmer, which are called automatically whenever a parameter called by name has to be evaluated. Such procedures must be capable of returning both the value of the parameter and also the address of the parameter should an assignment to that parameter be required.

7.2.6 Dynamic storage allocation

The discussions so far have concentrated on the management of static storage, where the compiler knows the location and layout of all variables.

Slight complications are introduced when the language allows the use of arrays whose sizes are not known until run time, but usually they can be handled with only minor modifications to the straightforward static variable allocation techniques. However, many languages also require a storage allocation scheme that can allocate space on request during program execution. In some languages, the storage requests may be implicit. For example, in SNOBOL4, a language that can handle variable length character strings, the space occupied by a variable can vary dynamically during execution as the length of the string referred to by the variable changes according to the operations performed on it. The implementation of SNOBOL4 has to include storage management facilities to allow this dynamic allocation and freeing of storage. LISP is another good example of a language where dynamic storage allocation is fundamentally important. In other languages, storage requests are explicitly issued by the programmer. For example, Pascal implementations include the *new* and *dispose* procedures which can be called by the programmer to acquire and release dynamic storage. These facilities allow the construction of dynamic data structures, such as linked lists and trees.

The space to satisfy these dynamic storage requests is taken from an area of storage often called the **heap**. Heap storage is distinguishable from stack-based allocation in that the pattern of storage allocation and return does not necessarily follow the pattern of procedure call and return. For example, a call to *new* in a Pascal procedure causes the allocation of storage that is not automatically released when the Pascal procedure terminates.

To implement these facilities for dynamic storage, it is likely that a general-purpose storage allocation package will be required that is capable of allocating variable sized blocks on request and also of handling the subsequent return of these blocks to the free pool. As may be expected, the details of such a storage allocation package will depend on the language being supported. It may be that the operating system can provide these facilities and that, in this case, assuming that the performance is adequate, the implementation of the language's storage allocation package is straightforward. Unfortunately, it is more likely that the language implementor will have to provide these facilities almost from scratch. Fortunately, a great deal has been published on the subject of storage allocation packages – for example, see Knuth [1973].

The characteristics of a language have a great impact on the techniques that can be used for storage return. In the case of Pascal, the return of dynamic storage for potential reuse is the responsibility of the programmer, via the *dispose* procedure. In other languages, it may still be possible to make use of explicit return of storage but without programmer intervention. The use of reference counts may also help to ensure the prompt return of free storage. It may also be necessary to implement a garbage collector, whose task is to reclaim dynamically allocated storage that has become inaccessible.

It is fairly easy to implement a simple yet efficient storage allocation package that does not attempt to optimize the use of storage. Introducing comprehensive storage reclamation facilities may result in a slightly more efficient use of storage, but this is at the cost of increased implementation difficulties and perhaps much slower execution.

7.3   Code Generation from a Tree

The task of the syntax analyzer is to produce a representation of the source program in a form directly representing its syntactic structure. This representation is usually in the form of a binary tree or similar data structure. The task of the code generator is to traverse this tree, producing functionally equivalent object code. It is possible to generate either target machine code directly from the tree or some form of intermediate code from which target machine code can be generated by a subsequent phase of the compiler. Both of these approaches have advantages. Generating target machine code directly simplifies the design of the compiler. In addition, there are some optimization techniques that are more easily applied to a tree than to a linear data structure. On the other hand, code generation via an intermediate code may help to achieve better compiler modularity and portability. But, logically, there is no difference between these two approaches, since the intermediate code can be considered as the target machine code for some abstract machine. In this section, we will be considering the generation of code for an abstract machine that is fairly close in design to most of the conventional processors in use today. There are also many similarities between this abstract machine and the intermediate codes (see Section 6.6), such as the three-address code described in Aho [1986].

7.3.1   An abstract machine

This section contains an informal description of an abstract machine that will be used in the code-generation examples in later sections. It has many similarities with some of the popular 16- and 32-bit microprocessors. In particular, it is close to the Motorola MC68000 series of processors.

The machine contains 16 general-purpose registers, called R0, R1, ..., R15. These registers can be used to store data values or addresses. Operations involving these registers are much faster than the same operations using main storage locations. Hence, when generating high-quality code, it is important that as many as possible of the frequently used operands are held in these machine registers.

The assembly language for this abstract machine supports the following conventions for specifying the operands for instructions:

Operand	Meaning
#<data>	immediate data, stored in the instruction
<register>	one of the 16 registers
(<register>)	the location pointed to by the specified register
<offset>(<register>)	the location pointed to by the specified register + <offset>
<name>	the storage location labelled <name>

Instructions can take up to two arguments. If there are two arguments, the first is interpreted as the source argument and the second as the destination argument.

The abstract machine supports a set of basic instructions including:

Instruction	Description
MOVE	move data from source (first argument) to destination (second argument)
ADD	destination := destination + source
SUB	destination := destination − source
MUL	destination := destination * source
DIV	destination := destination / source
AND	destination := destination & source (logical AND)
OR	destination := destination | source (logical OR)
EOR	destination := destination <exclusive or> source
ASL	destination := destination shifted left arithmetically by source places
ASR	destination := destination shifted right arithmetically by source places
NEG	destination := −destination
CLR	destination := 0
CMP	compare source with destination
B	unconditional branch
Bxx	branch if condition xx is true (after a compare) – the condition can be EQ, NE, LE, LT, GE or GT.

The destination operand in all the arithmetic and logical instructions must be a register.

Details such as the number of bits in each register and the size of the address space are of no real concern at this point, although such details

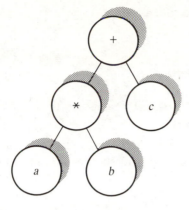

FIGURE 7.5

Tree for the expression
a * *b* + *c*.

would have to be taken into account when writing a code generator for a real processor. Furthermore, the larger instruction set of a real processor, explicitly including instructions designed to handle particular sizes of data items, would also add to the complexity of the implementation of a practical code generator.

7.3.2   Arithmetic expressions

As most of the programs running on computers today make extensive use of arithmetic calculations, the generation of good code for arithmetic expressions is essential for a good compiler. Furthermore, many of the techniques used for the code generation of arithmetic expressions are applicable to other language constructs.

The code generator operates on the arithmetic expression in the form of a tree produced by the syntax analyzer. For example, the expression *a* * *b* + *c* yields the tree shown in Figure 7.5. A code generator should traverse this tree, or some transformation of this tree, to produce code of the general form:

```
MOVE a, R0        ;R0 := a
MUL  b, R0        ;R0 := a * b
ADD  c, R0        ;result in R0
```

The aim here is to develop an algorithm that traverses the tree in such a way as to produce correct and, in some sense, 'optimal' code. If the abstract machine for which code is being generated uses stack-based operations, then the code-generation problem is simplified: a post-order traversal of the tree is performed [Knuth, 1973], which directly yields the instructions for the stack machine. In this example, a post-order traversal yields *ab* * *c* + and the code generated is:

```
PUSH a
PUSH b
MUL                ;multiply top two items of the stack
PUSH c
ADD                ;result at top of stack
```

This process is very simple, which explains the popularity of stack-based abstract (and real) machines. But the abstract machine described here is not stack based and so a somewhat more complex algorithm is required.

Suppose that the code generator operates on a tree whose nodes are defined in Pascal as:

```
type nodep = ↑ node;
     node = record
     nodetype : (operator, variable, constant);
     id : char;   (* representation of operator or variable *)
     val : integer;   (* value of constant if nodetype = constant *)
     left, right : nodep
end;
```

A simple code-generation procedure can now be written. This recursive procedure is based on a post-order tree traversal.

```
procedure code(p : nodep; register : integer);

begin
  if p ↑ .nodetype = operator then
  begin
    code(p ↑ .left, register);
    code(p ↑ .right, register + 1);

    case p ↑ .id of
      '+' : emit1('ADD', register + 1, register);
            (* generate instruction of the form ADD R1, R0 *)
      '−' : emit1('SUB', register + 1, register);
      '*' : emit1('MUL', register + 1, register);
      '/' : emit1('DIV', register + 1, register);
    end
  end
  else
  if p ↑ .nodetype = variable then
    emit2('MOVE', p ↑ .id, register)
      (* generate instruction of the form MOVE a, R0 *)
```

```
    else
  if p ↑ .nodetype = constant then
    emit3('MOVE', p ↑ .val, register)
      (* generate instruction of the form MOVE #3, R0 *)
  else
    error('Unknown nodetype')
end;
```

The parameter *register* to procedure *code* indicates the number of the machine register in which the result of the evaluation of the expression should be placed.

Consider now what output this elementary code-generation procedure produces for various simple arithmetic expressions, assuming that the result is required in R0.

EXAMPLE

The expression $a * b + c$ yields:

```
MOVE a, R0
MOVE b, R1
MUL  R1, R0
MOVE c, R1
ADD  R1, R0
```

The expression $a * b - c/d$ yields:

```
MOVE a, R0
MOVE b, R1
MUL  R1, R0
MOVE c, R1
MOVE d, R2
DIV  R2, R1
SUB  R1, R0
```

The expression $(a + b + c)/3$ yields:

```
MOVE a, R0
MOVE b, R1
ADD  R1, R0
MOVE c, R1
ADD  R1, R0
MOVE #3, R1
DIV  R1, R0
```

From these examples, it is easy to see that procedure *code* does not generate optimal code for the abstract machine. Its most obvious failing is that it does not recognize that the first operand of the ADD, SUB, MUL and DIV instructions need not be a register. This can be easily remedied by making an explicit check whether the source operand is a variable or a constant – that is, a leaf node in the tree. The procedure can be rewritten thus:

```
procedure code(p : nodep; register : integer);
var source : nodep;
    op : string;   (* defined appropriately *)

begin
  if p ↑ .nodetype = operator then
  begin
    source := p ↑ .right;
    case p ↑ .id of
      '+' : op := 'ADD';
      '−' : op := 'SUB';
      '*' : op := 'MUL';
      '/' : op := 'DIV';
    end;
    code(p ↑ .left, register);

    if source ↑ .nodetype = operator then
      (* behave as in previous version of code *)
    begin
      code(source, register + 1);
      emit1(op, register + 1, register);
    end
    else
    if source ↑ .nodetype = variable then
      emit2(op, source ↑ .id, register)
        (* generate instruction of the form ADD a, R0 *)
    else
    if source ↑ .nodetype = constant then
      emit3(op, source ↑ .val, register)
        (* generate instruction of the form ADD #3, R0 *)
    else
      error('Unknown nodetype')
  end
  else
  if p ↑ .nodetype = variable then
    emit2('MOVE', p ↑ .id, register)
  else
  if p ↑ .nodetype = constant then
    emit3('MOVE', p ↑ .val, register)
  else
    error('Unknown nodetype')
end;
```

Applying the modified algorithm to the earlier examples results in the following fragments of code.

EXAMPLE

The expression $a * b + c$ yields:

```
MOVE a, R0
MUL  b, R0
ADD  c, R0
```

The expression $a * b - c/d$ yields:

```
MOVE a, R0
MUL  b, R0
MOVE c, R1
DIV  d, R1
SUB  R1, R0
```

The expression $(a + b + c)/3$ yields:

```
MOVE a, R0
ADD  b, R0
ADD  c, R0
DIV  #3, R0
```

These examples show that the rewritten procedure is a great improvement over the previous version of *code* and, indeed, for these three examples, the code is optimal. However, as will be seen later, there are certain characteristics of the arithmetic operators that make further optimizations possible in some cases.

Use of a limited number of registers

In its present form, the *code* procedure does not make any restrictions on the use of registers in the code generation of arithmetic expressions. In the examples, *register* is set to zero when *code* is initially called. The registers are then used sequentially as required, until the code generation of the expression is complete. Of the three examples just given, the first and third use only one register while the second uses two registers. Obviously, more complex expressions require more registers. The abstract machine being used for these examples has 16 registers, but only a subset of these registers are available for the code generation of arithmetic expressions, the rest being dedicated to other functions such as a stack pointer or a display pointer. It is therefore easy to write programs containing expressions that would require more registers for their implementation than are available, and so other temporary storage locations must be found. Main memory can certainly be used for this purpose and often the stack is used as a source of these temporary storage locations.

One of the aims of the code generator writer must be to minimize the use of these temporary locations for reasons of both space and time efficiency. Therefore, it is important to look slightly more analytically at the process of code generation from a tree, so that temporary storage location requirements can be minimized. The analysis presented here is based on that in Horowitz [1978].

The optimization criterion is to minimize the use of temporary storage locations. In the context of the abstract machine, this is equivalent to minimizing the number of MOVE instructions that have a storage location as the destination argument. (It is assumed that the result of the expression is left in one of the registers.) To investigate techniques for achieving this optimization, it is useful to determine the minimum number of registers required for the evaluation of an expression without the use of temporary variables.

To define a function to calculate the minimum number of registers, consider the following two special cases:

(1)   If the expression consists of a single variable and no operators – that is, the tree consists of a single leaf node containing a variable – then the optimal code has the form:

```
MOVE a, R0
```

and only one register is required, which is used to hold the result of evaluating the expression.

(2)   If the expression contains a single operator, it must be of the form a **op** b. The tree has the form shown in Figure 7.6(a). The optimal code has the form:

```
MOVE a, R0
op   b, R0        ;where op is ADD, SUB, MUL or DIV
```

Again, only one register is required.

In the more general case, the tree has the form shown in Figure 7.6(b). Suppose that the minimum number of registers required to evaluate the left (L) and right (R) subtrees are n_L and n_R, respectively. It is assumed that the evaluations of these subtrees are independent; that is, the expression is represented as a well-formed binary tree with disjoint subtrees. Suppose also that the minimum number of registers required to evaluate the whole expression is n. It is clear that $n \geq \max(n_L, n_R)$.

(a)

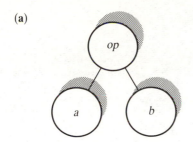

(b)

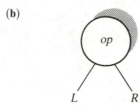

FIGURE 7.6

Tree for the expression
a **op** *b*.

Assume first that $n_L > n_R$; that is, more registers are required to evaluate the left subtree. In this case, the left subtree is evaluated first using n_L registers. One of these registers is used to hold the result of the evaluation, which leaves $n_L - 1$ registers free to be used in the evaluation of the right subtree. But it is known that $n_L > n_R$, hence $n_L - 1 \geq n_R$. Therefore, the $n_L - 1$ registers are sufficient to evaluate the right subtree and so $n = n_L$ in this case. A similar argument applies to the case where $n_R > n_L$ and the equality $n = n_R$ is obtained. So when $n_L \neq n_R$, $n = \max(n_L, n_R)$.

Finally, suppose $n_L = n_R$. If the left subtree is computed first, then n_L registers are used. If the right subtree consists of a single leaf node, then an instruction of the form:

```
op   rleaf, R0    ;assumes result of evaluation of left subtree
                  ;is left in R0. Result of evaluation of
                  ;complete expression is in R0
```

can be used and $n = n_L$. If the right subtree is not a single leaf, then $n_R (= n_L)$ registers are required for its evaluation and hence $n = n_L + 1$, since one extra register is required to hold the result of whichever subtree is evaluated first.

Horowitz [1978] summarizes this argument by defining the function $MR(P)$ as follows, where P is a node in a tree of depth ≥ 2:

$MR(P) = 0$ if P is a leaf node and the right child of its parent
$\quad\quad = 1$ if P is a leaf node and the left child of its parent
$\quad\quad = \max(n_L, n_R)$ where n_L and n_R are as defined and $n_L \neq n_R$
$\quad\quad = n_L + 1$ where n_L and n_R are as defined and $n_L = n_R$

(a)

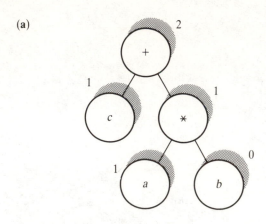

(b)

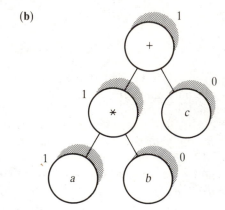

FIGURE 7.7

Trees for the expression
$c + a * b$.

Given an arbitrary tree defining an expression, it is now easy to determine the minimum number of registers required for its evaluation. Using the logic presented in the foregoing argument, it is also easy to write a simple code-generation routine that generates optimal code. The *MR* function is used in this routine to determine which subtree is to be evaluated first. Details of this code-generation routine are contained in Horowitz [1978].

Special properties of operators

In what sense is the code generated by such a routine 'optimal'? Obviously, the code is making use of registers rather than temporary storage locations if it possibly can. Because of the design of the abstract machine, this is equivalent to stating that 'optimal' implies the smallest number of MOVE instructions, and hence the smallest total number of all instructions. It is highly likely that this will yield the fastest code on most processors, given the indicated restricted instruction set.

But this code is not optimal when certain properties of the operators are taken into account. In particular, some operators are commutative, so

(a)

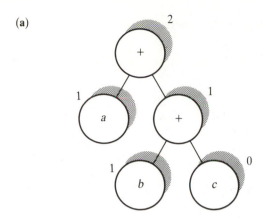

(b)

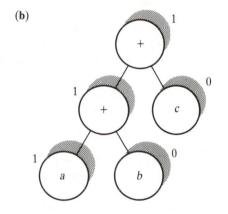

FIGURE 7.8

Trees for the expression
$a + b + c$.

that a **op** $b = b$ **op** a, while others are associative, so that a **op** (b **op** c) = (a **op** b) **op** c. As an example, consider the expression $c + a * b$, whose tree has the form shown in Figure 7.7(a). Each node is labelled with its *MR* value. Since the root is labelled 2, two registers are required for the evaluation of this expression, with no use of temporary storage locations. In an implementation where only one register is available for use in the expression evaluation, the optimal code generated for this tree would have the form:

```
MOVE a, R0
MUL  b, R0
MOVE R0, temp1    ;use temporary storage location
MOVE c, R0
ADD  temp1, R0    ;result to R0
```

As the + operator is commutative, the expression $c + a * b$ can be written as $a * b + c$. The corresponding tree and MR values are shown in

Figure 7.7(b). The code generated would now be:

```
MOVE a, R0
MUL  b, R0
ADD  c, R0          ;result to R0
```

Similarly, the expression $a + b + c$ can be interpreted as $a + (b + c)$ or as $(a + b) + c$. The two trees with MR values are shown in Figure 7.8. The two sets of generated code would be:

```
MOVE b, R0          MOVE a, R0
ADD  c, R0          ADD  b, R0
MOVE R0, temp1      ADD  c, R0
MOVE a, R0
ADD  temp1, R0
```

Fortunately, it is not too difficult to develop code-generation algorithms that take commutativity and associativity into account and generate code that is optimal under somewhat more relaxed conditions.

'Reverse' arithmetic instructions

Some processors support additional instructions that can make the code generated for some expressions a little simpler. The SUB and DIV instructions for the abstract machine are asymmetrical because subtraction and division operations are not commutative. Suppose that the machine supports the reverse operations RSUB and RDIV, defined as:

```
RSUB    destination := source − destination
RDIV    destination := source / destination
```

If the expression $a/(b + c)$ is evaluated without these instructions, it can be seen from the *MR* values in the tree in Figure 7.9(a) that two registers are required. The code generated would have the form:

```
MOVE a, R0
MOVE b, R1
ADD  c, R1
DIV  R1, R0        ;answer to R0
```

Using the reverse division operator, the tree and *MR* values are as in Figure 7.9(b); hence, only one register is required. The code generated becomes:

```
MOVE b, R0
ADD  c, R0
RDIV a, R0
```

(a)

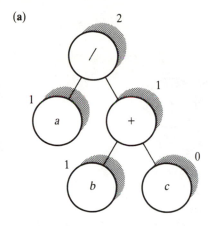

(b)

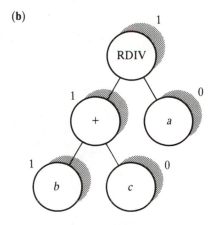

FIGURE 7.9

Trees for the expression
$a/(b + c)$.

producing a saving of one register and one instruction.

Directed acyclic graphs

So far, this section has been concerned with generating code for an expression represented in the form of a binary tree, where the left and right subtrees of any node are disjoint and both operands of any operator can be computed independently. However, it is possible to represent expressions, (as well as other programming language structures) using a similar type of data structure in which the restriction of disjoint subtrees is relaxed. This data structure is called the **directed acyclic graph** (**DAG**). Such structures can represent common sub-expressions. For example, consider the representation of the expression $a * (b + c) + d/(b + c)$ as a binary tree. This is shown in Figure 7.10(a). It can be represented in a somewhat more compact form as a DAG as shown in Figure 7.10(b). This structure recognizes the common sub-expression $(b + c)$ and it is represented only once.

(a)

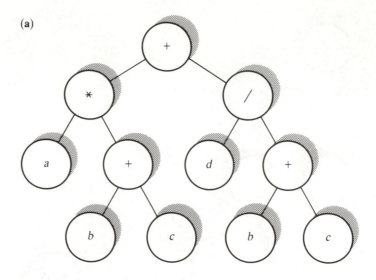

(b)

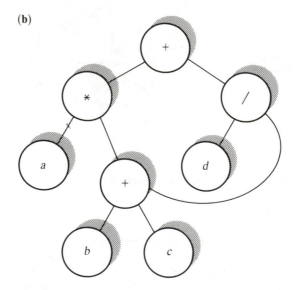

FIGURE 7.10

Representations of the expression $a * (b + c) + d/(b + c)$.

Unfortunately, constructing a DAG is not nearly as straightforward as constructing a binary tree. Furthermore, generating optimal code from a general DAG is complex and can be very time consuming. Fortunately, some heuristic algorithms have been developed that generate 'good' but not necessarily optimal code.

7.3.3 Boolean expressions

Boolean expressions can be handled in a very similar way to arithmetic expressions, except that different machine operations are used (AND, OR and EOR) and only two different values need be manipulated. Conventionally, TRUE is represented by a non-zero value – typically, this may be −1 or 1, but the choice may be governed by the language specification – and FALSE by zero. This allows Boolean operations to be implemented directly by the machine's bitwise logical instructions. For example, the expression (*p* **and** *q*) **or** *r* would cause the following code to be generated:

```
MOVE p, R0
AND  q, R0
OR   r, R0
```

Major optimizations may be possible in some cases. For example, the value of the Boolean expression (*a* > 0) **or** (*b* > 0) **or** (*c* > 0) is TRUE if any of the three comparisons yields TRUE. So, if *a* is found to be greater than zero, then the other two comparisons need not be executed. A similar argument applies to an expression of the form (*a* > 0) **and** (*b* > 0) **and** (*c* > 0). If *a* is found not to be greater than zero, the whole expression must have the value FALSE, removing the necessity for the evaluation of the other two conditions. So, in these examples, it may be possible to generate a conditional branch instruction to skip the code for the tests that need not be executed. As such short-circuited evaluation may be insisted upon, disallowed or left unspecified by the language definition, its use cannot be universal. The use of this method is illustrated in the code that could be generated for an expression of the form (*a* > 0) **or** (*b* > 0) **or** (*c* > 0):

```
    CMP   a, #0
    BGT   L1            ;branch if a > 0
    CMP   b, #0
    BGT   L1
    CMP   c, #0
    BGT   L1
    CLR   R0            ;result FALSE
    B     L2
L1: MOVE  #-1, R0       ;result TRUE
L2:
```

Although the original expression included three **or** operations, the generated code contains no OR instructions. Thus, the Boolean expression is not being evaluated using the logical operations; instead, it is being evaluated using a series of tests and jumps with the Boolean values of the sub-expressions determining the paths taken through the instructions. Any Boolean expression can be evaluated in this way with the sequence of instructions terminating with jumps to one of two locations: one reached if the value of the expression is TRUE and the other reached if the value of the expression is FALSE. In the example just given, the code in these locations simply loads R0 with the values −1 and 0, respectively, to indicate the Boolean value of the expression.

Thus, there are two approaches to the evaluation of a Boolean expression: one uses a numerical representation for TRUE and FALSE, which can be manipulated by the machine's logical instructions, and the other uses a conditional branching representation. Both these methods have their distinct advantages and both are used in real compilers. However, in the popular high-level languages, there is a frequent use of Boolean expressions in which the conditional branching representation seems more natural. In Pascal, for example, a Boolean expression is required in every **if**, **while** and **repeat** statement. But when code generating these statements, there is no need to introduce numerical representations of the results of the Boolean expressions.

EXAMPLE

The code produced for the statement:

> **if** $a < b$ **then** $a := a + 1$;

could take the form:

```
        CMP   a, b
        BGE   L1
        MOVE  a, R0
        ADD   #1, R0
        MOVE  R0, a
L1:
```

If a numerical value is calculated as the result of the expression $a < b$, then the following somewhat more verbose code may be the result:

```
        CMP   a, b
        BGE   L1
        MOVE  #-1, R0      ;TRUE if a < b
        B     L2
L1:     CLR   R0           ;FALSE if a >= b
L2:     CMP   #0, R0
        BEQ   L3           ;branch if Boolean result is FALSE
        MOVE  a, R0
        ADD   #1, R0
        MOVE  R0, a
L3:
```

In this case, the generated code corresponds more closely to the equivalent statement:

if $(a < b) = $ *true* **then** $a := a + 1$;

Unfortunately, this technique of short-circuiting the evaluation of a Boolean expression is not without its complications under some circumstances. Problems may arise because it may be impossible to predict in advance whether certain parts of a Boolean expression will be evaluated. If the expression contains calls to functions with side effects, then the program may behave in an unpredictable manner. For example, a statement of the form:

if *done* **and** *trans*(x) **then** …

may be implemented so that the Boolean function *trans* is only called if *done* has the value TRUE. If *trans* modifies a global variable each time it is called, then this statement may not have the effect that the programmer intended. This effect is of course a language specification issue – the language should specify the semantics of such a statement. Similarly, there are situations where the short-circuited evaluation of a condition may be essential. For example, a statement of the form:

while $(i <= 10)$ **and** $(a[i] = 0)$ **do** …

where a is declared as an array having an upper bound of 10 will fail if i has the value 11 and both sub-expressions are evaluated. Different high-level languages approach this problem in different ways, but the code generator writer must be aware of the language rules. Some languages do not specify whether this short-circuited evaluation is permitted and the choice of whether to use this technique is left to the implementor. Other languages state that short-circuited evaluation should always be applied and some languages even provide constructs that allow the programmer to specify which type of evaluation is required.

7.3.4　Conditional statements

if statements

Code generation for an **if** statement is comparatively easy, but the details depend on whether the Boolean condition is evaluated in terms of the logical values or as a series of tests and jumps. For example, if the condition in the generalized **if** statement (**if** c **then** $S1$ **else** $S2$) is evaluated as a numerical value (−1 for TRUE and 0 for FALSE), then the code could take the form:

```
        <evaluate c>        ;result to R0
        CMP   #0, R0
        BEQ   L1
        <code for S1>
        B     L2
L1:     <code for S2>
L2:
```

If the code generator is producing assembly language, as in the example just given, the management of the arguments to the branch instructions is easy because symbolic labels can be used. When the instruction BEQ L1 is generated, the code generator need not know the precise location of L1. However, if the code generator is producing some form of machine language, symbolic labels are not permitted. Furthermore, in a single-pass code generator, it is not possible to determine the addresses of the destinations of forward branches at the time of generation of the branch instruction. A technique commonly used to overcome this difficulty is known as **backpatching**. Here, the destination address is left unspecified in the branch instruction and a record is kept of the location of this incomplete instruction. When the address of the destination is known (the address of the destination of the BEQ instruction above is known when the code for S1 has been generated), the incomplete instruction can be modified to include the resolved address.

case statements

The other conditional statement supported by Pascal is the **case** statement. This is a multi-way branch and there are several feasible techniques for its implementation. The choice between these techniques depends to a large extent on the number and range of the **case** alternatives.

A simple approach is to interpret the **case** statement as a sequence of **if**...**then**...**else**...**if** alternatives. The code generated would then have the form:

```
        CMP   #k1, R0      ;case 1 has case label k1
        BNE   L1
        <code for case 1>
        B     L100
L1:     CMP   #k2, R0
        BNE   L2
        <code for case 2>
L2:     CMP   #k3, R0
          .
          .
          .
L100:                      ;exit from case statement
```

A similar and essentially equivalent alternative is to structure the code as follows, although it is quite difficult to produce code of this form in one pass of the code generator:

```
        CMP   #k1, R0
        BEQ   L1
        CMP   #k2, R0
        BEQ   L2
          .
          .
          .
L1:     <code for case 1>
        B     L100
L2:     <code for case 2>
        B     L100
          .
          .
          .
L100:
```

If the number of **case** alternatives is large, these techniques may result in inefficient and verbose code. It may be possible to implement a jump table if the numerical range of the **case** labels is not too large. This is a table of addresses or complete jump instructions which is indexed by the **case** index value to find the location of the appropriate code. The smallest and largest **case** labels are found and the difference between these values defines the size of the jump table required. Each location in the jump table corresponding to a **case** label value present in the **case** statement is filled with the address of the code handling that **case** alternative. Code is generated at the head of the **case** statement to use the **case** index value to index the jump table, thus rapidly selecting the section of code to be executed.

Yet another approach is to sort the values of the **case** labels and generate code to perform a binary chop using the value of the **case** index. Hash tables can also be used. Certain patterns of **case** labels may suggest further techniques, but the choice of implementation technique for each particular **case** statement may be quite difficult.

Whichever method is chosen, care has to be taken to handle unexpected **case** index values in a predictable manner. If the **case** index has a value at run time that is not equal to any of the **case** labels, then the generated code should not fail. Languages vary widely in their handling of this situation. In Pascal, an error should be reported, but many implementations support the use of an *otherwise* branch. If a jump table is being used for the implementation, then the unused entries in the table should contain the address of the code to handle this condition. Code should also be generated to ensure that the **case** index is within the appropriate range before it is used to index the jump table.

7.3.5 Repetitive statements

The code generation of these statements presents no special problems. For example, code generated for **while** *c* **do** *S* has the general form:

```
L2:    <evaluate c>        ;result to R0
       CMP  #0, R0
       BEQ  L1
       <code for S>
       B    L2
L1:
```

This code is slightly simplified if the condition is evaluated in terms of tests and jumps. **repeat** statements can be handled in a very similar way.

The translation of **for** statements can also be performed in this way, but most processors support instructions that make the translation somewhat more efficient and compact. Fast decrement, test-and-branch instructions (decrement register and branch if result is non-zero) are often available and these can sometimes be applied to this situation with advantage.

7.3.6 *goto* statements

The action of the **goto** statement is performed by a jump or branch instruction on the target hardware. The destination address of the branch is given by the value of the label; if it is a forward jump, then backpatching may be necessary. For a **goto** whose destination is within the current block, only a single branch instruction is required. But for a non-local **goto** where, for example, control is transferred from within a procedure to the enclosing main program, the value of the stack pointer has to be reset to point to the base of the stack frame of the destination block immediately before the branch instruction is executed.

7.4   Hardware Issues

In this chapter, several examples have been presented of the code generated for a simple abstract machine. Real machines are usually much more complicated with a much larger variety of instructions, more addressing modes and the capability of handling a range of different data types. Making efficient use of such instruction sets requires a carefully written code generator. But the compiler writer is seldom forgotten by the designers of today's processors. Regular instruction sets are provided which often include special instructions that mirror popular high-level language constructs. Modern techniques of processor and of code generator design give much better results than those obtained on the much more restricted processors designed over a decade ago.

7.4.1 Instruction sets

Many modern processors provide extended support for stack-based subroutine call and return. Rapid and compact implementation of subroutine operations are essential if the principles of structured programming are to be followed. Instructions such as PUSH and POP, saving and restoring of multiple registers, and stack space allocation and deallocation are frequently available. Some processors also make assumptions about the use of machine registers and stack locations for specific purposes, such as for the storage of return addresses, and static and dynamic chain pointers. This may make procedure implementation for some languages particularly simple and efficient. On the other hand, for some languages, the generality of the processor-supplied call and return instructions may be unnecessary and, in fact, a short sequence of simple instructions may perform more efficiently.

Instructions may be available that closely match the implementation of certain specific high-level language constructs. The use of decrement and branch instructions for the support of **for** statements has already been mentioned. Instructions to support the multi-way branching of **case** statements are occasionally found. The Motorola MC68020 processor includes instructions that check that the value contained in a register is within specified lower and upper bounds. These instructions are of immense assistance in language implementations that carry out range checking; for example, Pascal compilers should be capable of producing run-time checking code to check that array subscripts, subrange type variables and the like are always within permitted ranges. Performing this checking without special-purpose instructions can add greatly to code sizes and execution times.

The format of the operands of the instructions is important to the code generator writer. Processors vary in the maximum number of address arguments that can be contained within a machine instruction. Some processors require that the operands for certain instructions should be contained within registers. In some cases, just one of the two arguments has to be a register. Other processors have a much more orthogonal instruction set in which instruction arguments can be fetched by any of the addressing modes supported by the hardware. These regular instruction sets simplify the design of the code generator. Further simplification may be possible if the processor supports instructions that take up to three arguments, thus allowing statements such as $a := b + c$ (depending on the location and nature of a, b and c) to be translated into a single machine instruction. The DEC VAX-11 supports instructions of this form, in addition to the more common two-operand instructions.

7.4.2 Addressing modes

A rich set of addressing modes may allow the generation of more compact and efficient code. For example, the DEC PDP-11 series of computers introduced a wide range of addressing modes, most of which have been incorporated into more recent processor designs. Most instruction arguments can make use of the full range of addressing modes. Preferably, the instruction set should be symmetrical, so that any addressing mode is permitted when specifying the operand of an instruction. Restrictions may cause irritation to the code generator writer.

Indexed addressing is of particular importance to the compiler writer. If space for variables is allocated on the stack, then rapid access to these variables can be achieved by supplying the appropriate offsets from the current value of the stack pointer. This can be done on the PDP-11 by generating an instruction of the form:

```
MOV  6(R1), R0    ;R1 is used to point to the stack.
                  ;The value of the variable is placed in R0
```

The PDP-11 also supports **autoincrement** and **autodecrement** addressing which simplify code for accessing stacks, arrays and so on. For example, the instruction:

```
MOV  R0, (R1)+
```

stores the value of R0 in the location pointed to by R1, and R1 is incremented to point to the next location. The inverse operation is performed by:

```
MOV  -(R1), R0
```

which decrements R1 before using its contents as an address. These two instructions perform the PUSH and POP operations on the stack pointed to by R1. A compiler can make good use of these facilities when generating procedure call and return code for the PDP-11. These addressing modes can also be used in the generation of optimized code. For example, the statement:

for $i := 1$ **to** 1000 **do** $a[i] := 0$;

could be processed by the compiler so that the generated code (on the

PDP-11) has the form:

```
      <initialize loop counter>
      <set R2 to point to the start of array a>
L1:   <check for 1000 iterations>
      CLR  (R2)+       ;zero location and point to next
      BR   L1
```

The PDP-11 supports various other addressing modes, all of which are of use to the code generator writer, but being a comparatively simple machine, generating code to access high-level language data structures can be a little verbose. For example, high-level language programs frequently make use of arrays, but it is important that the code to access arrays is compact and efficient. To illustrate this, consider the implementation of a single-dimensional array where its name is associated with a location on the stack, which points to the first location of a contiguous area of storage, holding the elements of the array. To access an array element, two indexing operations have to be performed. The starting address of the array is obtained by reading the location at the appropriate offset from the current stack pointer. An index value is then added to this starting address to obtain the address of the required element.

The PDP-11 cannot support this type of access in a single machine instruction, but more recent processors, such as the VAX-11 and the Motorola MC68000, incorporate addressing modes that make array access much easier. Indeed, the VAX-11 offers index mode addressing, which provides a very powerful and flexible array access mechanism with array indexes being multiplied automatically by the size of each array element. This mode is only supported for array elements of sizes 1, 2, 4 and 8 bytes.

Stack-based addressing may be of assistance when generating code to evaluate constructs such as arithmetic expressions. The National Semiconductor Series 32000 processors support a top-of-stack addressing mode, which allows instructions to access values stored in a stack. The selected stack pointer is automatically incremented or decremented depending on the nature of the operation.

All but the simplest of the modern general-purpose processors support a very wide range of addressing modes and it may become difficult for a practical code generator to make effective use of all of these modes. However, there are code optimization techniques that can be applied to the output of a code generator which could possibly make good use of all the addressing modes available. These techniques are discussed in Section 7.5.

7.4.3   Reduced instruction set architectures

Reduced instruction set computers (RISCs) are becoming increasingly popular. These machines have simple instruction sets and they are capable of executing instructions extremely quickly. RISC architectures need high-level language support; indeed, RISC machines are primarily designed to run compiler-generated code since the complexities of the choice of instruction sequence and the efficient use of pipelining, where the hardware can be executing several instructions simultaneously, are much better handled by a compiler than by a human assembly language writer.

Code generator design for these machines poses no insurmountable problems. Many of these processors have large numbers of fast registers, thus easing the register-allocation problem. There is no need to include code in the code generator to handle the use of complex, special-purpose instructions or addressing modes. Straightforward code optimization techniques can also be used. These machines are examined in a little more detail in Chapter 8.

7.4.4 Data types

The design of a code generator is simplified and machine code complexity is reduced if the target machine includes instructions capable of manipulating the fundamental data types supported by the high-level language. Most of the earlier processors supported operations on logical data and integer values in a limited range. High-level language operations on objects such as large integers or floating-point numbers were therefore translated into comparatively complex sections of target machine code, simulating the operations on the programmer's data types in terms of operations on the simple hardware-supported data types.

Integer data

One of the most important characteristics of the target hardware, as far as the compiler writer is concerned, is the number of bits used by the hardware in performing integer operations. A short integer representation in the hardware may result in potentially unacceptable restrictions on the range of integer values allowed in an implementation of a high-level language on that hardware. For example, two's-complement 16-bit integer operations result in an integer range of -32768 to $+32767$, which the programmer may feel is too restrictive for some applications. Under these circumstances, the compiler writer is perfectly free to implement integer values used in the source program using 32 target hardware bits and to generate code to simulate the 32-bit integer operations in terms of 16-bit hardware-supplied instructions. A much larger integer range can be achieved but at the cost of slower and longer code. Fortunately, most modern processors directly support 32-bit (and sometimes larger) integer arithmetic.

Floating-point data

Floating-point data types are also candidates for hardware support. The algorithms for floating-point arithmetic are complex and it is only comparatively recently that fast and accurate floating-point hardware has become widely available. Indeed, the complexity of floating-point operations has in many cases made it impossible to include such operations in the instruction set of the commonly used microprocessors of today; instead, separate co-processors are used to provide these functions. Most of the floating-point co-processors provide both 32-bit (single-precision) and 64-bit (double-precision) arithmetic. Ideally, operands for the co-processor should be capable of being specified using any of the addressing modes supported by the main processor. Then, the code generation of floating-point operations becomes just as easy as for integer operations. Implementation problems are somewhat eased, however, because of the existence of standards for the internal representation of floating-point numbers.

Character and string data

Instructions operating on single bytes can be used to support character and string data types. If variable length character strings are required, their representation may be defined by the language or, alternatively, it may be left to the implementor. For example, the length of a string may be explicitly contained in a byte preceding the characters of the string or may be implicit by storing the string as a sequence of bytes terminated by a byte containing a special value, such as zero. The hardware may support special instructions designed for variable length string manipulation and, in this case, the representation may be influenced by the requirements of these instructions. The VAX-11 has a wide range of powerful character string instructions, some of which are very specialized and hence unlikely to be generated directly by a compiler.

Single-bit data

Single-bit data types, such as Booleans, are supported by some of the more recent processors, effectively allowing the direct addressing of single-bit fields. For example, the Motorola MC68020 supports variable length bit fields, up to 32 bits, using a group of instructions that perform operations such as bit insertion, extraction, setting, clearing, changing, testing and scanning. Facilities like this allow the compact and efficient implementation of data types such as Booleans and sets.

Binary-coded decimal data

To ease the implementation of some business-oriented software, support for binary-coded decimal (BCD) data is often found. For example, the

IBM 370 series supported this data type. Here, numbers are represented by storing one or two decimal digits in each byte. This representation is not as compact as the more conventional binary form, but it does offer advantages in speed of input and output conversion. Implementations of COBOL can make good use of this data type.

Regularity

Code generator complexity can be reduced if the instruction set is regular. Ideally, for each type of basic operation such as add or move there should be a consistent set of instructions, each member of which is designed to operate on a particular data type supported by the hardware. For example, the Motorola MC68000 processor series provides a set of instructions performing standard binary addition. These instructions have mnemonics `ADD.B`, `ADD.W` and `ADD.L` and are designed for 8-, 16- and 32-bit operands, respectively. The formats of the operands of these instructions are identical, which allows the code generator to select the operands and operator type independently from the operand type. If the format of the instruction is different for different operand types, the code generator has much more work to do. Most of the modern processors, other than those with RISC architectures, support this idea of regularity – for example, Motorola MC68020 and National Semiconductor 32016.

7.4.5   Use of registers

The code generator writer must decide at an early stage how the registers of the target machine are to be used by the generated code. The allocation will of course depend on hardware aspects such as the number of registers available, whether certain registers can only be used for specific purposes, such as address registers or stack pointers, and whether there are any constraints imposed by the addressing modes. The allocation will also depend on the comparative speeds, and indeed the availability, of register/register, register/store and store/store instructions. It is usually assumed that register access is significantly faster than store access, although, perhaps surprisingly, this is not the case for all processors.

Some registers should be allocated to facilitate access to stored variables. For example, if a stack-based storage allocation system is used to store local variables and to support subprogram call and return, then registers may have to be used as stack pointers, display pointers and static chain pointers. Furthermore, in this type of environment, it is usually a good idea to allocate a small set of registers for argument passing. The first few arguments to a subprogram can then be stored in the registers as well as on the stack. This arrangement can offer performance advantages, since arguments tend to be referenced quite often within a subprogram. If registers become in short supply later within the subprogram, then these argument registers can be redeployed.

Several registers must also be reserved for general-purpose use – for example, for the evaluation of expressions. However, the number of registers required for this purpose may not have to be particularly large as surprisingly complex expressions can be evaluated within a small number of registers without the use of temporary storage locations. A general aim of the code generator writer should be to attempt to keep as many as possible of the frequently accessed variables or values in fast machine registers.

Some languages allow the programmer to specify that certain variables should, if possible, be held in machine registers during program execution. For example, in C, a *register* declaration can be used to indicate to the compiler that the specified variables will be referenced frequently in the program. It can be argued that such declarations are unnecessary, since it should be the task of the compiler to recognize which variables should be held in machine registers. On the other hand, these declarations may make it much easier for the compiler to generate efficient code. In languages such as C and BCPL, any indirect assignment operation – that is, an operation that explicitly sets the contents of a specified address to a value – must invalidate the contents of all registers used for saving variables stored in main memory locations. In the case of C, the language definition states that it is illegal to attempt to evaluate the storage address of a register variable. Hence, indirect assignments are not allowed to such variables and so register variables need not be reloaded after an indirect assignment.

7.5   Code Optimization

The generation of 'good' code is still considered to be one of the major trademarks of a high-quality compiler. Even though hardware costs are falling and performance is rising fast, there is still a strong desire to make high-level language programs run as quickly as possible. Also, more and more complex high-level languages are being developed, requiring increasingly powerful techniques for the generation of efficient code. So, code optimization is still a topic of prime importance. A great deal of research has been done in this area and many complex techniques have been developed. Many of these techniques are beyond the scope of this book, but, fortunately, there are some comparatively straightforward optimizations that can result in a dramatic improvement in the quality of the target code.

Optimization techniques can be broadly classified into two categories:

(1) **Machine-independent techniques**, which can be applied on almost any conventional target hardware. These techniques are not concerned with the characteristics of particular processors, such as the number of machine registers and the form of the instruction set.

(2) **Machine-dependent techniques**, which make use of knowledge of the particular target hardware on which the generated code is to run. Register allocation and the use of particular machine instructions are of concern here.

This section on code optimization describes several techniques, most of which are machine independent. But we must start by taking a broad look at the aims of code optimization.

7.5.1 Aims of code optimization

Despite the use of the word 'optimization', compilers rarely produce optimal code. The aim of the code optimization phase of a compiler is to *improve* the generated code, subject to a few important constraints.

Although obvious, it is extremely important that the code optimization should not alter the meaning of the program. A code optimizer that produces compact but incorrect code is useless. It is surprising how many compiler bugs can be circumvented by simply disabling the compiler's optimization phase.

Ideally, code optimization should not impose an excessive overhead at compile time. There is little point in extending the compilation time by many minutes to simply save a few seconds of run time, especially if the program is only going to be run once. There are some optimization techniques that are noted for their large computation times. Because optimization can have a significant impact on compilation time, it should be possible for the user of a compiler to disable the optimization phase while a program is being debugged or when compiling small programs for which there would be negligible run-time savings. Optimization could be turned back on for debugged versions of larger or longer-running programs. An approach sometimes used to improve the overall benefit of optimization is for the compiler to attempt to identify those areas of the program that will contribute the most to the program's execution time. The compiler then makes efforts to optimize these sections only. Typically, these sections will be inner loops or subprograms called from inner loops. It is impossible for a compiler to make an accurate assessment of statement execution frequencies, but it is usually possible and fairly easy to make some reasonable guesses.

The term 'code optimization', as used in this chapter, describes the means by which code is improved so that it runs faster on the target hardware. It is quite possible to optimize code so that it occupies as little memory space as possible. Such optimization would be relevant when writing software for a small embedded system where memory space is at a premium. However, because of rapidly falling memory costs and increasing packing densities, space optimization is becoming less important. Nevertheless, the process of optimization for run-time speed should not cause the size of the target code to grow unduly. For example, it would not be appropriate for an optimizing compiler to generate code for the statement:

for $i := 1$ **to** 1000 **do** $p1$

by generating 1000 sequential copies of the code for procedure $p1$ to avoid generating code to perform the **for** loop testing and branching. On the other hand, if 1000 were 10 or less and if $p1$ was not long, the story may be different.

It is vital to have an intimate knowledge of the target hardware to be able to design some optimal code-generating algorithms. Knowledge of relative instruction timings is also needed, but these figures may be modified by operand values and hardware pipelining. Fortunately, these effects rarely need to influence compiler design.

Optimization can be carried out at several different levels. For example, low-level optimization can be performed when generating code for evaluating arithmetic expressions, by minimizing the number of memory references or instructions executed. At a slightly higher level, it may be advantageous for an optimization algorithm to have the effect of making small modifications to source language statements while retaining its meaning. For example, it may be preferable to code generate a statement as $i := j * i$ rather than $i := i * j$. It may also be possible to alter some sequences of statements so that better code can be produced. These are the levels at which code optimization is considered here. However, a compiler can theoretically optimize at a much higher level, by making alterations to the algorithms used by the programmer. For example, on examining a high-level language program, the compiler may recognize that it is an implementation of a slow algorithm for inverting matrices. The compiler can then generate the code for a much better algorithm! Such compiler technology, applicable to a general program, does not yet exist, and so such algorithm optimizations are still the responsibility of the programmer.

It is tempting to include more and more optimization techniques when writing a compiler and there must be an element of pride involved in producing high-quality code. But the benefits of optimization should always be kept in perspective.

The following sections present several techniques for code optimization. All of these, except for the peephole optimization, are machine-independent techniques, since they can be applied without detailed knowledge of the target machine's instruction set. These techniques are all interrelated in the sense that the application of one optimization can necessitate the application of another. For example, it may be possible to perform some sort of statement rearrangement after loop optimization has been carried out.

7.5.2 Elimination of redundant code

Perhaps the most obvious approach to code optimization is to detect redundant code and prevent its inclusion in the object program. There are circumstances where the detection of redundant code is comparatively easy. For example, a Pascal program might include code of the form:

> **if** *tracing* **then**
> **begin**
>
> .
>
> .
>
> .
>
> **end**

where *tracing* is defined as a constant with the value TRUE or FALSE. *tracing* may be set to TRUE if debugging output is required, but normally it will be set to FALSE. If *tracing* is FALSE, then there is no need for the compiler to generate any code for this statement, since there is no way in which it can be executed. Even if *tracing* is a variable, rather than a constant, it may be possible to eliminate redundant code if the compiler can determine that *tracing* definitely has the value FALSE at the beginning of the statement starting **if** *tracing* **then** ... .

It may be possible to remove redundant code in the evaluation of expressions. For example, in the unlikely event of a programmer writing an expression of the form:

$$(x - x) * (y * z + x)$$

the optimizer should be able to determine that one of the operands in the multiplication has the value zero and hence the value of the whole expression is zero. But the optimizer should not be too enthusiastic about making such simplifications. For example, consider a function *rand*, which returns a random number in some predefined range. A statement of the form:

> *ratio* := *rand*/*rand*

should not be simplified to code that sets *ratio* to 1. This problem occurs because the function *rand* has side effects. In most languages, the programmer can reasonably assume that if a call to a function with side effects appears n times in an expression, that function should be called n times.

Another method for eliminating redundant code is to recognize the existence of common sub-expressions in a program and, if possible, to evaluate the sub-expression once only. For example, the assignment:

$$x := a * a/(1 - a * a)$$

can be code generated as:

$$temp := a * a;$$
$$x := temp/(1 - temp)$$

where the temporary value *temp* need not be stored in primary memory; instead, it can be retained in a register. The expression can be represented as a DAG, which allows the common sub-expressions to be identified. As well as being applicable at a local level within a single statement or expression, it is possible to identify common sub-expressions at a more global level, by considering paths of execution through the program. A simple example is the recognition of the common sub-expression $x * x + y * y$ in the sequence of statements:

$$a := x/(x * x + y * y);$$
$$b := z/(x * x + y * y + z * z)$$

The pattern-matching algorithms used to detect common sub-expressions can be very complex and time consuming. The process is aided if expressions are represented internally in some canonical form. For example, the operands of commutative operators can be placed in the tree so that, for variable operands, the identifier representing the operand on the left-hand branch of the tree alphabetically precedes the identifier on the right-hand side of the tree; for example, $b + a$ can be represented as $a + b$. Similar rules could also apply to constant values appearing in expressions. When a new sub-expression tree is created, a search is carried out to determine whether an identical tree occurs elsewhere. If so, it may be possible to avoid the duplication of the tree. This ordering of leaves in the tree is important as it simplifies the identification of the common sub-expressions in expressions such as $a + b + b + a$.

The analysis of common sub-expressions can become quite complex when statement dependencies have to be considered. For example, if the sequence of assignments:

$$a := x/(x * x + y * y);$$
$$z := a * 2;$$
$$b := z/(x * x + y * y + z * z)$$

is encountered in a program, the sub-expression $x * x + y * y$ need only be computed once during the evaluation of the expression in the first assignment, since $x * x + y * y$ is not dependent on the value of z, which may be altered between the uses of the common sub-expression. However, if the sequence of assignments had the form:

$$a := x/(x * x + y * y);$$
$$y := a * 2;$$
$$b := z/(x * x + y * y + z * z)$$

then the sub-expression $x * x + y * y$ would have to be evaluated twice, since its value might change after the assignment to y. Techniques for handling these dependencies are presented in Tremblay [1985].

In the examples just presented, the programmer can force the recognition of common sub-expressions by rewriting the expressions. For example, the assignments to a and b can be rewritten:

$$t := x * x + y * y;$$
$$a := x/t;$$
$$b := z/(t + z)$$

This is in fact a widely used style, since it often results in shorter and clearer programs. However, there are circumstances when the programmer cannot have direct control over the identification of common sub-expressions, such as in the statement:

$$a[i, j] := a[i, j - 1] + a[i, j] + a[i, j + 1]$$

Array indexing may involve multiplication and can be quite time consuming. Therefore, if the compiler can optimize the indexing in this statement by recognizing common sub-expressions used in obtaining the addresses of the array elements, considerable time and code savings may result.

7.5.3 Folding of constants

It may be possible to evaluate some expressions or sub-expressions at compile time, thus removing the necessity for generating code to perform the evaluation at run time. For example, the assignment $j := i + 2 + 3$ can be simplified to $j := i + 5$. Similarly, assuming that a flow analysis has shown that the pair of assignments:

$$i := 5; \quad j := i - 2$$

can be treated as an indivisible unit – that is, there are no transfers of control directly to the second assignment – they can be replaced by:

$$i := 5; \quad j := 3$$

It may be possible to perform some type coercions at compile time. For example, suppose that x is a real variable and the assignment $x := 10$ appears in a program. Then, the compiler should ensure that the integer 10 is represented in the compiled code as the real value 10 so that a *float* (integer $\rightarrow$ real) operation need not be performed each time the statement is executed.

7.5.4   Loop optimization

There are several techniques that can be used to improve the code generated for statements within a loop. Any savings made within a loop are particularly worthwhile. A comparatively simple optimization is to search for code that can be executed outside the loop; in other words, the optimizer has to search for **loop invariants**, which are values that do not change within a loop. For example:

```
for i := 1 to 1000 do
begin
    t := i * i/(x * x + y * y);
    .
    .
    .
end;
```

If the values of x and y are not changed within the loop, then the value of $x * x + y * y$ should be calculated just once, immediately before the loop is entered.

A similar optimization may be applied to array access. For example, considerable savings are possible in the following statement if the address calculations associated with the i and j indices of array a are performed once outside the loop:

```
for k := 2 to kmax do a[i, j, k] := a[i, j, k] + a[i, j, k − 1]
```

If the number of times a loop is to be executed is small and can be determined at compile time, it may be possible to **unroll** the loop to avoid executing the loop-controlling code. For example, the statement:

```
for i := 1 to 3 do a[i] := 0
```

is interpreted as $a[1] := 0; a[2] := 0; a[3] := 0$. Here, there is a space/time tradeoff, since the improvement in execution time in unrolling the loop is traded against the probable and significant increase in the size of the object program.

A third approach to loop optimization is to attempt to perform **strength reduction**. This is the process by which one operation is replaced by one that can be executed more efficiently.

EXAMPLE

It may be possible to replace a multiplication within a loop by a faster executing addition. Hence:

```
for i := 1 to max do
begin
  j := i * 5;
  .
  .
  .
end;
```

is equivalent to:

```
j := 0;
for i := 1 to max do
begin
  j := j + 5;
  .
  .
  .
end;
```

It is possible to perform this strength reduction of multiplication to addition when one operand of the multiplication is a loop invariant and the other is an **induction variable** (the loop counter or a variable which keeps in step with the loop counter). Aho [1986] gives a detailed description of algorithms that can be used to detect induction variables and hence perform the strength reduction.

7.5.5 Expression rewriting and statement rearrangement

Section 7.3.2 examined the problems of code generation of arithmetic expressions. But the constraints under which these algorithms operate can be relaxed somewhat by introducing some additional rules of arithmetic. For example, the rule of distributivity allows the expression $x * a + x * b$ to be rewritten as $x * (a + b)$ (ignoring problems of overflow and so on which might occur during its execution), which may facilitate the generation of marginally better machine code. Similarly, there may be circumstances when the rule of commutativity ($a + b = b + a$) may help simplify an expression.

Other simplifications may be possible. Examples are:

$x + 0$ can be transformed to x

$x * 1$ can be transformed to x

$x/1$ can be transformed to x

$x * 2$ can be transformed to $x + x$

Expressions such as $x + 0$ are unlikely to be written in this form by most programmers, but they can occur in certain situations, such as after constant folding when symbolic constants are used. Such optimizations are easy to perform given a tree representation of the expression. Depending on the design of the target machine, it may also be appropriate to replace integer multiplications and divisions by a constant that is a power of two with bitwise shift operations, which are probably somewhat faster than the replaced multiplication or division. Before this can be done, however, the description of the target hardware has to be examined carefully to determine exactly what happens in the shift instructions in situations where one or more of the operands are negative, for example.

Code optimizations may also be possible by recognizing that code need not be generated independently for successive statements. For example, in a sequence of assignment statements, values calculated during the evaluation of one expression and placed in registers may simplify the calculation of the expression in the following assignment.

EXAMPLE

Given the three assignments:

$$a := b + c; \quad d := e; \quad f := a * c$$

the code generated for a single register machine could be:

```
MOVE b, R0
ADD  c, R0
MOVE R0, a        ;a := b + c
MOVE e, R0
MOVE R0, d        ;d := e
MOVE a, R0
MUL  c, R0
MOVE R0, f        ;f := a * c
```

If the original statements are rearranged to the functionally equivalent:

$$a := b + c; \quad f := a * c; \quad d := e$$

the code generated could be:

```
MOVE b, R0
ADD  c, R0
MOVE R0, a        ;a := b + c
MUL  c, R0
MOVE R0, f        ;f := a * c
MOVE e, R0
MOVE R0, d        ;d := e
```

which represents a saving of one instruction.

To apply this technique, the code generator must always keep track of the variable or expression whose value is being stored in each register. More complex examples with more dramatic code size reductions are quite easy to construct. However, statement rearrangement cannot be done in all cases, so a careful examination of statement dependencies must be performed.

7.5.6 Peephole optimization

The optimization techniques described so far are largely machine independent in that they all have a beneficial effect on the code generated for almost any target machine. In contrast, there are also code optimization techniques that are much more machine specific. For example, the algorithms for generating optimal code for arithmetic expressions outlined in Section 7.3.2 rely on a knowledge of the number of registers available in the target hardware.

Peephole optimization is another machine-dependent technique that, fortunately, is comparatively easy to understand and implement, yet can offer great improvements in the target code. A good peephole optimizer can make the application of some of the machine-independent optimizations unnecessary. The peephole optimizer works as a separate phase of compilation, acting on the machine code or assembly language produced by the code generator. The aim of this phase is to examine small groups of target instructions, through a **peephole**. By using a complete knowledge of the target machine's instruction set, repertoire of addressing modes and so on, the optimizer attempts to replace single instructions or groups of instructions by instructions that are either shorter or execute more quickly. The peephole is repeatedly passed over the code to be optimized until no more improvement is possible.

This approach can achieve optimization in several different ways. A simple and obvious optimization is to replace an instruction by one that executes more quickly. For example, if the optimizer encounters the instruction MOVE #0, R0, it would be appropriate to replace it by CLR R0. Similarly, ADD #1, R0 could be replaced by INC R0 (most processors support an increment instruction), MUL #4, R0 by ASL #2, R0, and so on. Many of the expression simplifications described in the last section can also be performed by the peephole optimizer. For example, instructions such as ADD #0, R0 or MUL #1, R0 can be deleted, assuming that these instructions do not have side effects such as the setting of condition codes on which subsequent instructions may depend.

Other optimizations are possible when pairs of instructions are examined. If a code generator operates by considering each high-level language construct or statement independently, there is a possibility that when code for two successive statements is juxtaposed, there is scope for optimization at the boundary. A simple case of this type is shown in the code generator of the statements $b := a$; $c := b$. A code generator might output the code:

```
MOVE a, R0
MOVE R0, b        ;b := a
MOVE b, R0
MOVE R0, c        ;c := b
```

In this case, the peephole optimizer recognizes that the third statement is redundant and can be omitted. By extending this idea, it may be possible for the optimizer to keep track of register contents so that a register reference is substituted for a memory reference, wherever possible.

The peephole optimizer can also collapse chains of jump instructions. When the destination of a jump instruction is another jump instruction, the destination address of the first jump can be set to the destination address of the second jump. Such chains of jumps can occur from the code generation of constructs such as conditional statements contained within repetitive statements. Redundant or unreachable code can also be removed by a peephole optimizer. It is fairly easy to recognize a section of code that is preceded by an unconditional jump and which is not the destination of any other jumps.

The peephole optimizer must make repeated passes over the code that it is trying to improve until no further improvements can be made. It may be possible to combine the improvements made in one pass with existing instructions to make further improvements. This type of optimizer is a logically simple, self-contained program, but skill is required in its coding to ensure efficient operation. Dramatic code improvements can be achieved using this technique and so such optimizers are often found in production compilers. A detailed description of the target hardware must of course be available to the optimizer, but it is possible to design the optimizer so that the target machine description is separated from the actual code of the optimizer. In this way, the optimizer can be adapted easily to different target machines. A description of such an optimizer is contained in Davidson [1980].

Peephole optimization can also be applied to intermediate codes with some success. If the intermediate code or target machine code is expressed in a text form, then macro processors, or even text editors, may be used to perform some peephole optimizations.

7.5.7 Problems of optimization

The primary aim of the optimization phase of a compiler is to improve the code so that it runs as quickly as possible on the target machine. A secondary aim is, presumably, to ensure that the code size does not increase too much. Unfortunately, the increased internal complexity of modern processors may make it very difficult for the code optimizer to select the optimal sequence of instructions to perform a particular task because of factors such as instruction pipelining, instruction timing depending on data values, parallel execution of instructions and so on. Parallelism, where operations can overlap in time, is a particular problem and exploitation of such facilities may cause serious complications in code generation. Fortunately, the requirement of squeezing the last drop of performance out of compiler-generated code in this way is rarely necessary. However, array processors and vector computers are now in widespread use and special techniques have to be used to recognize vector operations in the high-level language source program and translate them to the special vector instructions on the target machine [Fischer, 1980]. On the other hand, parallelism can remove the necessity for some optimizations. For example, common sub-expression elimination could be left undone.

Unfortunately, programs rarely work the first time they are run. A useful tool in the removal of errors is the **symbolic debugger**, which allows the programmer to set breakpoints in the running program, examine and modify data, and so on. Particular problems occur when symbolic debuggers are applied to optimized code because the optimizing transformations may have made it very difficult for the debugger to associate target machine instructions with source program statements and declarations. For example, the optimizer may have altered the arrangement of statements and thus the correspondence between successive source statements and successive blocks of target machine code will have been lost. A simple approach to this problem, and one frequently adopted, is to ignore it by ensuring that the debugger can only be used on code that has been produced without optimization. But this is not an entirely satisfactory solution since programs that are not optimized can work but when optimized can fail. So, a debugger should really be capable of handling optimized code. Techniques for allowing this are presented in Aho [1986] and in Hennessy [1982].

7.6   Automatic Production of Code Generators

An attractive approach for the production of code generators is to develop a system that accepts a description of the target machine and then generates a program that can be used to translate from some machine-independent intermediate language to machine code for that target machine. This aim can be achieved to some degree by writing the code generator so that the machine-independent algorithms are separated as much as possible from the machine-dependent algorithms and information. The task of writing a code generator for a new machine then becomes one of modifying the machine-dependent sections. However, more automated methods are clearly preferable, so that the effort required in producing the code generator can be minimized.

Aho [1986] describes a technique for transforming a detailed tree representation of the program into target machine code using a set of templates, particular to the target machine. A pattern-matching algorithm is repeatedly applied to the tree and the templates, and when a template matches, the appropriate code is output.

Several automated tools for the production of code generators are now available. Perhaps the most widely known work in this area is in the Production-Quality Compiler-Compiler (PQCC) system [Leverett, 1980], a project concerned with the production of high-quality optimizing compilers. Here, an optimizing table-driven code generator can be produced from a formal description of the target machine. This formal description is expressed in a language called ISP [Siewiorek, 1982]. An overview of this system appears in Tremblay [1985] and further details are contained in Cattell [1980, 1982].

SUMMARY

- The structure of the storage area holding the values of variables has to reflect the characteristics of the language being compiled. A stack-based allocation scheme is appropriate for the block-structured languages.

- Procedure call and return can also be handled cleanly using a stack-based approach. Each stack frame contains linkage information enabling the caller's environment to be restored on procedure return.

- Access to non-local variables is often achieved by using a display or via the static chain. Using machine registers to point to the current, the global and to carefully chosen intermediate stack frames can result in particularly efficient variable access.

- Argument passing can also be managed on the stack.

- Some languages require the support of a dynamic storage allocation package.

- Simple algorithms are available to generate optimal code from arithmetic expressions represented in the form of a tree. These algorithms can make use of any number of fast machine registers.

- If the language permits it, it may be possible to deduce the value of a Boolean expression without evaluating it all. But beware of side effects!

- If the target machine has a complex and irregular instruction set, the design of the code generator may become complex. However, a reasonable variety of addressing modes is essential for efficient code.

- Compilers can now generate code to make efficient use of RISC architectures.

- Hardware support for a variety of data types may help the compiler writer.

- Code optimization techniques are classified into two groups: machine dependent and machine independent. Machine-independent techniques include the elimination of redundant code, folding of constants, loop optimization, expression rewriting and statement rearrangement. Peephole optimization is an effective machine-dependent technique.

- Recent developments in the automated production of code generators from target machine descriptions look promising.

EXERCISES

7.1 Devise variable storage allocation schemes suitable for BASIC and for FORTRAN.

7.2 Suppose a Pascal compiler is being implemented on a machine with eight general-purpose registers. Suggest for what purposes these registers could be used in the code generated by the compiler. How would your answer change if only four registers were available, or 32 registers?

7.3 What advice would you give to the designer of a processor that was to be optimized for the rapid execution of Pascal programs?

7.4 Examine the characteristics of several of the current microprocessors and plan how the registers and the instructions could be used in an implementation of a language such as C or Pascal. Do any of the processors pose particular implementation difficulties? Do any of the processors support facilities that would make an implementation particularly efficient?

7.5 By considering specific processors, show how the run-time checking of ranges of array subscripts can be performed efficiently.

7.6 Devise a method for determining precisely how the Pascal **case** statement should be implemented on a particular processor given the set of different case labels. State whether you are aiming for compact code, efficient code or some combination of the two.

7.7 Obtain the specification of a RISC processor and develop code-generation algorithms for algebraic expressions stored in the form of a tree. Then write a peephole optimizer to cope with the lower level issues, such as pipelining and instruction rearrangement. Does this approach produce high-quality code?

7.8 Consult the references on peephole optimization and write a peephole optimizer for a particular processor based on a set of pattern-matching rules. If an instruction or a sequence of instructions is found on the input which matches one of the patterns, the corresponding transformation is applied to the instruction or instructions. If you have access to some general-purpose pattern-matching language such as SNOBOL, then the problem is simplified. Consider also the use of Lex or Yacc.

PART THREE

Implementation

Part Three examines some of the methods available for implementing a high-level language system. Writing a compiler can be an enormous software project and so techniques for reducing the effort required are particularly valuable. It is important to plan the implementation with considerable care and to make use of the wide range of software techniques and tools that have been used successfully for high-level language implementation.

CHAPTER 8

Approaches to Language Implementation

The implementation of a complete compiler for a non-trivial language is a major project. Compilers for the larger languages such as ALGOL 68 or Ada can easily take many man-years to implement, even when using today's comparatively powerful software development tools. Therefore, just as with any other large software project, the development and implementation of a compiler needs very careful planning. The aim of course is to produce an efficient and reliable compiler generating high-quality object code with the minimum amount of development effort. As has been seen, many standard techniques and software tools have been developed to assist the compiler writer. There are also several standard implementation methods that can help to minimize further the effort required to implement a new compiler. This chapter examines some of these implementation methods, outlines some of the issues raised by the use of less conventional target architectures and shows how some languages may be implemented using an interpretive approach.

8.1 Software Issues

Compiler implementation involves a wide range of software issues. Compilers are large and complex pieces of software, and so detailed program and data structure designs are essential before coding can begin. Extensive validation is required throughout the development process to ensure that a reliable piece of software is being produced. Once a compiler is in service, remaining bugs can have very serious consequences.

Two fundamental pieces of information are required as soon as a compiler project starts:

(1)   The form of the source language (for which language is this compiler being written?).

(2)   The form of the target language (on which processor should the code produced by this compiler be run?).

These fixed requirements form the starting point when deciding on an implementation plan.

8.1.1 Choosing an implementation plan

A useful and crucial question to ask is 'In which programming language should I write the compiler?' There are many characteristics of a suitable language, including the following:

- It must be suitable for the development of large pieces of software. Ideally, it should support modularity (Standard Pascal fails here).

- It should support the straightforward manipulation of characters, since much of the compilation process is concerned with character handling.

- It should itself be capable of efficient implementation, otherwise a slow compiler will result.

- The compiler writer should enjoy writing programs in that language.

- The implementation of a language in its own language – for example, writing a C compiler in C – is a key to portability.

One of the most popular compiler implementation languages is C. Although this is partly due to the design of the language itself, it is also because the UNIX operating system offers a very attractive compiler development environment and C is so well integrated into UNIX and the allied compiler-generating tools. Even seemingly inappropriate languages such as FORTRAN, but extended with character-handling facilities, have been used successfully for the coding of compilers. Fortunately, it is now

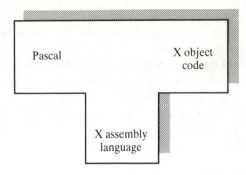

FIGURE 8.1
T-diagram.

unusual to write a new compiler in an assembly language, since such languages are now rarely considered appropriate for large software projects.

The development of a compiler can be made much easier by utilizing compiler development tools. It may then be possible to generate at least parts of the compiler modules automatically. The development of these compiler-generating tools is a fruitful area for computer science research and a few of the more popular systems are described in Chapter 9.

Despite the advantages offered by software development in high-level languages, it may appear in some circumstances that the coding of a compiler in a low-level language is an appropriate course of action. For example, consider the problem of implementing a Pascal compiler on a new piece of hardware (a computer called X) on which assembly language is the only programming language already available. Under these circumstances, the obvious approach is to write the Pascal compiler in assembler. Hence, the compiler in this case is a program that takes Pascal source as input, produces machine code for the target machine as output and is written in the assembly language of the target machine. The languages characterizing this compiler can be represented as:

Pascal → [X assembly language, running on X] → X object code

showing that Pascal source is translated by a program written in X assembly language (the compiler) running on machine X into X's object code. This code can then be run on the target machine. This notation is essentially equivalent to the **T-diagram** described in Bratman [1961]. The T-diagram for this compiler is shown in Figure 8.1. The language accepted as input by the compiler is stated on the left, the language output by the compiler is shown on the right and the language in which the compiler is written is shown at the bottom. The advantage of this particular notation is that several T-diagrams can be meshed together to represent more complex compiler implementation methods. This compiler implementation involves a great deal of work since a large assembly language program has to be written for X. Note also in this case that the compiler is very machine specific; that is, not only does it run on X but it also produces machine code suitable for running on X. Furthermore, only one computer is involved in the entire implementation process.

The use of a high-level language for coding the compiler can offer great savings in implementation effort. If the language in which the compiler is being written is already available on the computer in use, then the process is simple. For example, Pascal might already be available on machine X, thus permitting the coding of, say, a Modula-2 compiler in Pascal. Such a compiler can be represented as:

Modula-2 → [Pascal, running on X] → X's object code

If the language in which the compiler is being written is not available on the machine, then all is not lost, since it may be possible to make use of an implementation of that language on another machine. For example, a Modula-2 compiler could be implemented in Pascal on machine Y, producing object code for machine X:

Modula-2 → [Pascal, running on Y] → X's object code

The object code for X generated on machine Y would of course have to be transferred to X for its execution. This process of generating code on one machine for execution on another is called **cross-compilation**.

At first sight, the introduction of a second computer to the compiler implementation plan seems to offer a somewhat inconvenient solution. Each time a compilation is required, it has to be done on machine Y and the object code transferred, perhaps via a slow or laborious mechanism, to machine X for execution. Furthermore, both computers have to be running, and inter-linked somehow, for this approach to work. But the significance of the cross-compilation approach can be seen in the following example.

Suppose that a Modula-2 compiler is required for machine X, but that the compiler itself is to be coded in Modula-2. Coding the compiler in the language it is to compile is nothing special and, as will be seen, it has a great deal in its favour. Suppose further that Modula-2 is already available on machine Y. In this case, the compiler can be run on machine Y, producing object code for machine X:

Modula-2 → [Modula-2, running on Y] → X machine code

This is the same situation as before except that the compiler is coded in Modula-2 rather than Pascal. The special feature of this approach appears in the next step. The compiler, running on Y, is nothing more than a large program written in Modula-2. Its function is to transform an input file of Modula-2 statements into a functionally equivalent sequence of statements in X's machine code. Therefore, the source statements of this Modula-2 compiler can be passed into itself running on Y to produce a file containing X's machine code. This file is of course a Modula-2 compiler, which is capable of being run on X. By making the compiler compile itself, a version of the compiler that runs on X has been created. Once this machine code has been transferred to X, a self-sufficient Modula-2 compiler is available on X; hence, there is no further use for machine Y for supporting Modula-2 compilation.

This implementation plan is very attractive. Machine Y is only required for compiler development and once this development has reached the stage at which the compiler can (correctly) compile itself, machine Y is no longer required. Consequently, the original compiler implemented on Y need not be of the highest quality – for example, optimization can be completely disregarded. Further development (and obviously conventional use) of the compiler can then continue at leisure on machine X.

This approach to compiler implementation is called **bootstrapping**. Many languages, including C, BCPL, Pascal, FORTRAN and LISP, have been implemented in this way. The next section shows how to extend this bootstrapping approach to simplify compiler implementation even further and to enhance the compiler's portability.

8.1.2   Compiler portability

Section 4.1 introduced the idea of a compiler being split into two distinct phases. The first phase is concerned with the analysis of the source program while the second phase is concerned with the synthesis of the target machine code. The analysis phase consists primarily of the lexical and syntax analyzers and it can be written in a manner that is target machine independent. This phase is concerned with the structure of the input to the compiler rather than the structure of the target machine on which the object code will run. The synthesis phase, on the other hand, is target machine dependent. If the compiler can be designed so that the interface between these two phases is 'visible' and comparatively simple, such as via some form of intermediate code, then implementation and portability problems are greatly simplified. This is because the accessibility of the intermediate language can offer a convenient method for compiler implementation.

As an example, consider a Pascal compiler implemented in this fashion. The compiler consists of two parts: the machine-independent front end (the analysis phase) and the machine-dependent code generator and optimizer (the synthesis phase). The interface between these two parts is via an intermediate code called Pcode. Implementations of the compiler on different machines all include identical front ends, but each target machine requires its own code generator. The restriction on machine dependencies in the synthesis phase has the effect of reducing the amount of work required to produce a new implementation of the language, since the front end can remain unchanged in all implementations of the compiler. Both parts are written in Pascal.

The steps required to implement such a Pascal compiler on machine X, assuming that this compiler is already available on machine Y (producing code for machine Y), are as follows. A code generator is written in Pascal on machine Y, which takes Pcode as input and produces X's machine code as output. This can be tested by obtaining the Pcode for various test programs using the front end of Y's Pascal compiler and passing this Pcode through the new code generator. The target machine code can be transferred to X for testing.

Once a working code generator for X has been developed, the bootstrapping of the new compiler can start. The Pascal source of the front end of the compiler, which is common to all implementations, is passed through the running front end on machine Y to produce a Pcode version of the front end. This Pcode can then be passed through the new code generator developed on Y to produce a version of the front end in X's machine code. Similarly, the Pcode of the new code generator can be obtained by passing the source of the code generator through the running front end on machine Y. This Pcode can be passed through the new code generator, again on machine Y, to produce a version of the Pcode → X's machine code generator in X's machine code. Thus, the complete compiler is available in X's machine code and it can be transferred to X to produce a complete stand-alone system.

Fortunately, it is possible to perform a rapid and fairly stringent test of a new compiler implementation of this type. The compiler can be made to compile itself. The source versions of the front end and the code generator can be passed through the compiler running on X, thus obtaining a machine code version of the compiler for X on X. This new compiler should be identical to the existing compiler on X. Although this is obviously not an exhaustive test of the compiler, it does give some reassuring evidence for correctness.

Splitting up a compiler into two distinct sections with an intermediate code interface between the sections and coding the compiler in the language it is to compile is a popular implementation technique. By developing a simple and clear intermediate code, it is possible to make the compiler implementation process comparatively straightforward. As before, gradual improvement of the code generator is possible without the aid of the original host machine.

An example of a portable compiler tool kit is described in Tanenbaum [1983]. In this system, a front end is required for each of the source languages to be compiled. The front end translates the source language into an intermediate code, which is the machine code for a hypothetical stack-based machine called EM (encoding machine). This intermediate code is then optimized and can be passed into the back end, which is a code generator and an optimizer translating EM code into target machine code.

The back end is designed to be as machine independent as possible, to enhance the portability of the system. The back end is a table-driven program, the contents of which indicate how each EM instruction should be translated into target machine code. EM interpreters are also available to assist in the rapid implementation of this portable compiler system on a new machine. The use of intermediate code interpreters is described in the next section.

This idea of having an intermediate language common to a large range of source high-level languages is not new. A language called UNCOL (UNiversal Computer-Oriented Language) was proposed in the late 1950s [Sammet, 1969]. However, practical difficulties prevented its development at the time.

8.1.3   Other implementation routes

The implementation technique just described depends on the simultaneous availability of two machines: a machine on which there is already an implementation of the language and the target machine. In circumstances where a host machine is not available for developing a code generator for the target machine, all the implementation development must take place on the target machine.

This section is again concerned with the problem of implementing a portable compiler on a new machine and it shows how an implementation kit can be put together to ease the transfer.

Suppose again that the problem is to implement a Pascal compiler on machine X. This Pascal compiler is coded in Pascal and consists of two distinct phases, which are linked by a Pcode interface. To make a transfer to a new machine possible, the implementation kit must include, at the very least, the Pascal source of the front end together with the front end translated into Pcode. Remember that this front end, and hence the Pcode version of it, is the same for all machines and implementations.

The implementation of Pascal on machine X can then proceed as follows. A code generator to translate Pcode into X's machine code is written on X in a language already available on X – in assembly language, if really necessary. This code generator allows the production of a version of the front end of the compiler in X's machine code, using the Pcode in the implementation kit. This version then makes up a complete compiler. As before, the code generator written on X need not produce optimized code for the minimal implementation. Once the complete compiler is running on X, it is perfectly possible to recode the code generator in Pascal and continue its development in that language.

Although this is a simple-sounding approach, it may be a major project implementing the code generator on X in a language, such as assembler, that may not be well suited to the purpose. An alternative approach involves the writing of an interpreter for the intermediate code on X. If Pcode is a simple language, then this interpreter will also be simple, since all it has to do is to read the Pcode instructions one by one and simulate their execution. The effort required to write such an interpreter is considerably less than that required for the development of a code generator. Furthermore, it can be coded in any appropriate language available on X. This interpreter offers the facility for executing programs expressed in Pcode and, once the interpreter has been written, a complete Pascal system has been implemented. The Pascal front end can be run by interpreting its Pcode and hence any Pascal program can be translated into Pcode by running that front end interpretively. The newly produced Pcode can then be passed through the interpreter, thus executing the Pascal program.

This interpretive Pascal system may be simple to implement but it suffers from slow execution times, as interpreting Pcode is normally much slower than executing the corresponding machine code on the target hardware. Therefore, the use of the interpreter should be seen as a temporary measure, until the development of a code generator written in Pascal can be undertaken. This code generator can be developed using the interpretive Pascal system on X and, once a working version has been produced, the interpreter is no longer necessary.

Several languages have been implemented in this way. For example, the BCPL distribution kit contains the compiler sources (in BCPL) together with their translations into an intermediate language called INTCODE [Richards, 1980]. This particular intermediate language has been specifically designed for the purpose of BCPL compiler bootstrapping and an interpreter for INTCODE can be written in a language such as FORTRAN in at most a few days. This allows an interpretive implementation of BCPL to be completed extremely rapidly. Development of a code generator can then proceed.

8.1.4 Run-time libraries

The preceding sections may have given the impression that the implementation of a new language system ends with the successful porting of the compiler. Alas, this is rarely so. Programs written in a new language will want to make use of the operating system facilities on the target machine by performing input and output, making storage allocation requests and so on. A convenient way of providing this interface between the compiled code and the operating system is via a **run-time library**; that is, a set of routines that can be called by the compiled code to perform all the machine- and operating system-dependent functions required by the user's high-level language program. For example, when a Pascal program calls the *writeln* procedure, the run-time library is called, firstly, to perform the translation of the arguments into the appropriate output format. It then either places the data to be output into an internal buffer and returns or calls the operating system to perform the required output operation. A Pascal run-time library can also handle the storage management routines *new* and *dispose* and the mathematical routines such as *sin* and *sqrt*. It may also perform any initialization required before the code produced by the compiler is entered, such as the setting up of stack pointers, opening default input and output streams and space allocation.

It is likely that at least part of the run-time library will have to be written in a low-level language, to make use of particular machine and operating system facilities. The coding of small, frequently executed sections of the library in assembler may also contribute towards an efficient implementation of the run-time library. It may be possible to write a part of the run-time library in a high-level language. For example, most implementations of BCPL make use of a run-time library made up of two sections: a small section containing the low-level routines written in assembly language and a larger section containing all the other routines, written in BCPL. Hopefully, most, if not all, of this high-level language part can be made machine independent.

8.1.5   Performance issues

The compiler writer has to be aware of any performance constraints on the running of the generated code or on the running of the compiler itself. The compiler can influence the execution speed of the target code, primarily via the design of the code generator and any associated code-optimization phase. Optimizations performed during earlier phases, such as in the syntax analyzer, can also have a significant impact on execution speed. But these optimizations do not come free. The development and implementation of optimizing transformations is not particularly easy, and so the cost of developing a high-performance optimizing compiler can be high. Furthermore, extensive target code optimization can result in long compilation times. For this reason, some optimizing compilers offer the programmer the choice of optimized code and long compilation times or less efficient code and rapid compilation. Nevertheless, it is possible to implement many optimizing transformations within the compiler with minimal cost to compilation speed while having a major influence on target code speed. Many of these simple transformations, which can be applied during code generation or optimization, have already been described in Chapter 7.

A good compiler should also perform as much validity checking as it possibly can on the source program. For example, type checking should be applied ruthlessly by a compiler for a strongly typed language. This may help to reduce the amount of checking that has to be applied at run time. A general principle quoted by Gries [1971], which should be carefully noted, states *'never put off till run time what you can do at compile time'*.

Compilation speed is also influenced by many other aspects of compiler design. For example, the choice of parsing technique has a significant impact here. Some parsers are comparatively easy to write, but leave much to be desired in their efficiency. The number of passes or phases also has a large bearing on compilation speed. A multi-pass compiler using disk files to communicate between the passes is unlikely to run rapidly. But, again, there may be a tradeoff: such a compiler may be easier to develop and maintain and may even produce better target code than a single-pass compiler.

A compiler can spend a large proportion of its execution time within the lexical analyzer. Therefore, the efficient coding of the lexical analyzer is essential for an efficient compiler. Care must also be taken with design aspects such as data structures for symbol lookup and the internal representation of symbols.

Another issue affecting compiler performance is that concerned with error detection and recovery. A major factor in compiler design is the production of accurate and informative error messages, indicating incorrect source programs, so that the programmer can isolate the errors and correct them as easily as possible. As has already been seen in Chapter 6, the choice of a parsing method influences the ease by which accurately placed and informative error messages can be produced.

8.1.6   Debugging, validation and maintenance

When designing any large software project, plans for debugging and maintenance have to be considered very carefully. Debugging is simplified if the individual compiler modules can be debugged separately. At the very least, this will involve the incorporation of code to display the output of each module in a human-readable format. In this way, it is possible, for example, to develop and debug the lexical analyzer before starting work on the syntax analyzer. The output of other tracing information, such as the sequence in which the syntax rules are used by the parser, will also doubtless speed debugging. Such debugging code should never be removed, since the debugging of a compiler can never really be complete!

Several approaches can be used to debug a compiler. For example, the compiler writer can write simple source programs as test input to the compiler and then verify that the code generated by the compiler has the expected effect, or that appropriate error messages are output. In addition, as discussed earlier, the compiler can be made to compile itself in some circumstances, which can form a good test for the correct operation of the compiler. But such simple, unstructured tests cannot really be used to give any accurate picture of the reliability of a compiler, so it is essential to undertake a more rigorous testing programme. Such a programme should involve the testing of the compiler on a large structured suite of test programs, each carefully designed to check out specific aspects of the compiler. Such suites can indicate how closely the compiler adheres to the language definition, as well as ensuring that functionally correct code is being produced. The production of these validation suites is an extremely taxing task, requiring a detailed knowledge of the language definition and its interpretation together with an accurate appreciation of the aspects of the language that can cause difficulties for the compiler writer. The programs must help ensure that the compiler correctly interprets both the syntax and the semantics of the source language. Some of the programs must also contain deliberate errors, to check the compiler's facilities for error detection and recovery. Fortunately, such validation suites are now available for several programming languages. When a new compiler for one of these languages is developed, the correct results from each of the programs in the suite indicates that reasonable faith in the compiler's reliability is justified. Many national and international standards organizations have been taking an active part in the production and use of validation suites and the importance of compiler validation is now well recognized. A detailed examination of validation techniques, concentrating on Pascal compiler validation, is contained in Wichmann [1983].

Once a compiler has been released for general use, it is very likely that modifications to remove bugs and improvements will be demanded. Furthermore, if changes are made to the language definition, it may also be necessary to make the corresponding modification to the compiler. Correcting or modifying a well-structured compiler should not be an excessively difficult task; in fact, the effort involved may prove to be insignificant when compared with the effort required to issue updated copies of the compiler to all its users!

8.1.7 Language issues

The major controlling element in the design of a compiler is of course the nature of the source language. For some languages, the use of a compiler may be unnecessary or inappropriate, so an interpreter may be used instead (see Section 8.3). For example, most implementations of BASIC are interpreted – indeed, BASIC's GOTO statement poses particular compilation problems. LISP can also be implemented very simply using an interpreter – further details can be found in MacLennan [1983].

Some languages incorporate constructs that require special implementation techniques. For example, some languages like Concurrent Pascal and Ada provide facilities for specifying concurrency. The way in which the compiler writer implements such concurrent processes depends on the nature of the target hardware and any operating system already running on it. For example, the compiler may be able to map the concurrent processes specified within the program on to processes understood by the operating system on the target hardware. Appropriate operating system calls can then be generated to control their execution. In other environments, it may be more appropriate to incorporate process management facilities within the language's run-time library. Hardware issues may also be important. For example, consider the implementation of an occam program on a set of transputers [Inmos, 1984]. The transputer is a simple but powerful processor that is specially designed with communication facilities to make multi-transputer systems easy to develop. occam is specially designed to reflect these communication paths, supporting concurrency and process interaction. The design of occam emphasizes the support of concurrency and communication while retaining simplicity.

8.2   Hardware Issues

Chapter 7 discussed many of the hardware issues affecting code generator design in terms of fairly conventional machine architectures, reflecting the structure of most of today's computers on which compiled languages run. But hardware design has progressed well beyond this traditional processor, so it is appropriate to look briefly at some of the hardware issues that may affect the language implementor.

8.2.1   Microprocessor issues

The development of the microprocessor from the early and elementary 4-bit designs to the powerful and complex 32-bit systems of today has been extremely rapid. Although looking slightly dated when compared with today's technology, the 8-bit processor still has many attractions and is still used in a wide range of applications. These processors generally have a comparatively simple instruction set with a few general-purpose and/or special-purpose registers and they can only perform arithmetic and other operations on 8 (or occasionally 16) bits at a time. For example, a single machine instruction may have the effect of adding the contents of one 8-bit memory location to an 8-bit accumulator. For many practical applications, 8-bit operations are far too limiting, so routines have to be developed to manipulate 16- or 32-bit quantities.

The implementation of high-level languages on 8-bit processors poses some special problems. For example, the compiler may have to translate the simple statement $i := j + k$ into a comparatively large number of machine instructions, since it is extremely unlikely that the Pascal programmer will find just 8-bit representations of the integers i, j and k acceptable. There are no major difficulties in actually performing this translation, but the effect is that a very large quantity of code will be produced for the simplest of programs. There are two practical alternatives to this problem. The first is for the compiler to generate calls to subroutines to perform these multi-byte operations. As these subroutines only need to appear once in primary memory, probably in the run-time library, code sizes can be significantly reduced. The code generated by the compiler in such a case consists mostly of the setting up of arguments and calls to subroutines. The second alternative is logically very similar. The compiler does not generate target machine code, but instead it generates an intermediate, fairly low-level code, where each instruction can be thought of as corresponding to a single subroutine call in the first approach. The program is translated into this intermediate form, stored in primary memory and then a small interpreter program runs on the microprocessor, interpreting the intermediate code instruction by instruction. With care, the intermediate code can be designed so that it is simple and compact. Furthermore, if the interpreter is coded tightly in assembly language, an efficient implementation is produced, although not quite as efficient as compiled target code, requiring much less memory than a conventionally compiled solution.

Many successful interpreted implementations have been developed for 8-bit systems. Perhaps the most famous of these is the **UCSD p-System**, which is a portable collection of compilers and other utilities together with a set of machine-specific interpreters.

8.2.2 Microprogramming

Most processors have a fixed instruction set determined by the manufacturer. Although the design of this instruction set may have been influenced by the needs of the compiler writer, any specific compiler has to be structured in such a way as to produce this particular form of target language, which is wholly defined by the hardware. An alternative approach is to implement a 'soft' instruction set; that is, an instruction set that can be modified or augmented by defining the new instructions in terms of **microcode**. The latter is a sequence of very low-level instructions indicating the sequence of operations that have to be performed by the hardware in executing the new member of the instruction set. This facility allows instruction sets to be redesigned to suit the application and is of special significance to the compiler writer, since the constraint of one particular target architecture has been dropped. For example, each high-level language implementation can have its own set of target machine instructions reflecting the particular needs of that particular high-level language. It may be possible to make the hardware interpret an existing intermediate code, which is an interesting and potentially attractive method of language implementation. Another possibility is to allow the target machine's instruction set to be reconfigured dynamically. Several research groups are actively working in these areas.

8.2.3   High-level language architectures

Allowing a programmer access to a processor's microcode is an attractive proposition, but it does have its disadvantages. Writing microcode is usually very difficult as well as time consuming, while debugging microcode often presents major problems; so, the effort required to develop the microcode for a particular application may be considerable. Furthermore, there may be security implications in allowing the user direct access to the microcode; for example, it may be possible to circumvent the virtual address translation mechanism by writing in microcode, and hence memory protection may be lost. So there must be mechanisms to prevent such problems.

Many processor designers now feel that it is more satisfactory to produce processors with large and, hopefully, regular instruction sets designed to fulfil all the reasonable needs of the compiler writer. Most of the larger processors in widespread use today fall into this category, some of which have already been mentioned in the last chapter. They provide high-level language support by offering a wide range of addressing structures, including stack-based addressing, operations on many different high-level language data types and so on.

Inevitably, the designs of the instruction sets for these processors are somewhat of a compromise. For example, the designs cannot be language specific, since they are intended to be acceptable target machines for any high-level language. Another approach to hardware design is to bring the design of the processor nearer to the design of a particular high-level language. Then, instructions are supported that correspond directly with the constructs of the high-level language. LISP processors have been built this way, offering high performance because all the fundamental list operations are handled directly by the hardware. There is also great interest in logic machines to support PROLOG. Processors directly supporting FORTH and BASIC-like languages, used primarily for the fast development of simple real-time control systems, are also now available.

The primary design aim of most of these processors is to execute compiled code rapidly, the emphasis here being placed on run-time rather than compile-time efficiency. But it is now possible, at least in theory, to develop a processor that includes a microcoded or, conceivably a hardwired, compiler. This processor translates a high-level language program into an equivalent machine language version, which is then executed. As far as the user of this processor is concerned, the high-level language is the processor's machine language. The most significant advantage of this form of processor is that compilation can be performed very rapidly, with pipelining offering overlapped execution of the compiler's phases. Furthermore, efficient execution is possible if the internal machine language is designed carefully. However, there is a major disadvantage. Implementing a compiler in microcode or hardware is not simple, as indicated at the beginning of this section. (Note that the necessity for writing a compiler has not disappeared; in fact, the problem has to be solved at a lower (and less hospitable) level.) Nevertheless, research continues in this area, with some promising results being obtained.

8.2.4   RISC machines

The approaches to processor design described in the last section suggest that processor complexity is a prerequisite for the rapid execution of compiled code. Indeed, most of the processors currently in popular use seem to have followed an evolutionary development path in which their complexity increased as improvements were made. But this increased complexity does have drawbacks. The processors are costly to design and build and they often contain design errors which are only discovered after the processor has been put into widespread use. In contrast with this steadily increasing complexity, there has been a recent rapid development of interest in very simple processors running at high instruction rates. These are the reduced instruction set computers. The advocates of RISC architectures state that high performance is more likely to be obtained by executing many simple instructions very quickly on a RISC architecture rather than by executing fewer more complex instructions not quite so quickly on a complex instruction set computer (CISC) architecture.

Many RISC developments have been made at Stanford University and at the University of California at Berkeley. Development has been very rapid, with RISC architectures now being found in a wide range of commercially available computer hardware. In particular, many UNIX-based high-performance workstations now use RISC technology.

RISC designs can offer high performance for several different reasons.

- RISC instruction times are short, since each instruction performs a very simple operation and can therefore be completed in a very small number of machine cycles.

- RISC designs usually have little or no microcode and a large number of fast registers, thus reducing the necessity for memory/register transfer operations.

- Complex addressing modes are not supported.

- The precise design of the instruction set takes into account the operations most frequently carried out by high-level language programs and those that can be feasibly implemented in hardware.

- Most modern high-performance processors incorporate some form of pipelining, allowing the processor to execute several instructions simultaneously. For example, as one arithmetic instruction is being executed, the next instruction in sequence can be fetched from memory. This overlapping of instruction execution can make a significant difference to the effective instruction execution rates. CISC architectures, in contrast, have to incorporate complex hardware interlock mechanisms to ensure that no pipelining conflicts take place. For example, if one instruction attempts to operate on data calculated by a previous instruction, the second instruction must be held up until the first instruction has completed.

The approach usually adopted in RISC systems is to transfer the burden of pipeline management to the compiler. No hardware interlocking in the pipeline is necessary because the compiler takes care never to generate adjacent instructions that could cause a clash in the pipeline. For example, if the compiler found that it was necessary to generate a pair of instructions where the second relied on the result generated by the first, it would separate these two instructions by a no-op instruction (an instruction performing no useful work), thereby ensuring that there would be no pipeline clash. A subsequent phase of the compiler would attempt to rearrange the instruction sequence, if possible replacing these no-op instructions with other instructions performing useful work.

Although such requirements place stringent demands on the design of the compiler, recent experiments have shown that the rewards can be high; the performance of these simple processors together with the optimizing compilers can be much greater than that of the more conventional CISC architectures. A detailed examination of the methods by which the compiler can manage pipeline constraints appears in Hennessy [1983].

8.3   Interpreters

An **interpreter** is a piece of software that directly executes a source program. This source program can be in the form of the original text, as input by the programmer. In such a case, the interpreter parses and then executes each statement in the appropriate sequence. However, a much more common method for implementing an interpreter involves a two-phase process: the source program is translated into an internal-coded form and then the interpreter executes the program in this internal form. In effect, this is just like conventional compilation except that the target code is interpreted by software rather than directly by the hardware processor. Interpreters can sometimes be an alternative to the use of a compiler for high-level language implementation. Also, as has already been seen in Section 8.1.3, interpreters can be used to simplify the process of compiler implementation.

Many of the techniques used for interpreter implementation are also used for compilers. For example, if the source program is translated into an internal form before being interpreted, a translator program is required to incorporate lexical and syntax analysis. This section examines some of the issues concerning interpreters. A much more detailed and comprehensive treatment, including practical information, appears in Brown [1979].

8.3.1   Levels of interpretation

Interpreters can be written to execute source program statements directly. Each time a statement is executed, the interpreter has to parse the statement to determine what action it must take. This may lead to a very inefficient implementation, since the compiler may spend a lot of time repeatedly analyzing statements that are executed frequently. A much better approach is to perform the analysis of each statement of the program just once. In interactive implementations of some languages, it may be possible to perform this analysis as the statements are being input to the computer. Once the complete program is available in this translated form, the interpreter can start program execution. There are several advantages in interpreting an internal form of the program rather than the original source form. Obviously, execution efficiency is improved, since statements need only be parsed once. As the internal form of the program is likely to be much more compact than the original source form, less run-time storage will be required. Run-time storage requirements may be further reduced if the source analysis/translation phase is separated from the interpretation phase – the code to perform the translation into the internal form need not be present while the interpreter is executing the program. If the internal form is designed well, then the interpreter itself can be simple and compact. Most microcomputer implementations of BASIC recode all the BASIC keywords and other special tokens in a compact form, such as a single byte, before program storage. This can make a great deal of difference to the storage requirements and execution speeds of BASIC programs.

An extremely useful facility in an interpretive language system requires the easy reconstruction of the source program from the internal form. If the interpreter detects an error during the running of a program, the interpreter must report the error to the user and ideally display or at least identify the source statement in which the error was detected. If the source program is being interpreted directly, then the display of a source statement after an error is trivial, since the entire source is available in memory. If an encoded internal form is being interpreted, then the translation back to the source form may be very much harder. Therefore, to facilitate this reconstruction of the source program, the internal form should not be too far removed from the source form. Execution efficiency may suffer as a result, but there are great gains in the ease of debugging.

These source reconstruction facilities are also required in interactive language implementations, to allow the programmer to list programs already input.

It is worth noting that the implementation of a compiler can be considered to be an interpretive system. The source program is translated into an internal form – the machine code of the target hardware – and the target hardware acts as the interpreter of this internal form. Logically, there is very little distinction between the direct use of the hardware as an interpreter and the coding of an interpreter in microcode. It may be possible to implement a very high-performance interpreter by making use of microcode to implement a virtual machine whose object code is the same as the internal form of the language being interpreted.

8.3.2   Why use an interpreter?

The choice of whether to implement a high-level language using a compiler or an interpreter is not always easy, since both approaches have their own distinct advantages. It is possible to write interpreters for most programming languages and, indeed, there are some languages for which the use of an interpreter is much more appropriate. Some languages such as SNOBOL allow the type of a variable to change dynamically during execution. For example, an integer value can be assigned to a variable and then later in the program the variable can be used to hold a character string. Compiling efficient code to handle such dynamic typing is difficult as the type of any variable is not known at compile time. However, an interpreter can handle this situation much more easily and potentially more efficiently. Languages such as BASIC that were designed for highly interactive use are somewhat more suited to interpretation because the programmer has greater control over execution.

An interpreter can offer very powerful debugging facilities. It is much easier to implement comprehensive debugging facilities in an interpreter than in a compiled language system. At any time, the interpreter has access to the source program in its original form or in an internal form, together with symbol tables containing variable names and values. This allows diagnostic information to be output in a form that is easily understood by the programmer since, on an error, source statements can be identified, values of variables can be output and so on. It is also easy for the interpreter to output tracing information as the program runs. For example, the interpreter can be told to output a message each time the value of a particular variable is changed in addition to the source statements causing the changes. Tracing of all subroutine calls or program jumps may also be useful. Interactive software development is supported in languages such as BASIC, where the interpreter is usually incorporated with facilities for program input and editing.

Another major advantage of the interpreter over the compiler is that an interpreter is usually much smaller and easier to write than a complete compiler. An interpreter is just concerned with the analysis and subsequent execution of the source program, not with the synthesis of the object program.

Despite these advantages of an interpreter, the execution of compiled object code is likely to be much more efficient than the use of an interpreter. If speed of execution is of primary concern, then an optimizing compiler is required. If a computer system supports both a compiled and an interpreted implementation of a language, then it is more appropriate to use the interpreter for programs whose execution times are short, since the interpreter is likely to spend less time performing source program translation than the compiler.

Most of today's microcomputer systems support an interpretive BASIC system, often closely integrated with the operating system. Interpreted language systems are very appropriate for these computers because ease of use and debugging are usually of the utmost concern, execution speed is rarely critical, and a compact interpreter and compact storage of the source program is important. The BASIC interpreter is often an integral part of the hardware, being stored with the operating system in read-only memory.

8.3.3   Implementation techniques

Since interpreter systems may incorporate some of the techniques used by compilers, particularly for lexical and syntax analysis, many of the algorithms used for program analysis are relevant. The formal specification of the source language is just as important for an interpreted system as for a compiled system. The interpreter itself is usually based on a large multiway branch, where each branch deals with one particular type of statement. If the internal language being interpreted has a simple structure, then it may be appropriate to code the interpreter in a low-level language. This may allow the direct use of hardware facilities to speed the interpreter's execution, but this is gained at the expense of portability.

An interpreter must be concerned with run-time storage management. The mechanisms used can be very similar to those used for run-time storage management of variables used by compiled language systems, but the choice depends primarily on the nature of the source language. Simple non-recursive languages may allow the use of a simple symbol table that includes symbol values. A stack-based scheme is the natural choice for other languages.

Well-documented examples of complete interpreters (coded in Pascal) appear in Welsh [1986] and Brinch Hansen [1985]. These interpreters are designed to execute intermediate languages generated from Pascal source programs.

SUMMARY

- Implementing a compiler in an appropriate high-level language rather than in a low-level language is most strongly recommended.

- Portability can be enhanced by writing a compiler in its own language and by subdividing the compiler into a machine-independent analysis phase and a machine-dependent synthesis phase.

- A run-time library can form an interface between the language and the operating system.

- Interpretive implementations of high-level languages are often successful on the less powerful, primarily 8-bit, microprocessors.

- The development of hardware that directly supports high-level languages is an active research area, with powerful working systems already having been produced. RISC hardware can also offer high-performance implementations.

- High-level languages can also be implemented using interpreters. There are many advantages to the interpretive approach and, for some languages, this is the only practical implementation route. Interpreted implementations tend to be much slower than compiled code.

EXERCISES

8.1 Explain some of the techniques that can be adopted to make a compiler portable. List the steps required for the implementation of a portable compiler on a new processor.

8.2 Use the T-diagram notation to describe the Pascal implementation path outlined in Section 8.1.3.

8.3 What are the advantages and disadvantages of writing a Pascal compiler in Pascal? Is Pascal a good compiler implementation language?

8.4 How would you manage the testing of a new compiler?

8.5 Write an interpreter for a simple subset of Pascal.

CHAPTER 9

Software Tools

Writing a compiler is not a simple project and anything that makes the task simpler is worth using. At a very early stage in the history of compiler development, it was recognized that some aspects of compiler design could be automated. Consequently, a great deal of effort has been directed towards the development of software tools to aid the production of compilers. Many packages have been implemented, but most of these have disappeared into obscurity as they were designed for use in only a very restricted application area or were never completed. However, some packages have stood the test of time and are still in widespread use. Two best-known software tools for compiler construction are Lex (a lexical analyzer generator) and Yacc (a parser generator), both of which are available under the UNIX operating system. Their continuing popularity is partly due to their widespread availability, but also because they are powerful, easy-to-use tools with a wide range of applicability. This chapter describes these two software tools.

9.1   Lex

Chapter 5 described lexical analyzers and showed how regular expressions can be used to define the tokens to be recognized by a lexical analyzer. The process of converting regular expressions into programs to recognize regular expressions is not particularly easy to do by hand. In particular, it is very easy to introduce errors into the recognizing programs. Lex [Lesk, 1975] is a software tool that takes as input a specification of a set of regular expressions together with actions to be taken on recognizing each of these expressions. The output of Lex is a program that recognizes the regular expressions and acts appropriately on each. If the input to Lex defines the syntax of the basic tokens of a programming language, the output of Lex can be used as the lexical analyzer for a compiler for that language. Lex produces a program containing a table-driven recognizer for the regular expressions together with user-supplied code defining the actions to be taken on recognizing each expression.

The input to Lex takes the form:

> *definitions*
> *%%*
> *rules*
> *%%*
> *user routines*

Any of these three sections may be empty but the %% separator between the definitions and the rules cannot be omitted. The format and purpose of the *definitions* section will not be described here, but further details concerning this and other aspects of Lex can be found in Lesk [1975] and Schreiner [1985]. The *user routines* section defines routines used in the rule actions and is copied directly to the output. The key part of the Lex input is contained in the *rules* section. This section defines a set of rules as regular expressions and corresponding actions, each rule starting on a new line. The actions are coded as C statements. Lex supports a very powerful range of operators for the construction of regular expressions. For example, a Lex program to remove all digits from its input has the form:

> *%%*
> [0-9]+ ;

Here, the regular expression [0-9]+ matches a string of one or more characters in the range 0 to 9. The null action (;) in this rule signifies that on recognizing the pattern in the source, nothing further should be done. Lex automatically includes a default pattern so that all unrecognized input characters are copied unchanged to the output, so this Lex program will only affect those characters in the range 0 to 9.

EXAMPLE

A Lex program to replace sequences of blanks or tabs by a single space has the form:

    %%
    [\t]+ *printf*(" ");

In the regular expression, \t denotes a tab character.

Another useful expression is:

    [A-Za-z][A-Za-z0-9]*

which represents an arbitrary string of letters and digits, starting with a letter, suitable for matching identifiers in many programming languages.

It is possible to include context-sensitive rules in Lex input. For example, the expression:

    xy/z

matches xy only if followed by a z. It is also possible to specify a left context that has to be satisfied for a rule to be executed. This lookahead allows lexical analyzers for FORTRAN to be constructed comparatively easily.

A large number of other operators and facilities are provided by Lex to allow the specification of even the most complex of patterns. For example, there are simple rules for the handling of ambiguity. If more than one expression matches the input, Lex automatically chooses the expression yielding the longest match. If ambiguity is still present, the rule specified first in the Lex program is used.

Given a familiarity with Lex and C, a lexical analyzer for almost any programming language can be written in a very short time. All the tokens of the language are identified, corresponding matching expressions are defined and the simple action of returning the token identity, perhaps with an additional value, is associated with each expression. However, if the number of rules is large, there is a danger that Lex will generate a large lexical analyzer. Consequently, if a language includes a set of reserved words that are lexically similar to identifiers, such as in Pascal, code size is reduced if both reserved words and identifiers are matched by the same pattern expression and the code specified in the action part of the rule determines whether the string matched is a reserved word, and if so, which.

Lex does not have application solely in the generation of lexical analyzers. It can also be used to assist in the implementation of almost any text pattern-matching application, such as text editing, program pretty-printing, code conversion and so on.

9.2   Yacc

Yacc (Yet Another Compiler-Compiler) [Johnson, 1975] assists in the next phase of the compiler. Given a set of grammar rules, Yacc will attempt to create a table-driven LALR(1) parser (see Section 6.3.3), which will be output in a form suitable for inclusion in an application program such as a compiler. Fortunately, Yacc and Lex mix together well and it is easy to construct a lexical analyzer using Lex, which can be called by the parser constructed by Yacc.

The basic structure of the input to Yacc is very similar to that for Lex. The input to Yacc takes the form:

> *declarations*
> *%%*
> *rules*
> *%%*
> *programs*

Just as with Lex, the first *%%* separator and the *rules* section cannot be omitted. Each rule is made up of a BNF-style grammar rule followed by an optional action, which is executed if that rule is matched by the source input. For example, the BNF rule:

> <expression> ::= <expression> + <term> | <term>

can be expressed in Yacc syntax as:

> *expression : expression* '+' *term* | *term* ;

This example can be made into a complete Yacc program by preceding it with a line containing *%%* and also by including a rule defining a term. Yacc automatically assumes that *expression* and *term* are non-terminal symbols in the grammar. Names representing terminal symbols (returned by the lexical analyzer) have to be declared explicitly in the declarations section.

EXAMPLE

```
%token identifier
%%
term : identifier |
   '(' expression ')' ;
```

Actions can be specified by following the grammar rule by one or more C statements enclosed within curly brackets. For example:

```
expression : expression '+' term
{ printf("Addition expression detected\n"); } ;
expression : term
{ printf("Simple expression detected\n"); } ;
```

In a real parser, these actions can be used to construct the parse tree or to generate code directly. To do this, Yacc provides a facility for associating values with the symbols used in a grammar rule. Yacc defines the pseudo variables $1, $2 and so on to have the values of the first, second and subsequent symbols on the right-hand side of the grammar rule. Values can be passed to other grammar rules by performing an assignment in the action part to the pseudo variable $$, which associates a value with the symbol on the left-hand side of the rule.

Yacc has particularly useful facilities for handling ambiguity and conflicts in the grammar rules. Whenever such problems arise, the user is notified, but Yacc's default action may well produce a parser with the desired effect. One of the traditional examples of this concerns the parsing of the **if** statement with an optional **else** part (see Section 6.2.1). Yacc will warn of the ambiguity inherent in this structure, but its default action is to accept the longest possible string at any stage, which has the normally desired effect. Some other ambiguity problems are also handled neatly by Yacc. For example, defining an arithmetic expression in BNF as:

```
<expression> ::= <expression> + <expression>
              | <expression> − <expression>
              | <expression> * <expression>
              | <expression> / <expression>
              | identifier
```

may cause the less powerful parsers a great deal of trouble, since they have no way of determining the associativity or precedence of the operators. As was seen in Chapter 6, the conventional way of handling this situation is to rewrite the rules by introducing new non-terminal symbols, so that the rules of associativity and precedence become implicitly defined by the rules. Yacc offers a somewhat simpler approach: associativity and precedence of operators can be specified explicitly in the declarations section.

EXAMPLE

```
%token identifier
%left '+' '−'
%left '*' '/'
%%
expression : expression '+' expression
           | expression '−' expression
           | expression '*' expression
           | expression '/' expression
           | identifier ;
```

This has the effect of defining the operators '+', '−', '*' and '/' to be left-associative with '*' and '/' having precedence greater than that of '+' and '−'. Precedence is indicated implicitly by the order in which the declaration statements occur. Similarly, declarations introduced by *%right* define right-associative operators and those introduced by *%nonassoc* are non-associative.

Error detection and recovery is an important concern when constructing parsers. Yacc allows the user considerable freedom in choosing error recovery actions appropriate for each situation. But even with the facilities provided by Yacc, error handling remains a difficult area.

The power and utility of Yacc should not be underestimated. The effort saved during compiler implementation by using Yacc, rather than a handwritten parser, can be considerable.

An example of the use of Lex and Yacc for the development of an interpreter for a very simple programming language is given in the appendix.

9.3   Other Compiler Construction Tools

There have been many research projects concerned with the development of compiler-compiler packages. Some of these projects have concentrated on the production of parser generators, but much of the more recent work has been directed towards tools assisting with the production of code generators and code optimizers. There is little doubt that it will soon be possible to integrate these tools, thereby enabling the rapid production of compilers for a wide range of languages using just a definition of the syntax and semantics of the source language and a similar definition for the target language.

An early, but still interesting project was the ANALYZER program designed for producing the tables for a mixed-strategy parser from a set of BNF grammar rules [McKeeman, 1970]. Several more recent projects have concentrated on the automated use of attribute grammars for parsing. Automating the synthesis of instructions for the target machine is now a flourishing research area. Cattell [1982] identifies three categories for the classification of work in machine-independent compilation:

(1)   **Retargetable code generators**, which are designed so that the target machine-specific information is confined to a (hopefully) small section of code and data. The rest of the code generator is machine independent. Many of today's compilers are written using this philosophy.

(2)   **Template-based code generators**, which take the retargetable idea a little further so that all the target machine-dependent information is confined to data tables that control the actions of the code generator. The data tables consist of sets of templates which are matched against the parse tree. When a template matches, the corresponding code can be output. It may be quite difficult and/or time consuming to generate optimized code using this approach.

(3)   **Artificial intelligence-based code generators**, which just require the specification of the target machine in some formal language and automatically generate code to fulfil these specifications. Obviously, this is a most desirable aim and promising research has been carried out in this area. Development of such code generators is still at a very early stage and it will be some years before these techniques become other than experimental.

One of the more well-known tools to help automate the production of code generators and optimizers is the Production-Quality Compiler-Compiler (PQCC) system developed at Carnegie-Mellon University. This system has already been mentioned in Section 7.6, where references to more detailed information were given.

9.4   Programming-Support Tools

Support for a programming language is not complete once a compiler or interpreter has been implemented. If a programmer has access to other language-support tools, the cost of software development in that language can be reduced significantly. These additional facilities include tools for program editing, debugging, analysis and documentation. Ideally, such tools should be closely integrated with the language implementation so that, for example, when the compiler detects syntactic errors in the source program, the editor can be entered automatically with the cursor indicating the position of the error.

The rapid production of syntactically correct programs is a major goal. Formal program design methodologies can help a great deal towards this goal, but conventional text editors provide little support when entering the program into the computer. The use of syntax-driven editors is increasing and they can assist the user in eliminating syntax errors as the program is being input. Such an editor only accepts syntactically correct input and prompts the user, if necessary, to input only those constructs that are syntactically correct at the current position. These editors can considerably improve run time by removing the necessity for repeated runs of the compiler to remove syntax errors.

By integrating an editor with a compiler, incremental compilation may be possible. As each statement is input, it is compiled into some internal form and stored for subsequent code generation or interpretation. Incremental compilation may be particularly difficult for languages that allow the routine use of forward references; for example, compiling a statement incorporating variables whose types have not yet been declared is comparatively difficult. Subsequent editing of the program may also cause problems; for example, if the type of a globally declared variable in Pascal is changed, then many consequent changes may be necessary to the code generated for the rest of the program.

Debugging tools should also be integrated with the programming language. Debugging compiled code using a debugger operating at the machine code level can be particularly frustrating, since it relies on the programmer having a knowledge of the low-level architecture of the target machine and also of the form of the code generated by the compiler. Debugging at the source code level is much more appropriate, but such debugging tools are not easy to implement.

Integrated program development environments are now being considered as an important aid for the rapid construction of correct software. An important example of such an environment is the Cornell Program Synthesizer which provides facilities for program editing, execution and debugging. These facilities provide an interactive and integrated program development environment. By using syntax-directed editors, syntactic errors are reported as programs are input or edited. Code is generated incrementally. Further details are contained in Teitelbaum [1981]. Another widely used example of such an environment is the POPLOG system [Barrett, 1985] developed at the University of Sussex. This is an interactive environment directly supporting software development in POP-11, LISP, PROLOG, SML and other languages via incremental compilation. It incorporates a powerful device-independent editor called VED, which is used for accessing help and teaching information as well as for program input and editing.

Considerable progress has been made over the last decade in the provision of powerful software tools to ease the programmer's burden. The application of the basic principles of language and compiler design will help continue this development.

SUMMARY

- Lex is a program that translates a set of regular expressions, together with corresponding actions, into a complete recognizing program, suitable for use as the lexical analyzer for a compiler.

- Yacc is the corresponding parser generator. It takes the specification of a grammar as a series of productions, together with actions to be taken when each production is applied. It constructs a complete, table-driven LALR(1) parser for the grammar.

- Several systems assisting in the production of code generators are available. For example, the PQCC system produces a table-driven code generator from a formal description of the target machine.

- There are now many integrated programming support environments in use. These systems provide facilities such as syntax-directed editing, interactive editing, execution and debugging of programs, multi-language support and so on.

EXERCISES

9.1 Use Lex and Yacc to implement the desk calculator program introduced in Exercise 4.10 and Exercise 6.11. Compare the time taken
to complete Exercise 6.11 with the time taken to complete this
question.

9.2 Examine the outputs of Lex and Yacc for the desk calculator grammar rules and try to understand what these programs have produced.

9.3 Write a translator from BASIC to Pascal or C.

9.4 Which part of a compiler would you most like (or least dislike)
writing, and why?

9.5 The last and most obvious question that should be included in this
book is 'design a language and write a compiler for it!' This is not a
project to be undertaken lightly, but with appropriate constraints it
can be accomplished without undue effort. For example, if the
language is suitably simple, such as a subset or a 'small' version of
Pascal, the target machine is a carefully designed, simple abstract
machine and high-quality code is not essential; then, the project can
be achieved quite rapidly. An alternative approach is to take an
existing compiler and introduce additional language constructs. If
the original compiler is well designed, this should be a feasible
project. Writing a good compiler for a large language producing
object code for a complex processor is a project that may require
many man-years of effort!

APPENDIX

Example of the Use of Lex and Yacc

This appendix presents a very simple example of the use of the lexical analyzer generator Lex and the parser generator Yacc. The example is a rudimentary desk calculator operating on integer values. Although the code is very simple, it does show the power and convenience of using Lex and Yacc. A more complex example, such as a front end or even a complete compiler for a simple language, was not chosen to avoid the danger of obscuring the Lex and Yacc facilities by a large quantity of C code.

The specification of the desk calculator is that it should accept expressions in normal infix format and support the binary operations '+', '−', '*', 'div' (integer division) and 'mod' (the modulus operator). Parentheses are supported. It should also accept the unary operator 'sqr' which produces the square of its operand. Unary minus is not required.

The design of the lexical analyzer for this calculator is straightforward. The lexical tokens should be the operators, integer numbers and the newline character indicating the end of an expression to be evaluated.

A suitable input file for Lex to return these tokens is as follows:

```
%%
[ \t] ;    /* ignore blanks and tabs */
[0-9]+ { yylval = atoi(yytext); return NUMBER; }
"mod"  return MOD;
"div"  return DIV;
"sqr"  return SQR;
\n |.  return yytext[0];   /* return everything else */
```

The first rule recognizes spaces and tab characters. Since there is no corresponding action, they are ignored. The second rule recognizes an integer constant as a string of one or more digits. The C function *atoi* converts the string representation of the constant into an integer and returns it to the syntax analyzer via the variable *yylval*. It also returns the fact that it has recognized a *NUMBER*. The next three rules recognize the three multi-character operators while the final rule passes all other single characters back to the syntax analyzer. The explicit inclusion of the new-line character ('\n') in the rule is necessary since it is not recognized by '.'.

The single-character operators such as '+' are not explicitly recognised in this lexical analyzer – they are passed on automatically by the last rule. Therefore, this lexical analyzer does no error detection: it does not detect the input of an illegal character. It is up to the syntax analyzer in this example to do the error detection and recovery.

The syntax rules defining the form of acceptable expressions are contained within the input to Yacc:

```
%{
#include <stdio.h>
%}

%token NUMBER

%left '+' '-'
%left '*' DIV MOD
   /* gives a higher precedence to '*', DIV and MOD */
%left SQR

%%
comm:     comm '\n'
        | /* empty */
        | comm expr '\n' { printf("%d\n", $2); }
        | comm error '\n' { yyerrok; printf("Try again\n"); }
        ;

expr:     '(' expr ')'       { $$ = $2; }
        | expr '+' expr      { $$ = $1 + $3; }
        | expr '-' expr      { $$ = $1 - $3; }
        | expr '*' expr      { $$ = $1 * $3; }
        | expr DIV expr      { $$ = $1 / $3; }
        | expr MOD expr      { $$ = $1 % $3; }
        | SQR expr           { $$ = $2 * $2; }
        | NUMBER
        ;
%%

#include "lex.yy.c"
yyerror(s)
char *s;
{ printf("%s\n", s);
}
```

```
main( )
{ return yyparse( );
}
```

Five operators are defined to be left-associative with the precedence of '*',
DIV and *MOD* being greater than that of '+' and '−'. *SQR* is a unary
operator with the highest precedence.

   The rule defining *comm* (a command) starts with two alternatives,
which effectively allow empty commands. The next alternative recognizes
a command containing a valid expression and the action is to print the
value of the expression. The final alternative handles error recovery. If an
error is detected in the parse, the parser skips to a newline character, the
error status is reset (*yyerrok*) and an appropriate message is output.

   The alternatives defining *expr* should be self-explanatory. Note that
the specification of the associativity and precedence of the operators
removes the inherent ambiguities in this grammar.

   The final section of the Yacc input contains the C code required by
the parser. Yacc has access to the names of the Lex tokens because of the
#include directive. The routines *yyerror*, which is called whenever the
parser detects an error, and *main* have to be supplied by the user. Only the
simplest of versions of these routines are required in this application.

   These two specifications can be converted into a complete calculator
program as shown below. The file *calc.l* contains the Lex source and the
file *calc.y* contains the Yacc source. A little evidence that *calc* works is also
shown. Commands input by the user are shown in Bold.

```
% lex calc.l
% yacc calc.y
% cc y.tab.c -ll -o calc
% calc
1+1
2
3 + 4 * 5
23
(3+4)*5
35
sqrsqr2+3
19
25 mod 7
4
(3))
syntax error
Try again

↑C
%
```

Annotated Bibliography

This bibliography presents the details of a few textbooks containing more specialized or detailed information than that contained within this book. The fields of high-level languages and compiler design contain an enormous amount of published material and these references only form a minute and personal subset.

Programming languages

There are now many textbooks that present a comparative description of several programming languages. Such comparative studies can be much more illuminating that the individual detailed language manuals.

Ghezzi, C. and Jazayeri, M. (1987), *Programming Language Concepts*, Second Edition, John Wiley & Sons: New York.

Horowitz, E. (1983), *Fundamentals of Programming Languages*, Springer-Verlag: Berlin.

Horowitz, E. (1983), *Programming Languages: A Grand Tour*, Springer-Verlag: Berlin.

MacLennan, Bruce J. (1983), *Principles of Programming Languages: Design, Evaluation and Implementation*, Holt-Saunders International: New York.

Sammet, J. E. (1969), *Programming Languages: History and Fundamentals*, Prentice-Hall: Englewood Cliffs, NJ.

Detailed information about the many techniques that have been used for the definition of programming languages is contained in:

McGettrick, A. D. (1980), *The Definition of Programming Languages*, Cambridge University Press.

Compiler construction

There are a few large textbooks that cover most of the field of compiler construction in some detail. For example:

Aho, A. V., Sethi, R. and Ullman, J. D. (1986), *Compilers – Principles, Techniques and Tools*, Addison-Wesley Publishing Company: Reading, MA.

Tremblay, J.-P. and Sorenson, P. G. (1985), *The Theory and Practice of Compiler Writing*, McGraw-Hill Book Company: New York.

Waite, W. M. and Goos, G. (1984), *Compiler Construction*, Springer-Verlag: New York.

A more formal approach to automata theory and grammars is taken in:

Hopcroft, J. E. and Ullman, J. D. (1979), *Introduction to Automata Theory, Languages and Computation*, Addison-Wesley Publishing Company: Reading, MA.

A practical and thorough treatment of syntax analysis is contained in:

Gough, K. J. (1988), *Syntax Analysis and Software Tools*, Addison-Wesley Publishing Company: Sydney.

Further practical implementation on compiler design and on language implementation is found in:

Bornat, R. (1979), *Understanding and Writing Compilers*, Macmillan: London.

Brown, P. J. (1979), *Writing Interactive Compilers and Interpreters*, John Wiley & Sons: Chichester.

Brief descriptions of compiler construction tools are made in many textbooks. A detailed and practical description of the use of Lex and Yacc, avoiding much of the theoretical background, is in:

Schreiner, A. T. and Friedman, H. G., Jr. (1985), *Introduction to Compiler Construction with UNIX*, Prentice-Hall: Englewood Cliffs, NJ.

Finally, there are now several excellent books that examine the details of specific compilers or which look at techniques for the compilation of specific languages. The source versions of many high-quality compilers are available in the public domain and the study of such programs is undoubtedly the best way of learning how to write other compilers.

Barron, D. W. (1981), *Pascal – The Language and its Implementation*, John Wiley & Sons: Chichester.

Brinch Hansen, P. (1985), *Brinch Hansen on Pascal Compilers*, Prentice-Hall International: London.

Richards, M. and Whitby-Strevens, C. (1980), *BCPL – The Language and its Compiler*, Cambridge University Press.

Welsh, J. and Hay, A. (1986), *A Model Implementation of Standard Pascal*, Prentice-Hall International: Englewood Cliffs, NJ.

References

Abelson, H., Sussman, G. J. and Sussman, J. (1985), *Structure and Interpretation of Computer Programs*, MIT Press: Cambridge, MA.

Adams, D. (1979), *The Hitch Hiker's Guide to the Galaxy*, Pan Books: London.

Aho, A. V. and Ullman, J. D. (1972), *The Theory of Parsing, Translation and Compiling*, Vol. 1, Prentice-Hall: Englewood Cliffs, NJ.

Aho, A. V. and Ullman, J. D. (1979), *Principles of Compiler Design*, Addison-Wesley Publishing Company: Reading, MA.

Aho, A. V., Hopcroft, J. E. and Ullman, J. D. (1983), *Data Structures and Algorithms*, Addison-Wesley Publishing Company: Reading, MA.

Aho, A. V., Sethi, R. and Ullman, J. D. (1986), *Compilers – Principles, Techniques and Tools*, Addison-Wesley Publishing Company: Reading, MA.

ANSI – American National Standards Institute (1974), *USA Standard COBOL*, X3.23-1974, New York.

ANSI – American National Standards Institute (1978), *ANSI FORTRAN*, X3.9-1978, New York.

Barrett, R., Ramsey, A. and Sloman, A. (1985), *POP-11: A Practical Language for Artificial Intelligence*, Ellis Horwood: Chichester.

Barron, D. W. *et al.* (1963), 'The Main Features of CPL', *Computer Journal*, **6**, pp. 134–143.

Berry, R. E. (1981), *Programming Language Translation*, Ellis Horwood: Chichester.

Birtwistle, G. M. *et al.* (1973), *SIMULA Begin*, Petrocelli/Charter: New York.

Bratko, I. (1986), *Prolog Programming for Artificial Intelligence*, Addison-Wesley Publishing Company: Wokingham.

Bratman, H. (1961), 'An Alternate Form of the UNCOL Diagram', *Communications of the ACM*, **4**(3), p. 142.

Brinch Hansen, P. (1975), 'The Programming Language Concurrent Pascal', *IEEE Transactions on Software Engineering*, SE-1, **2**, pp. 199-207.

Brinch Hansen, P. (1982), *Programming a Personal Computer*, Prentice-Hall: Englewood Cliffs, NJ.

Brinch Hansen, P. (1985), *Brinch Hansen on Pascal Compilers*, Prentice-Hall International: London.

Brown, P. J. (1979), *Writing Interactive Compilers and Interpreters*, John Wiley & Sons: Chichester.

Byte (1981), Special Issue on Smalltalk, *Byte*, **6**.

Cattell, R. G. G. (1980), 'Automatic Derivation of Code Generators from Machine Descriptions', *ACM Transactions on Programming Languages and Systems*, **2**(2), pp. 173–190.

Cattell, R. G. G. (1982), *Formalization and Automatic Derivation of Code Generators*, UMI Research Press: Ann Arbor, MI.

Clocksin, W. F. and Mellish, C. S. (1981), *Programming in Prolog*, Springer-Verlag: Berlin.

Dahl, O. J. and Nygaard, K. (1966), 'SIMULA – An ALGOL-Based Simulation Language', *Communications of the ACM*, **9**(9), pp. 671-678.

Davidson, J. W. and Fraser, C. W. (1980), 'The Design and Application of a Retargetable Peephole Optimizer', *ACM Transactions on Programming Languages and Systems*, **2**(2), pp. 191–202.

Dijkstra, E. W. (1968a), 'GOTO Statement Considered Harmful', *Communications of the ACM*, **11**(3), pp. 147–148.

Dijkstra, E. W. (1968b), 'Cooperating Sequential Processes', in *Programming Languages*, (F. Genuys, ed.), Academic Press: New York.

Earley, J. (1970), 'An Efficient Context-Free Parsing Algorithm', *Communications of the ACM*, **13**(2), pp. 94–102.

Farber, D. J., Griswold, R. E. and Polonsky, I. P. (1964), 'SNOBOL – A String Manipulation Language', *Journal of the ACM*, **11**(1), pp. 21–30.

Fischer, C. N. (1980), 'On Parsing and Compiling Arithmetic Expressions on Vector Computers', *ACM Transactions on Programming Languages and Systems*, **2**(2), pp. 203–224.

Floyd, R. W. (1963), 'Syntactic Analysis and Operator Precedence', *Journal of the ACM*, **10**(3), pp. 316–333.

Gries, D. (1971), *Compiler Construction for Digital Computers*, John Wiley & Sons: New York.

Griswold, R. E., Poage, J. F. and Polonsky, I. P. (1971), *The SNOBOL4 Programming Language*, Prentice-Hall: Englewood Cliffs, NJ.

Griswold, R. E. and Griswold, M. T. (1983), *The ICON Programming Language*, Prentice-Hall: Englewood Cliffs, NJ.

Hennessy, J. (1982), 'Symbolic Debugging of Optimized Code', *ACM Transactions on Programming Languages and Systems*, **4**(3), pp. 323–344.

Hennessy, J. and Gross T. (1983), 'Postpass Code Optimization of Pipeline Constraints', *ACM Transactions on Programming Languages and Systems*, **5**(3), pp. 422–448.

Hoare, C. A. R. and Wirth, N. (1973), 'An Axiomatic Definition of the Programming Language Pascal', *Acta Informatica*, **2**, pp. 335–355.

Hoare, C. A. R. (1981), 'The Emperor's Old Clothes', *Communications of the ACM*, **24**(2), pp. 75–83.

Horowitz, E. and Sahni, S. (1978), *Fundamentals of Computer Algorithms*, Pitman: London.

Hyman, A. (1984), *Charles Babbage – Pioneer of the Computer*, Oxford University Press.

Inmos (1984), *occam Programming Manual*, Prentice-Hall International: Englewood Cliffs, NJ.

Iverson, K. E. (1962), *A Programming Language*, John Wiley & Sons: New York.

Jensen, K. and Wirth, N. (1975), *The Pascal User Manual and Report*, Second Edition, Springer-Verlag: New York.

Jensen, K. and Wirth, N. (1985), *Pascal User Manual and Report*, Third Edition, *ISO Pascal Standard*, Springer-Verlag: New York.

Johnson, S. C. (1975), *Yacc – Yet Another Compiler-Compiler*, Computing Science Technical Report 32, AT & T Bell Laboratories, Murray Hill, NJ.

Kernighan, B. W. and Richie, D. M. (1978), *The C Programming Language*, Prentice-Hall: Englewood Cliffs, NJ.

Knuth, D. E. (1965), 'On the Translation of Languages from Left to Right', *Information and Control*, **8**(6), pp. 607–639.

Knuth, D. E. (1967), 'The Remaining Troublespots in ALGOL 60', *Communications of the ACM*, **10**(10), pp. 611–617.

Knuth, D. E. (1973), *The Art of Computer Programming*, Vol. 1, *Fundamental Algorithms*, Addison-Wesley Publishing Company: Reading, MA.

Lesk, M. E. (1975), *Lex – A Lexical Analyser Generator*, Computing Science Technical Report 39, AT & T Bell Laboratories, Murray Hill, NJ.

Leverett, B. W. *et al.* (1980), 'An Overview of the Production-Quality Compiler-Compiler Projects', *IEEE Computer*, **13**(8), pp. 38–49.

Lindsey, C. H. and van der Meulen, S. G. (1971), *Informal Introduction to ALGOL 68*, North-Holland Publishing Company: Amsterdam.

Lindsey, C. H. (1972), 'ALGOL 68 with Fewer Tears', *Computer Journal*, **15**(2), pp. 176–188.

MacLennan, B. J. (1983), *Principles of Programming Languages: Design, Evaluation and Implementation*, Holt-Saunders International: New York.

McCarthy, J. (1960), 'Recursive Functions of Symbolic Expressions and Their Computation by Machine', *Communications of the ACM*, **3**(4), pp. 184–195.

McCarthy, J. *et al.* (1965), *LISP 1.5 Programmer's Manual*, MIT Press: Cambridge, MA.

McGettrick, A. D. (1980), *The Definition of Programming Languages*, Cambridge University Press.

McKeeman, W. M., Horning, J. J. and Wortman, D. B. (1970), *A Compiler Generator*, Prentice-Hall: Englewood Cliffs, NJ.

Morrison, P. and Morrison, E. (1961), *Charles Babbage and His Calculating Engines*, Dover Publications: New York.

Naur, P. (1960), 'Report on the Algorithmic Language ALGOL 60', *Communications of the ACM*, **3**(5), pp. 299–314.

Naur, P. (1963), 'Revised Report on the Algorithmic Language ALGOL 60', *Communications of the ACM*, **6**(1), pp. 1–17.

Nori, K. V. *et al.* (1981), 'Pascal-P Implementation Notes', in *Pascal – The Language and its Implementation*, (D. W. Barron, ed.), John Wiley & Sons: Chichester.

Pemberton, S. and Daniels, M. C. (1982), *Pascal Implementation: The P4 Compiler*, Ellis Horwood: Chichester.

Perlis, A. J. and Samelson, K. (1958), 'Preliminary Report – International Algebraic Language', *Communications of the ACM*, **1**(12), pp. 8–22.

Rees, M. and Robson, D. (1987), *Practical Compiling with Pascal-S*, Addison-Wesley Publishing Company: Wokingham.

Richards, M. (1969), 'BCPL: A Tool for Compiler Writing and Systems Programming', *Proceedings of the AFIPS Spring Joint Computer Conference*, Boston, Massachusetts **34**, pp. 557–566.

Richards, M. and Whitby-Strevens, C. (1980), *BCPL – The Language and its Compiler*, Cambridge University Press.

Sammet, J. E. (1969), *Programming Languages: History and Fundamentals*, Prentice-Hall: Englewood Cliffs, NJ.

Schreiner, A. T. and Friedman, H. G., Jr. (1985), *Introduction to Compiler Construction with UNIX*, Prentice-Hall, Englewood Cliffs, NJ.

Siewiorek, D. P., Bell, C. G. and Newell A. (1982), *Computer Structures: Principles and Examples*, McGraw-Hill: New York.

Steele, G. L. (1984), *COMMON LISP: The Language*, Digital Press.

Stroustrup, B. (1985), *The C++ Programming Language*, Addison-Wesley Publishing Company: Reading, MA.

Tanenbaum, A. S. (1976), 'A Tutorial on ALGOL 68', *ACM Computing Surveys*, **8**(2), pp. 155–190.

Tanenbaum, A. S. *et al.* (1983), 'A Practical Tool Kit for Making Portable Compilers', *Communications of the ACM*, **26**(9), pp. 654–660.

Teitelbaum, T. and Reps, T. (1981), 'The Cornell Program Synthesizer: A Syntax-Directed Programming Environment', *Communications of the ACM*, **24**(9), pp. 563–573.

Thompson, K. (1968), 'Regular Expression Search Algorithm', *Communications of the ACM*, **11**(6), pp. 419–422.

Tremblay, J.-P. and Sorenson, P. G. (1985), *The Theory and Practice of Compiler Writing*, McGraw-Hill Book Company: New York.

USASI – United States of America Standards Institute (1966), *USA Standard FORTRAN*, USAS X3.9-1966, New York.

USDoD – United States Department of Defense (1980), *Ada Programming Language*, MIL-STD-1815.

van Wijngaarden, A. *et al*. (1969), 'Report on the Algorithmic Language ALGOL 68', *Numerische Mathematik*, **14**, pp. 79–218.

van Wijngaarden, A. *et al*. (1975), 'Revised Report on the Algorithmic Language ALGOL 68', *Acta Informatica*, **5**, pp. 1–236.

Wegner, P. (1972), 'The Vienna Definition Language', *ACM Computing Surveys*, **4**(1), pp. 5–63.

Welsh, J., Sneeringer, M. J. and Hoare, C. A. R. (1977), 'Ambiguities and Insecurities in Pascal', *Software – Practice and Experience*, **7**(6), pp. 675–696.

Welsh, J. and Hay, A. (1986), *A Model Implementation of Standard Pascal*, Prentice-Hall International: Englewood Cliffs, NJ.

Wichmann, B. A. and Ciechanowicz, Z. J. (1983), *Pascal Compiler Validation*, John Wiley & Sons: Chichester.

Winston, P. H. (1984), *Artificial Intelligence*, Addison-Wesley Publishing Company: Reading, MA.

Wirth, N. and Hoare, C. A. R. (1966), 'A Contribution to the Development of ALGOL', *Communications of the ACM*, **9**(6), pp. 413–431.

Wirth, N. (1971), 'The Programming Language Pascal', *Acta Informatica*, **1**(1), pp. 35–63.

Wirth, N. (1977), 'Modula: A Language for Modular Multiprogramming', *Software – Practice and Experience*, **7**, pp. 3–35.

Wirth, N. (1982), *Programming in Modula-2*, Springer-Verlag: New York.

Wirth, N. (1984), 'History and Goals of Modula-2', *Byte*, **9**(8), pp. 145–152.

SOLUTIONS TO SELECTED EXERCISES

Most of the exercises in this book are of a qualitative nature and so it is not appropriate to present complete solutions here. However, some guidelines are presented which may help the reader to develop fuller answers.

Chapter 1

1.3 There are several language features that can facilitate the writing of obscure code. If layout characters such as spaces and newlines are not significant in a program, inappropriate layout can confuse the reader. Yet again, the FORTRAN statement of the form `DO 1 I = 1.10` can be used as an example. Some languages do not adopt the concept of reserved words. For example, PL/I programs can use variables with names such as `IF, DO, FOR` and so on. Extensive use of such names can easily render a program unreadable. Support for address manipulation can also be used to confuse. Such support may give access to machine- or implementation-dependent effects, which can be extremely difficult to explain!

1.4 The support of low-level facilities is essential for a language to be used in applications such as the implementation of an operating system. The provision of address-manipulation operators (such as in BCPL and C) can help, as can the occasional relaxation of rigid type checking rules. Access to machine instructions may be achieved fairly cleanly by allowing the calling of subroutines, coded in assembly language, from the high-level language program. Some language implementations support the inclusion of assembly or machine language code, delimited appropriately, within the high-level language source.

Chapter 2

2.1 Consider the problem of numerical overflow and what happens when x, y and z are integer values with x and z both very large and positive, and y very large and negative.

2.2   The key to distinguish between these two types of parameter passing is that in call by reference, there is only one copy of the parameter, whereas in call by value-result, a local copy of the parameter is made. For example:

```
procedure p(a);
begin
    a := a + 1;
    a := a * x
end;
```

If x is a global variable, and is used as the actual parameter for a call to p, then the result left in x will depend on whether the parameter is passed by reference or by value-result.

Chapter 3

3.1   A useful starting point in answering this question is the catalogue of Pascal defects contained in Welsh [1977]. It is also instructive to consider the differences between Pascal and its descendants, such as Modula-2. Application-dependent shortcomings have to be considered too. For example, an engineer may complain about the poor support for complex arithmetic while a systems programmer may complain about the lack of access to low-level facilities. Proposing extensions to Pascal is something of a heresy – Pascal was designed to be a small yet powerful language.

3.2   There are several issues to be considered. To what value should the variables be initialized? In Pascal, zero may be appropriate for numerical values and nil for pointers, but for other types, such as the enumeration types, the choice of initialization value is not so obvious. Another issue concerns large data structures. For example, the overhead in initializing a large array may be considerable and also wasted if the array is subsequently initialized by the programmer.

3.4   One possible model for a solution is the *printf* routine supplied by C. But Pascal's lack of support for user-defined procedures with variable numbers of arguments can cause some implementation problems.

3.10   Pointers are generated in Pascal using the *new* function, which allocates space from the heap. So, if *new* is called within a procedure, the space allocated by *new* is still in existence, even after that procedure has finished execution, assuming that the pointer to that space has been retained in a non-local variable. Hence, the pointer stays valid. A security problem would be introduced if Pascal supported an 'addressof' operator. This operator could be used within a procedure to pass back the address of a locally defined data structure to the caller of the procedure. When the procedure exits, the local variables of that procedure effectively disappear and hence the pointer becomes invalid. There is, however, a problem in Pascal in that a pointer may be used which refers to space for a data structure that has already been released (using *dispose*).

3.11 There is usually a tradeoff between user friendliness and flexibility. For example, a programming language interface to a database management system may allow the programmer to implement complex application packages but does little for the casual user who wishes to make simple database queries.

Chapter 4

4.4 The key productions have the form:

<expression> → <term> | <term> * <expression>

<term> → <primary> | <primary> + <term>

4.7 The canonical parse is the rightmost derivation in reverse:

$a + b * c$

<primary> + $b * c$

<term> + $b * c$

<expression> + $b * c$

<expression> + <primary> * c

<expression> + <term> * c

<expression> + <term> * <primary>

<expression> + <term>

<expression>

4.9 The grammar can be defined using BNF rules of the form:

<letter> → a | b | c | d | e | f | g | h | i | j | k | l | m |
          n | o | p | q | r | s | t | u | v | w | x | y | z
<digit> → 0 | 1 | 2 | 3 | 4 | 5 | 6 | 7 | 8 | 9
<letterordigit> → <letter> | <digit>
<identifier> → <letter>
          | <letter> <letterordigit>
          | <letter> <letterordigit> <letterordigit>
          | <letter> <letterordigit> <letterordigit> <letterordigit>

Chapter 5

5.2

	input symbol			
state	(	*	)	other
1	2	1	1	1
2	2	3	1	1
3	3	4	3	3
4	3	4	5	3
5		finished		

State 1 is the starting state.

5.5 It is often useful to consider end-of-line and end-of-file as special characters rather than as states to be tested for by calling the Pascal *eoln* and *eof* functions. This reflects a stream-oriented view of character input.

5.6 Checking for overflow can be carried out as an integer constant is being read. Using the code in Section 5.4.3 as a model, the possibility of overflow should be checked for before *intval* is updated. If *intval* is currently greater than ($maxint\ div\ 10$), where *maxint* is the largest positive integer value representable in this implementation, then overflow is certain. If *intval* is equal to ($maxint\ div\ 10$), then a check has to be made on the current input character. If this single digit is larger than the last digit of *maxint*, then overflow also occurs. This algorithm may need extension on systems where the absolute value of the largest negative integer is not equal to the largest positive integer. For example, conventional two's-complement 16-bit arithmetic allows numbers in the range -32768 to $+32767$.

Chapter 6

6.3 If the grammar contains alternatives and it is not immediately obvious which alternative to select, given a current input symbol, there may be a need for backtracking. This is not impossible to implement, but it is irritating. It may be easy to transform the original grammar to avoid the need for backtracking – for example, by using factoring. Left-recursive rules also cause problems, but the grammar can be transformed to remove such rules.

In this question, factoring is needed in the rule for <value> and the left recursion has to be removed in the definition of <expr>.

6.4

	P	F	C	(	)	a	%	.
P				≐				
F				>	≐			
C				>	>		≐	
(		≐	<·	≐	<·			
)				>				
a				>	>	≐	>	
%			≐		<·			
.					≐			

Since there are no clashes of precedence in the table, this is a precedence grammar.

6.6

Stack	Input	Relation	Handle
	[x + x + x * x]		
[	x + x + x * x]	<·	
[x	+ x + x * x]	>	x
[P	+ x + x * x]	>	P
[F	+ x + x * x]	>	F
[T	+ x + x * x]	≐	
[T +	x + x * x]	<·	
[T + x	+ x * x]	>	x
[T + P	+ x * x]	>	P
[T + F	+ x * x]	>	T + F
[T	+ x * x]	≐	
[T +	x * x]	<·	
[T + x	* x]	>	x
[T + P	* x]	≐	
[T + P *	x]	≐	
[T + P * x	]	>	P * x
[T + P	]	>	P
[T + F	]	>	T + F
[T	]	>	T
[E	]	≐	
[E]	empty		S
S	empty		

Hence, this parse succeeds. The parse fails in the second example:

Stack	Input	Relation	Handle
	$[x + x * + x]$		
$[$	$x + x * + x]$	$<$	
$[x$	$+ x * + x]$	$>$	x
$[P$	$+ x * + x]$	$>$	P
$[F$	$+ x * + x]$	$>$	F
$[T$	$+ x * + x]$	$\doteq$	
$[T +$	$x * + x]$	$<$	
$[T + x$	$* + x]$	$>$	x
$[T + P$	$* + x]$	$\doteq$	
$[T + P *$	$+ x]$	error – no entry in table	

Chapter 7

7.2 The answer to this question depends to a great extent on the design of the target machine's instruction set and its addressing modes, as well as on the overall design of the run-time implementation. Eight registers could be used as follows: one could be used for a stack pointer, one for a pointer to the current display, one for a pointer to the outermost stack frame (for fast access to globally defined variables) and the remaining five for arithmetic, miscellaneous working storage and so on. With four registers, the allocation could be: one for a stack pointer, one for a display pointer and two for working storage. This would imply much storing and reloading of registers. With 32 registers, there is much more freedom in the allocation and several could be used as pointers to intermediate stack frames (effectively holding the contents of the display in registers). Many more could be used for miscellaneous working storage (reducing the need for the use of main storage locations for intermediate values) and for the storage of frequently used variables or other values.

7.3 Much relevant information is contained in *A Pascal Machine* by J. M. Bishop, reprinted in *Pascal – The Language and its Implementation* by D. W. Barron, John Wiley & Sons, Chichester, 1981.

Chapter 8

8.1 The most important aspect of portability is that the software – in this case, the compiler – must be coded in a 'portable' language. Then, the implementor must follow all the conventional rules for the coding of portable software, such as avoiding machine-dependent or operating system-dependent language extensions, avoiding making assumptions about machine characteristics (such as the number of bits used to represent an integer), avoiding reference to specific character sets, and so on.

8.3   Writing a compiler in the language it is to compile has many attractions (see text). Whether Pascal is a good language for writing a compiler is, of course, an important question and the answer depends to a large extent on personal prejudice. Many compilers have been successfully implemented in Pascal.

8.4   Wichmann [1983] is a good source of information for the testing of Pascal compilers.

Index

abstraction 4, 8
  data abstraction 71
  type abstraction 72
Ada 70–73
  rendezvous 72
  task 72
Ada Augusta 5
addressing modes 256–257
  autodecrement 256
  autoincrement 256
  indexed 256
ALGOL 58 57
ALGOL 60 57–60
  hardware representations 60
  publication language 59
  reference language 59
ALGOL 68 62–65
ALGOL W 61–62
algorithm optimization 263
algorithms 4
ambiguity 166–167, 181
analytical engine 5
ANALYZER 307
APL 82
application generators 89
applicative languages 20
argument passing, *see* parameter
    passing
arithmetic expressions 237–248
array bound checking 218
arrays 216–218, 257
artificial intelligence-based code
    generation 307
assembler 7
assembly language 7
associativity 31, 105, 245
atom 79
attribute grammars 113, 201–202, 307

augmented transition network
    grammar 113
autocodes 6

B 76
backpatching 252, 254
backtracking 120, 162
Backus-Naur Form 15, 102–106
BASIC 54–55
BCPL 73–77
binary operators 32
block number 205
block structured languages 57, 215
BNF, *see* Backus-Naur Form
Boolean expressions 249–251
bootstrapping 283
bottom-up parsing 118, 120–122,
    180–199
bounded-context parsing 198–199

C 76–77
C++ 77–78
call by copy-restore 232
call by name 24, 233
call by reference 23–24, 232
call by result 24
call by value 23, 231
call by value-result 24, 232
canonical derivation 122
canonical parse 122
case statements 252–253
character constants 151–152
Chomsky classification 109–110
CISC, *see* complex instruction set
    computers
class 77, 87
closure 109
COBOL 51–52

333